Illustrating Fashion
*Concept
to Creation*

This book is dedicated to my parents

Executive Editor: Olga T. Kontzias
Assistant Acquisitions Editor: Jason Moring
Associate Production Editor: Elizabeth Marotta
Art Director: Adam B. Bohannon
Director of Production: Priscilla Taguer
Editorial Assistant: Suzette Lam
Copy Editor: Jenn Plum, Words & Numbers
Cover Design: Adam B. Bohannon
Cover dress by Oscar de la Renta 2001

Second Edition, Copyright © 2005
Fairchild Publications, Inc.

First Edition, Copyright © 1996
Fairchild Publications, formerly a division of Capital Cities Media, Inc.

Third Printing 2000
Second Printing 1999

Library of Congress Catalog Card Number: 2004 109882

ISBN: 1-56367-371-1
GST R 133004424

Printed in the United States of America

Illustrating Fashion
Concept to Creation

Second Edition

Steven Stipelman
Fashion Institute of Technology

Fairchild Publications, Inc.
New York

Contents

The Fashion Figure

The Fashion Details

Rendering

The Extras

Preface

It has been nearly thirty-five years since I taught my first class, but the memory of that day is still very vivid. There I was, standing in front of a group of students, ready to teach them everything I knew about fashion illustration. It would have been very simple if teaching was just about dispensing facts, but I knew—even then—that there was a greater responsibility ahead of me.

I thought back to when I was accepted to the High School of Music and Art. For the first time in my life I felt that I belonged. Everyone around me was an artist. We all were there for similar purposes. We were all creative, full of energy, passionate about our work. The teachers inspired us, pushed us to the peak of our creativity, and opened up worlds that we never even knew existed. That was my first experience with this kind of learning. It was very different from the math and science classes that came before. Projects—no matter how complex—no longer seemed like a burden. I always wanted to expand on them, do more, push myself to greater levels.

After high school graduation, I attended the Fashion Institute of Technology, where I majored in Fashion Illustration. I knew that this would be my career. The fantasy lessened and reality started to set in—I was studying the subject that was to be my future. There were more rules, more restrictions, more realistic responsibilities. Even so, there were a handful of teachers that went beyond the classroom work and helped to bring out my fullest potential. When I think back, I don't exactly remember all facts that they taught me, but I remember that they cared, guided, and inspired me. Many years later, I became a recipient of the Mortimer C. Ritter alumni award an I am sure that their support and inspiration was at least partly responsible for this. In 2000 I received the Chancellors Award for Teaching Excellence from F.I.T. In 2004 I was selected for inclusion in Who's Who Among America's Teachers.

I remembered all these things as I started teaching my first class. Although I was younger than most of the students in the class, I was now standing in front of the room. The first years of teaching became tremendous learning experiences for me. After some time, I began to figure out what this "teaching" thing was all about. It is not just facts and lessons. It is the inspiration and curiosity that you bring to the classroom. It is guiding and directing, helping to make the students curious and passionate about the subject matter. Above all, teaching is about seeing each student as an individual—not just one amongst the many. Each student brings a particular point of view, talent, and an ability to learn. Each student has a personal life in and out of the classroom, with problems, insecurities, and levels of learning skills. And it is my responsibility to form a relationship with each and every one of them.

Many times, I have to divorce my own personal taste and feelings and see things the way that the students do. This, I know, will help them to reach their own potentials. It isn't always easy to accept that we—the student and myself—are from two different worlds, two different taste levels, two different ages. Because I resented the teachers that didn't understand me, I work to really understand my students. I try to establish trust and understanding because I have to guide them into their world. I have to teach them the facts without killing their creativity. To do this, I have to enter into and understand their world, and they must be open to mine.

The creative process has many levels. It begins with the "raw energy" that students bring with them. Over the years, the work becomes less raw—more polished, the taste level more refined. I sometimes think that it is sad that the raw energy and the sophistication do not take place at the same time. However, the teacher and the student must work together to try bring these two levels together. Is this always simple? No. Does it always work? No. But I try to reach every student and I feel that I am more successful than not.

Because fashion is alive and constantly changing, it is not an easy subject to learn or teach. Studying the facts and rules are the way that one begins. These are very important, but this is not always enough to guarantee a successful career. Understanding the concepts and "growing" the student's creativity must happen at the same time. You must know "why" before you can know "how," but as you are learning the "whys," you must constantly practice the "hows." This is what my book is about.

Writing this book brought back many of my early fears about teaching. Now I would be going out of the classroom, putting my methods and experiences in print. My artwork would be studied. I had to be aware of how different teachers and students would interpret this information. I had to remember that this book would also be used by very competent teachers who had their own points of view and methodologies. Because learning how to teach never ends, I wanted my book to offer many methods, techniques, and additional insights that I have learned through teaching. I did not want my book to offer only "one way." I have many years of teaching and diverse professional experiences. My artistic background comes from many areas, all of which helped me to write this book. I wanted my book to impart all of these to the student.

My first professional illustration job was as staff illustrator for Henri Bendel, which at the time was one of the most chic stores in the world. I drew the artwork for all the newspaper advertising. At the time, I was exposed to the finest designs, the most exquisite clothing. Many times, I could be found in the stockroom of the designer salon, studying all the fashions from Norell, Galanos, and Trigère, to name but a few. I could not believe that I was actually touching a Norell suit! It cost $850 in 1964! I know that I was extremely fortunate to be surrounded by this level of fashion at such an early period of my career.

After Bendel's, I went to *Women's Wear Daily*, where I was a fashion artist for the next twenty-five years. I drew the clothing of the best designers in the world—often from sketches before the clothing was actually made. I sketched the finest garments from the collections in New York and I also covered many couture shows in Paris, sending sketches by wireless to New York for publication. Additionally, I did portraits of such fashionable women as Babe Paley, Jacqueline Kennedy Onassis, and Nancy Reagan—all in their chicest clothes.

My freelance accounts kept me in touch with international apparel designers, advertising agencies, and the cosmetic industry, and my work has appeared in newspapers, magazines, and trade publications. I was fortunate to experience on a day-to-day basis what was once just a dream.

Despite the "glamour" of the fashion world, some of the most rewarding and satisfying moments in my career have been in the classrooms and lecture halls of the college campuses throughout the country. I am on the faculty of the Fashion Institute of Technology,

and have taught at Parson's School of Design, and Marist College. Additionally, I have lectured and taught workshops at schools that include Mount Mary College, Drexel University, Cornell University, Shannon Rodgers and Jerry Silverman School of Fashion Design and Merchandising, Colorado State University, University of Nebraska, and Stephens College. Teaching has afforded me the opportunity to transfer my knowledge and skills, which I believe has helped my students to optimize and experience new aspects of their art and work.

It is important to not only reach the "A" student, but it is sometimes even more satisfying and rewarding to reach those that have more difficulty in understanding the concepts or the actual drawing. What a thrill it is to see them produce something beautiful after all their hard work! I want all my students to achieve accuracy in the details in their drawings and sketches, but still maintain spontaneity and excitement, It is very important that they bring their own points of view, feelings, and emotions to their artwork. This is what will give their work the magic and that "special something" that separates their art from the crowd. Above all, I want to arouse a curiosity about fashion art and to challenge the student to develop their talents to the fullest. This is one of the reasons that I chose to vary the approaches to drawing fashion art in this book. I feel that by offering more than just one way, the student will not feel pressures or locked into any one style or technique. To support this, as I was drawing the illustrations for this book, I tried to suit the technique to the garment. Even so, all the drawings are still recognizably mine—a fact that I hope will show students that while there are many drawing techniques, they can still maintain their own particular, unique style.

Because I want this book to serve as a textbook for the beginning fashion student as well as a reference book for the more advanced student, I have included the facts and basic concepts of fashion art in addition to more complex, abstract, difficult topics. Each chapter begins with an overview of the subject. Whether it is a brief fashion history, or the relationship of the sleeve to the arm, each chapter first explains what will follow. Throughout the book, I have drawn designer garments that I thought were important and that could help the student understand a specific concept. These fashions will help the student become acquainted with the designer's name and the garment's place in fashion history. I hope that it shows that a well-designed garment can look beautiful forever. It is also my belief that without a knowledge of the past, it is impossible to design for the future.

As I have stated before, I do not believe that there is ever just "one way" or "one approach" to artwork. Because of this, I have left the choice of art supplies and techniques quite open, so that the student will never feel locked in. Many times, I have shown alternative ways of approaching or understanding a subject. For example, I am not a very strong believer in the "ten-head" approach to drawing a figure, but I realize its importance for many students, as well as teachers. Therefore I have included it as one of many techniques, which include the cutting, tracing, and blocking methods. I want students to understand that by "borrowing" a little bit from one chapter and applying it to another, they can develop their own technique, which—above all—should work for them.

This new edition has four new chapters including a color chapter that will help students learn important illustration techniques. The book is divided into four parts. Before the first part, there is and introduction called *Getting Started*. In this, I discuss the concepts of fashion art, developing your own talent, the different qualities of line, and art supplies. This beginning, I hope, will guide the student as well as help them relax and not worry.

The first part, *The Fashion Figure*, is divided into fourteen chapters which cover the basic concepts of drawing the fashion figure. Some of the subjects covered are proportion, balance lines, center front, the fashion face, and figure types. In this first part, we cover the various techniques of achieving a fashion figure, which include cutting, tracing, and blocking. Also examined is the concept of how to see and plan the fashion figure. The two new chapters teach how to draw the turned and profile figure and how garments shape the body. After going through these initial chapters and practicing all the techniques and learning the concepts, I am confident that the student will be able to draw a fashion figure.

The second part, *The Fashion Details*, covers drawing fashions on the figure. This part is divided into thirteen chapters, which include subjects from the fashion silhouette (and history) to necklines and collars, to sleeves and blouses, hemlines and skirts, pants,

drapery, tailored clothing, and accessories. Additionally, many of these chapters include a "drawing glossary" of various styles and garment details that are essential (but may be obscure) for the student to recognize. These chapters will help the student not only to draw these garments, but to identify fashions and garment details, as well as understanding the history behind the clothing.

The third part, *Rendering*, has only four, but very important, chapters—*Stripes and Plaids, Rendering Concepts, Rendering Techniques* (in color)*, and Knits*. This part has been included for the more advanced student, who is ready to take on the many difficulties of rendering. I also believe that these chapters will also help the beginning student to understand some of the more difficult aspects of fashion artwork.

The fourth part, *The Extras*, includes everything else that I believe a fashion artist must know. These six chapters cover menswear, drawing children, volume and manipulating the figure. The new chapter, The Walking Figure, demonstrates how to draw the walking figure or runway pose. Also included in this part is the essential chapter on "flats," which every fashion artist must know how to draw if they are to be successful.

Last, I briefly discuss the concept of "style." I am asked about this more than any other subject. It is my hope that by the time the student reaches the end of this book, they will have an understanding of the concepts of fashion drawing, both basic and advanced techniques, of their own talents, goals, and a glimmer of their own personal style.

I believe this book can be used as a textbook from the beginning to the end of a course of study. It can also be kept as a reference book to be used after the student is out of school. Teachers can use it as a text or to supplement what they already teach. Additionally, merchandising students can use it to help them with their courses in fashion and fashion art.

As I have said before, teaching is a great responsibility. I remember teachers that said the wrong thing to me at the wrong time. The results could have been devastating, but fortunately I had teachers that were deeply concerned and who are greatly responsible for my career. I care very deeply about the process of learning and the quality level for the students and teachers that are involved in the process. In the short time that we are involved with a student, a teacher has to create a minor miracle. A teacher must not only impart the facts, but help to expand the student's world and bring out the best potential and talent of the student.

My hope is that this book will be of some help. I hope it will help students to conquer their fear of drawing and teach them how to take the rules and concepts and make them their own. And in making them their own, they will be able to draw a beautiful, rewarding piece of artwork that is—above all—personal and unique.

Acknowledgments

I was very fortunate to have parents that nurtured and encouraged my artwork as long ago as I can remember. I want to thank them for sending me to art school, letting me study what made me happy, and for supporting me throughout my career. Watching my mother make beautiful clothing was one of my inspirations to study fashion.

There have been many teachers—some who are no longer with us—that have been very special to me from the very beginning. I want to thank all of them, but especially Julia Winston, Mae Stevens Baranik, Ruth McMurray, Ana Ishikawa, and Beatrice Dwan. A most special thanks to Frances Neady and Bill Ronin, two teachers that taught me that caring, inspiration, and guidance were as important and as necessary as the subject matter.

Thank you to Geraldine Stutz who hired me for my first illustration job at Henri Bendel. From my years at *Women's Wear Daily*, a very special thanks to Rudy Millendorf, the art director who was greatly responsible for the early years of my career, and fashion editors Tibby Taylor and June Weir for their guidance, as well as all the exceptionally talented fashion illustrators that I worked with over the twenty-five years that I spent at *WWD*.

To Sandi Keiser, Barbara Borgwardt, and Sister Aloyse of Mount Mary College, Robert Hillstead of the University of Nebraska, and Elizabeth Rhodes of the Shannon Rodgers and Jerry Silverman School of Fashion Design, a special thanks for their support.

I wish to express my gratitude to Linda Tain, professor at Fashion Institute of Technology, for all her input during the writing and drawing of this book.

Thanks to Dawn Oertel of Mount Mary College for knitting the wonderful swatches for the chapter on knits and to the Brown Sheep Yarn Company for supplying the yarn.

A grateful thanks to Aaron Duncan and Pablo Hernandez for teaching me how to use a computer—something that frightened me much more than writing this book!

For their support and encouragement, I would like to thank Josephine Vargas, Karen Scheetz, Susanna Luckey and Lincoln Hess.

Thanks to Charles Kleibacker and Mary Eliott for their help in setting up the historical clothing to be photographed and to Tom Etter and Jay Westhauser for their beautiful photographs. Also, thanks to Roy Wright for his photographs of the knitting and fabric swatches used in several chapters of this book.

I would like to thank the following people for their constructive, helpful, and thoughtful reviews of the preliminary chapters: Diane Ellis, Meredith College; Annette Fraser, Ph. D.; Lisa Gellert, Helen Lefeaux School of Fashion Design; Betsy Henderson, University of Minnesota. This book benefited greatly by their input.

When I was made an honorary member of the International Textile and Apparel Association, Olga Kontzias and Pamela Kirshen Fishman of Fairchild Books and Visuals suggested that I write this book. I am grateful for the opportunity and the confidence that they had in me. An additional thanks to Elizabeth Marotta and Monotype Composition who handled the production of this new edition.

A special thank you to Jenn Plum, who edited and gave order to the entire book and who helped to enrich it more than I had envisioned. It was a joy to work with her.

And last, to the hundreds of students who were (and are) in my classes; if not for their questions and curiosity, this book would never have been. A million thanks!

Steven Stipelman

Getting Started

What is Fashion Art?

Fashion art is the combination of clothing (which has its own life) and the figure (with its own life) becoming one. The fashion artist can take a garment and transform it—convey a mood—set a style—or give it an attitude. The fashion artist can create that one woman wearing that one garment and make it perfect.

Fashion art is an historical record of a piece of clothing and a period of time. The earliest cave art showed people wearing certain garments. Throughout history, whenever someone was painted or sketched, what they wore became an important indication of their station in life. When we look at the portraits by Sargent or Gainsborough, the men and women they painted were wearing the clothing that they thought best represented them.

In contemporary times, we have seen how the great fashion artists of the day illustrated the most fashionable women in their best clothing. Eric and Bouché's drawings of the elegant women of the 40s and 50s—for example the Duchess of Windsor or Marlene Dietrich wearing Schiaparelli, Dior, or Balenciaga—showed us the ultra-sophistication of that period. Kenneth Paul Block's drawings of Babe Paley, Gloria Guiness, and Jacqueline Kennedy helped us sense the polish of the early 60s. Antonio's illustrations of the 70s and 80s showed us the new, young, modern women breaking the rules and setting their own styles.

Fashion art was also used by department stores to project their images. Their illustrations often identified the store before the customer even saw the logo or name. In the 50s and 60s Dorothy Hood's wash drawings became the symbol for Lord and Taylor and Esther Larson's brush and ink drawings identified Bergdorf Goodman, Kenneth Paul Block and J. Hyde Crawford's charcoal illustrations were Bonwit Teller's image in the 60s and 70s.

When I was at *Women's Wear Daily*, the Paris couture was always covered by artists, because photographs were not permitted until a certain amount of time had elapsed. All retail advertising was done with artwork as well.

Fashion art plays a major role in the design world. Before beginning a collection, the fashion designer does a series of drawings called *croquis*. *Croquis* is the French word for a small, rough sketch. They lack specific detail, but still show the proportions and silhouettes of the clothing with a sense of style and flare.

The next stages include more detailed artwork that begins to focus on fabrication and details. The final stage is a finished piece of art—with all the elements of detail, fabrication, proportion, and accessories—as if the clothes were on the runway or in a magazine.

Besides the traditional fashion illustration, there are other roles for the fashion artist, as well. For example, the flat[1] is another form of fashion artwork. These are sketches of the clothing without a figure, often drawn with rulers and French curves. The line is exact and all the pieces are in proportion to each other. Many items in sportswear, menswear, and children's wear are designed only in flats. Additionally, a "spec" (or specification) is a flat with the various garment measurements indicated, for example, center back, shoulder, and sleeve lengths.

Today, with more overseas manufacturing, the role of the fashion artist is even greater. Finished sketches, flats, and specs travel thousands of miles to be worked on by people who do not speak similar languages. Artwork is the universal means of communication. Because of this, accuracy, proportion, and detail are vital.

To be a fashion artist, you must understand concepts, have flexibility in drawing, plus an open mind that is always ready to accept change. You need all the technical knowledge of anatomy and clothing details, as well as a knowledge of fashion—both historical and contemporary. With time and practice, a sense of fantasy, passion, and the right amount of common sense reality, you will see that there are no limits to what can be achieved.

See Chapter 35, Flats, p. 426

How Artists Develop

Drawing is a combination of three elements: the brain, the eyes, and the hands. When you look at a blank piece of paper you know exactly what you want to see on it—a beautiful and exciting piece of artwork. In the beginning, your hands do not have the technical skills, nor your brain the wealth of knowledge to achieve this.

Growth involves time. No matter how much you practice, the element of time is most important. If you sat for one week and drew nothing but heads, they would certainly improve, but over a period of one year they would become drawings with much more substance.

As your work develops, you reach different levels of acceptance. At the beginning, you are probably happy to get anything that even resembles a figure! Let's call this level one. As time goes on, you want something better. This becomes level two. The frustrating thing is that there is no smooth transition between these levels and you cannot get there in one step. You draw something, rip it up and throw it away—one after another. It is extremely frustrating until you realize that you are not losing your talent—you are just not ready to reach level two. The positive part, however, is that level one is no longer acceptable.

The most valuable thing to do at this time is to relax and practice what you do well—a head, a garment detail, or a specific rendering technique. Not only will you improve your skills, you will build the necessary confidence that will enable you to advance to the next level.

You finally reach level two and after a while, the same thing happens again. This process goes on all our lives. If it doesn't, there is no growth. The good part is that you begin to build a reserve bank of the techniques and skills you do very well and that you can refer to when you reach these plateaus.

In all the years that I have been an illustrator, I have accumulated a huge reserve bank of resources that I can use at any time. When I reach a level that is frustrating to me, I have many techniques and solutions that can get me through. Does the world know this? Not at all! I have developed enough of my skills to do a drawing that will always be acceptable on a certain professional level.

Am I completely satisfied with my art? Not always. I know that it is impossible to do the most perfect, wonderful, creative drawing every single time, no matter how long you've worked or how talented you are. The most you can do is the best possible level of work at the time you are doing it. We all have areas in which we are best and those that are more difficult, which require extra studying and practice. It is essential to accept the fact that there are techniques and concepts that will take years of practice to achieve even mediocre results.

A piece of artwork is not about attacking a piece of paper, nor should it be an accident. Granted, along the way an accident can produce an interesting result, but consistency is what your ultimate goal should be. Consistency comes from understanding concepts and developing skills. It is the combination of seeing, analyzing, making decisions, and solving problems. It is setting the best possible—but not impossible—standards.

If you have no standards to look to, or no past to compare your work to, then how far can you reach? If everything is acceptable, ultimately nothing is acceptable. Over the years and with hard work, you polish your skills and develop your technique so that your work will grow technically and creatively. Your concepts will become more sophisticated.

Let's hope this process never stops.

Line Quality

Think of writing. Writing is the most personal form of line quality. Write your name. You are not aware of dark, light, thick, thin, or how you are holding the pencil. A signature has the kind of line quality that is unique to you alone. It comes from within and seems quite natural. Was it always that simple? No!

Think back to when you were first learning how to write in script. The teacher was writing the letters on the blackboard. You were desperately trying to follow her, at the same time thinking of how you were holding you pencil. Never, never, will I ever be able to do this—you were saying to yourself—as you were also trying to stay between the lines of the ruled paper.

But one day, with much practice, you began to write easily. You were not using ruled paper anymore—but the words were on a straight line. You became more aware of what you were writing than how you were writing. In fact, after a while, you were not even writing with all the loops and dots that you were taught originally. Everyone developed an original way of writing, and yet, you were all able to read what the others wrote. It became your own natural and unique line—your signature.

After a time, you used a bold line when you wanted to make an emphatic statement or a more gentle line when you wanted to write a gracious thank-you note. It came from within. You were at one with all the elements of writing without being aware of it.

The same principle applies to drawing. How can you make it look effortless and still have control at the same time? The line should come from within. You should feel comfortable, as if you are "at one with the pencil or marker."

In art, line quality is the sensitivity to what you are drawing. Capturing the thicks, thins, darks, lights, hards, softs, as well as the gentle and the bold. It is capturing the essence of a garment, using only line. Line quality is different than rendering. When you add tones you begin to render. The line brings us into the kind of garment it is, the rendering gives us the specifics. However, if you do not capture the line quality—no rendering in the world will make it correct.

Some of you have a light touch and would do well with extra fine or fine markers, harder pencils, and softer brushes. Others—with a heavier touch—will feel more comfortable with supplies that can be pressed down on without fear of breakage. Bolder markers, softer pencils, and bristle brushes would be preferable for them. It is extremely important that you feel very comfortable with the supplies you are using.

To begin to draw, hold you pencil or marker in a similar manner to the way you write. This is the way you have been doing it for most of your life and is the easiest way. It should move around in your hand naturally as you draw. Unless you are very comfortable with your supplies, you cannot get a smooth and flowing line. The most important thing is not how you hold your pencil—but the results that you are getting with it.

If at any point you are not satisfied, or feel inhibited with the kind of line you are drawing, consider changing that particular supply, or even the way you are working with it.

Developing Line Quality

Think of a line as the tool to interpret the garment you want to draw. Before actually putting your hand to the paper, think about the line necessary to illustrate the garment.

- Silk crepe would require a "slow" line.
- Taffeta would need a short, bouncy line.
- Satin would demand a smooth, round line.
- Mohair would be best with a fuzzy, soft line.
- Lace would be beautiful in a flowing, lyrical line.
- Chiffon would need a gently flowing line.

After thinking and deciding what kind of the line is appropriate and "right" for you and your drawing, begin to make these same gestures or movements in the air, almost as if you were working on a sheet of paper. Try to think "if I had to represent this garment with only one line, what would be the most perfect one?" Fast and quick, slow and smooth, soft and shadowy, or hard and crisp? Keep doing this until your gestures begin to imitate the line that best represents the garment. Slowly, bring this down to a sheet of scrap paper and start scribbling in the garment, keeping it abstract. When you feel a certain rhythm taking place, begin to draw. In the beginning, the line will be self-conscious, but time and practice will slowly make it more natural.

A bad habit to develop is to draw one line by drawing many lines. Don't use ten strokes to make a line, try to get it with just one. Students generally use many more lines than are necessary. As an easy exercise, study a garment—either from life or a photo—and see how long you can draw before it becomes necessary to break the line.

Let the line capture the character of the design, the fabric from which it is made, and the sense of its characteristics. However, under no circumstances should the skin or exposed parts of the body have a textured or interesting line quality. It should remain as smooth as possible. All the very interesting lines should be reserved for the garment and fabrication.

Study the differences between the different textures of the garment and try to capture a different line quality in each of the parts, for example the fabric, buttons, or trim. First, draw an entire outfit that consists of many textures with just one marker or pencil. Let your strokes and movements give each part its own character. Next, draw abstract lines to indicate the feeling of taffeta ruffles, a big satin skirted ballgown, or a luxurious mohair sweater. Don't always think of the obvious—sometimes it might be interesting to draw lingerie with a heavy marker and mohair with a fine marker. Above all—economy of line will give you the best results.

You will know that you are successful when you are not aware of the line quality at all, but are more involved with what you are actually drawing.

Remember, the best line of all is the most natural—and the most personal.

Art Supplies

Art supplies are a means of enhancing or explaining a piece of artwork. Remember:

- Just a simple piece of paper and a pencil are all you need to do a drawing.

- No art supply will cover up a bad piece of artwork.

- No art supply will give you a style.

Not everyone can work well within all mediums. Many factors determine how well we work with certain supplies. Some artists have a heavier touch and work better using something that they can press down with. Others have light, delicate touch and do well with fine pens and pencils. Some achieve better results with water color, others do better with markers. The most important thing to keep in mind it that you have to feel comfortable with the supplies you are using.

School should expose you to the many different kinds of supplies and their uses. Through practice and experimentation, you will learn those that work best for you and those with which you work best. However, what doesn't work well for you at one time in your life might work very well at another.

Every time you go to an art store there are new and different supplies. In the following section, I have broken then down into categories and have explained the different types of supplies and their uses.

Pencils

The most common supply is the lead pencil ("lead" pencils are made of graphite and are not a danger to the student or artist). This is what we grew up writing with. Leads come in gradations that range from H (or hard)—which is used for more technical purposes or to sketch a figure before rendering—to B, which is soft and used more for sketching and shading.

There are gradations that range from H to 9H and from B to 8B, all of which afford different hard or soft gradations. Many students find mechanical pencils—which can be filled with different leads—work very well. Additionally, I strongly suggest that you have a small, battery-operated pencil sharpener because it is much easier than the small, hand-operated ones. It doesn't break the pencil point and allows the artist to have a very sharp point at all times.

Colored Pencils

I find colored pencils to be some of the most useful art supplies. They can work well on their own of be the perfect complement to markers, wash, or watercolor. Because they can be sharpened to a fine point at all times, they are wonderful for fine details, for example, topstitching, pockets or seams, as well as shadows and details on the face and hair.

Colored pencils come in hard and soft varieties, and in sets ranging from 12 to over 100 pencils. They are also sold separately, so a particular color can be purchased on its own.

Powdered Eye Shadows

When used with its foam rubber applicator, powdered eyeshadows produce velvety, soft lines with no distinct edges. The gray colors are good for shadows. The brown tones can be used for face and skin shadows. Colors produce wonderful effects for sheers and soft prints.

Erasers

I believe in the eraser. It can be very helpful in refining an underdrawing. Students are lead to believe that the first line must be perfect and because of this pressure they become very uptight when drawing. Erasing can make it much easier to achieve a good result, especially at the beginning. There are many pink and white erasers that are good for general use. Mechanical pencils have refillable erasers and there are erasers that come in a mechanical pencil form, which can be clicked up to give you an additional amount.

I find the kneaded eraser the most useful. It can remove lines from a light preliminary drawing without hurting the paper. I also find it excellent to lightly erase my line drawings before using color. It removes the top layer of lead and leaves just enough outline to guide me in my work. It can also be used to create a highlight and to clean up the paper after you finish the art.

Markers

Markers are an invention of the 1960s. We are very used to selecting from an infinite variety of them in every conceivable point size. It is difficult to imagine doing any artwork without them now.

Black ink markers come in many widths, ranging from extra fine to bold. The most important consideration is that the marker be comfortable in your hand and easy to manipulate. Try them out before purchasing them. Most markers are waterproof, but whenever using any water with them, do not test on a scrap—before you work on your original.

Colored markers come in such variety that it is often difficult to make a choice. They come in many different nibs—fine, medium, broad, and chiseled. Some markers have all the tips in one.

Now, there are also "blenders." These are clear markers that blend marker colors together, making it possible to achieve various effects. Also, gray markers come in both warm and color ranges, from 1 to 9, with 1 representing the lightest, and 9 representing the darkest.

Just remember, before using any marker draw a box to see if the color bleeds out. This will enable you to determine how close to the edge of your drawing you can go.

Brushes

The best possible brush is made from sable hair. They are very costly, and, at the beginning, not that necessary. There are many synthetic sable brushes that work very well. A number 6, 7, or 8 brush with a pointed tip is a good one for starters. For very fine work, you can use a 00, 0, or 1. Because these very fine brushes are not that expensive, in this case, it pays to buy one made of sable one. In addition to sable or synthetic sable, bristle brushes also work well with acrylics.

When you begin to add to your brush collection, you can experiment with different sizes and shapes. After using a brush, shake the excess water off and create a point. Never store a brush with the hair side down—rest them with the hairs up or laid on their side.

Pens and Inks

In recent years, markers have largely replaced pens. Sometimes, however, a pen is just what is necessary to use for a specific rendering. They are available from very delicate coquille to much broader nibs and can be inserted into a pen holder. Fountain pens (pens that are filled with ink) are very suitable for an unbroken line. There are also many inexpensive, disposable fountain pens that work very well. These fountain-type pens should be filled with inks appropriate for them. India ink is the most popular for washes and for dipping pens. Washes also can be executed with India ink.

Watercolor

Watercolor comes in both cake and tube forms. The prices vary greatly, but student-quality watercolors are quite good. Purchase the kind with which you feel most comfortable. Some students find the tube colors easier to mix. There are good quality cake sets, with the colors arranged according to the color chart. Mixing dishes are very expensive, and water can be put in any container or cup on hand.

Gouache

Gouache gives a more opaque color than watercolor, and is available in tubes. There is a wide range of colors available.

Paper

Paper can serve many needs, from very inexpensive varieties (that we can put ideas on) to very expensive ones (for elaborate finishes). They come in many sizes—5x7, 8x10, 9x12, 11x14, 14x17 or 18x24. Different sizes serve different needs. Various types of paper include:

- Photocopy paper. I find this wonderful for underdrawings and idea sketching. Because it is less expensive than tracing paper and can still be transparent, it does not inhibit the creative process as a more expensive paper might.

- Tracing paper, which is a thin, transparent paper that is very easy to see through. It is also used for corrections ad for protecting finished art.

- Vellum. This is a very heavy, transparent paper. It is good for certain renderings and takes different media very well. Color can be applied from the back for interesting results.

- Marker paper, which is made to work well with markers. It is slightly see-through to enable you to be able to trace.

- All-purpose paper. Usually this is a very acceptable-quality white paper. For a relatively low price, you get many sheets, which take both pencil and markers well.

- Bristol paper, which is a shiny, heavier paper. It has an extremely smooth surface and can be used for mounting vellum or other artwork.

- Illustration board. This is a board rather than a paper, which works well with different media and is sold in sheets of various sizes. It comes in colors as well and is good for mounting your work.

- Newsprint, which is a lesser-quality paper that is very off-white in color. Generally, it is used for sketching rather than finished art.

- Watercolor paper, which has either a smooth or a textured surface. It is sold in both pads and sheets. The prices vary greatly, but a less-expensive quality works just as well for a student or beginner. Additionally, a good-quality watercolor paper can be used on both sides.

Other Supplies and Equipment

These include pastels, oil pastels, acrylics, conte crayon, charcoal, watercolor and pastel pencils, luma dyes, as well as others. These all are used for specific needs. In addition to these supplies, there is other equipment that you will need to either buy or develop.

Swipe Files

A swipe file is your reference file and is one of the most helpful tools you can own. Each time you look through a fashion magazine or newspaper, clip what you like, what inspires you, or what you think is important. Buy manila envelopes in uniform sizes and label them—faces, collars, poses, hairstyles, and so forth, and place the appropriate photo or drawing in it. This must be started from day one. That way, whenever you have to refer to a specific pose, for example, a profile view of a face, you will have it on hand. Remember that if you need to see a certain style (for example, a plaid, a neckline, or a shoe), it might not be in a current fashion magazine.

Fashion Magazines – Collection Issues

These come out several times a year. Often they are expensive, but they almost always have runway photos from the many fashion collections. It is a quick way to find a good pose, and also serves as a very good reference for specific fabrics that might not be easy to find.

Pattern Counter Books

Check with local fabric stores for the less-current counter books issued by the various pattern companies. They have very clear, simple poses, with good examples of fashion details.

Pattern Magazines

These are good for a very quick reference to carry with you. The poses tend to be simple and clear, with many photos of different fabrics.

These are the basic supplies and equipment used in fashion art. However, there are many more supplies—enough to fill an entire book and they are constantly changing and being refined! By the time this book is in print, there will be an entire new crop. Therefore, it is very important to visit art stores regularly to see what is new.

Just remember, art students tend to "overbuy" art supplies. Often, too many can be too confusing. The three most valuable art supplies are your brain, your eyes, and your hands. When these three work well with each other, you have the best beginning. Remember, a good artist can work wonders with any art supply.

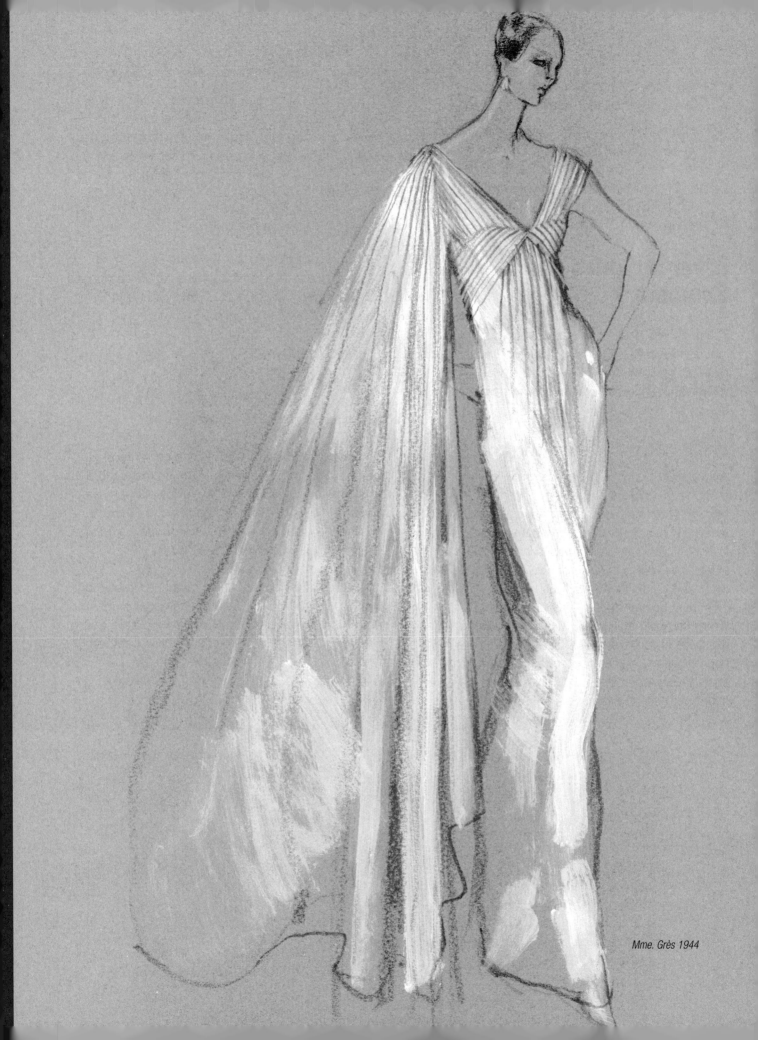

Mme. Grès 1944

Part 1

The Fashion Figure

Oscar de la Renta/Balmain 2002

Proportion and the Fashion Figure

One of the most difficult concepts to grasp in fashion art is the determination of the right proportion for the fashion figure. The human body, whether in fashion or in life, basically has been the same throughout time—always two legs, two arms, a torso, and a head.

The fashion figure is that person whose look and body represents the perfect proportion at a given time. Everyone has a different idea of how many "heads" high the fashion figure should be. We can only think "generally" as opposed to "definitely," because we, as fashion artists, are drawing the ideal figure of the moment. For example, Michelangelo made his figures 9-, 10-, or even 12-heads high to achieve a harmony and grace not found in nature. When you look at old films, paintings, or magazines, the fashion figure seems to take a different focus in each decade.

To grasp this concept, you must be completely open to change, because the figure that worked in the 1940s will not work in the 2000s. The clothing and fit—as well as the undergarments—determine the proportions of the fashion figure. Sometimes something considered the "ideal" of the moment during one period looks very different in another. When looking at photos of Marilyn Monroe from the 1950s, many might find her a bit heavy and untoned by today's standards.

Marilyn Monroe aside, in the 1950s, the ideal fashion model was about five foot nine and bone thin. The underpinnings that would further change the body (for example, girdles, waist cinchers, and padded bras) would make them appear even thinner and more perfect for the clothing of the period. The model looked sophisticated and aloof. When studying the photographs of that period, you can see that their poses were the result of the restrictions the garments placed on them. Often, only one leg was in front of the other and the arms were placed on the hips. The look was tall and willowy and the poses had studied movement.

Audrey Hepburn, Jackie Kennedy, and the Duchess of Windsor

Legs became the fashion focus of the 1960s

The look of the early 1960s was based on polish and perfection. Audrey Hepburn and Jacqueline Kennedy were forging the way to a younger sophistication. Givenchy designed the perfect clothing for them to wear. They became the ideals of the moment—thin and elegant. They were worldly and sophisticated with a hint of glamour and youth. Their look was studied, but had a less formal and more casual quality to it. This was in marked contrast to the very serious and formal style set by their predecessors, such as the Duchess of Windsor. They brought a new life to the fashion ideal.

The middle of the 1960s gave us one of the most dramatic changes in the fashion focus. Mary Quant gave us the miniskirt and never has the attitude of fashion been freer. The short skirt allowed the fashion model the ability to leap across the pages of the fashion magazines. Photographers such as Richard Avedon and illustrators such as Antonio gave new movement to the fashion figure. Suddenly women wanted to look younger. The unapproachable look of the 1950s models, as with Dovima and Suzy Parker, gave way to Twiggy, Jean Shrimpton, and Penelope Tree. They were young and spirited and their bodies were virtually free of all underpinnings. Skirts were barely there and the figure seemed to be all legs. The fashion figure was less curvy and the look was more "girl" than "woman." The makeup was less serious—more fun. Falls gave hair more volume than ever before.

From the 1960s on, the fashion figure became more natural. Makeup looked less artificial and instead of underpinnings, the "perfect" fashion figure was exercised, toned, and healthy—no longer the thin, clothes-hanger, but a woman with a more real body. She was neither ultrasophisticated nor little-girlish—instead, a liberated woman, completely at ease with herself.

We must learn from this to be flexible about what the ideal proportion is and to accept the fact that it is open to change. Remember, what looks perfect in one decade looks quite strange in another.

Even "retro" does not duplicate a decade perfectly. The inspiration might come from a certain time, but we bring our own time to it and change it just enough to look comfortable and "right."

A woman who is 5'7" can have a perfectly proportioned body, but can a woman that is 5'5" or 5'2". A fashion figure, however, must be taller than the average woman so there is more of her with which to overpowering blouse with big sleeves, big collar, and a lot of bodice detail—the figure might have to be a bit longer waisted and have a longer neck.

To show an exaggerated batwing sleeve, the arms might have to be a bit longer. To show a short miniskirt, the legs might have to be somewhat longer. Different clothing requires different focus. Different focus requires different exaggerations. As artists, we are choosing the most perfect of the perfect.

Let's look at the three figures on page 22, all in the same dress, all wearing a belt at the "waistline." The first one has a narrow belt, which sits on the waist. The second has a wider belt, which sits above the natural waist. The third has a wide belt, which sits below the natural waist. You can see in all three cases that the definition of "waistline" changes. More important, the relationship between the top and bottom of the dress changes as well.

A fashion figure must be taller than average

show the clothes—more to exaggerate and give great drama on the runway, either in a photograph or in artwork. When a model walks down a runway, the space she is in is larger than life. You are seeing her in a large, unnatural environment and if she were not tall, she would disappear in that space.

I have found that for now the 10-head fashion figure works best. Does this mean a 9- or 11-head figure is completely wrong? Absolutely not.

Let's imagine a room filled with the most perfect models. Even among the perfect, each one will have something that another does not. Some will have longer legs, others a longer neck or torso, or perhaps squarer shoulders.

In a drawing, we want to represent the best possible figure for the clothing and so—to show an

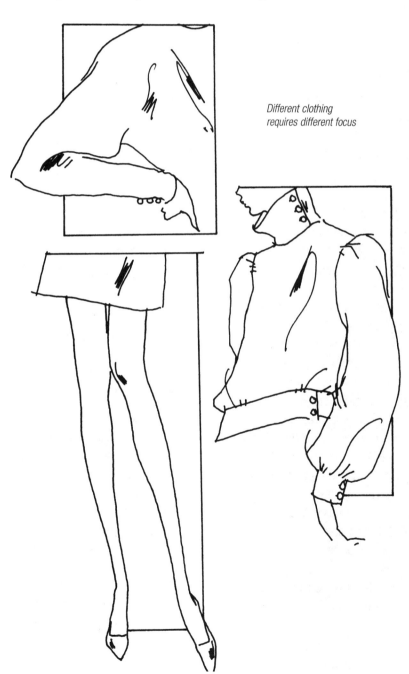

Different clothing requires different focus

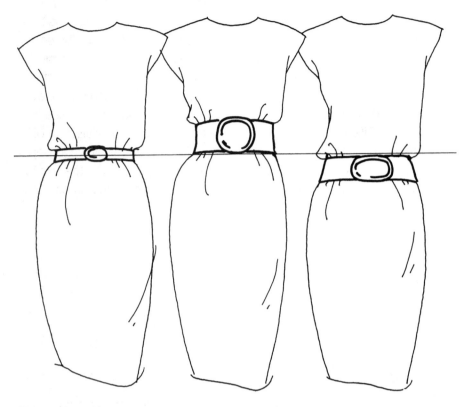

The same dress with three different waistlines

Many factors influence proportion. So, be open and flexible.

In this next section, we will discuss the fashion proportions of this century. You will see that in each decade, different parts of the body became more or less focused upon, for example small waists or no waists; emphasis on the breasts, the hips, or the shoulders; or a more curvy figure.

As new dress forms are made each year, the measurements are determined by the ideal body type of that year. When you line up size 8 dress forms over the last 10 years, you can see the most amazing variations of the same-size figure.

Clearly, the following criteria determine the "ideal" figure of a specific time:

- The model or celebrity of the moment.
- Focus on certain parts of the body, also the posture of the figure.
- Fit of the clothing and any undergarments, shoulder pads, or other devices—or lack of them.

Think back to Jean Harlow in the 1930s, Katharine Hepburn in the 1940s, Grace Kelly and Marilyn Monroe in the 1950s, Audrey Hepburn in the 1960s, Madonna in the 1980s, Princess Diana in the 1980s, Madonna in the 1990s, and Nicole Kidman and Halle Berry in the 2000s. Each is a perfect example of their time. The clothes they wore perfectly suited their look. It would be hard to imagine any one of them reversing places with each other.

The following is a very general overview of the way the fashion silhouettes of this century have changed the proportion of the body.

At the turn of the century, the body was almost completely covered. The corset gave the figure a very small waist. Skirts molded over the figure and touched the floor, often with bustles and trains. Hats were quite elaborate and gave great importance to the head. The stance of the figure took on a "S" curve. The major designers of this period were Charles Frederick Worth (the "father of couture"), Paul Poiret, Paquin, Doucet, and Fortuny.

The 1920s brought one of the most major changes to the fashion silhouette in the 20th century. Women showed their legs for the first time in this century. They threw off the elaborate corsets that gave them a very unnatural silhouette and began to wear undergarments of knitted elastic that gave their bodies a flattened, boyish look. The straight silhouette was the most popular of the period. During this time, the waistline moved down to the hips. Chanel's "little black dress"—in wool jersey or silk crepe—was the look. Other important designers of this decade were Vionnet, Lanvin, and Patou.

The 1930s brought us such glamorous movie stars as Greta Garbo, Marlene Dietrich, Joan Crawford, and Ginger Rogers. The depression made women long for the glamour that their lives did not have. The bias-cut gowns of Madeleine Vionnet gave women a very feminine silhouette. Coats were trimmed with fur, lounging pajamas became fashionable, and suits were smartly tailored, with hemlines longer at the beginning of the decade and shorter at the end. The look was glamorous and chic. The zipper was born. Schiaparelli, Molyneux, Grès, Mainbocher, Balenciaga, and Lelong were among the important designers of this decade.

World War II brought major changes to the world of fashion. When the Germans occupied France, most of the couture was at a standstill. War-time restrictions on fabric gave clothing a short, tailored silhouette. Adrian gave movie stars a padded-shoulder silhouette, clothing had a definite "military" influence, and the hat became one of the really creative parts of an outfit. Platform shoes brought new emphasis to the legs. In 1947, Christian Dior's New Look returned to the Paris couture the extravagance the war had taken away. Boned bodices, cinched waists, padded hips, and yards of nearly ankle-length skirts with elaborate petticoats brought the fashion silhouette back to almost what it was at the turn of the century. Other French designers of this decade were Jacques Fath, Maggy Rouff, and Pierre Balmain. The 1940s also gave American fashion a solid start. Designers such as Pauline Trigère, Norman Norell, Hattie Carnegie, and Charles James put Americans on the fashion map.

Redfern 1905

Chanel 1927

Schiaparelli 1935

Adrian 1945

Vionnet 1933

Charles James 1950s

Cardin 1961

Courrèges
1964

Balenciaga 1957

Dior 1947

Gernreich 1968

Saint Laurent 1978

Montana 1985

Saint Laurent 1977

Perry Ellis 1982

Armani 1990

Armani 1995

Ralph Lauren 2003

Versace 2003

Proportion and the Fashion Figure

The silhouette of the early 1950s gave us a fitted-waist shirt-waist, a more relaxed blouson, and a fitted sheath. It was in 1957 that fashion was to have its next revolution—Balenciaga introduced the chemise or sack dress. These dresses hung straight, had no waistline, and the hemline was beginning to shorten toward the knee. The chemise, (also interpreted by Givenchy, as well as the "trapeze" introduced by Yves Saint Laurent) allowed the clothing to fall away from the body, which now moved within the garment. The silhouette was geometric and the body was lost under these shapes. Other important designers of the 1950s were Americans—Claire McCardell, Anne Klein, Bonnie Cashin, and Vera Maxwell, who were bringing sportswear into its own.

The silhouettes of the early 1960s were continuations of the late 1950s—lightly fitting the body and slowly inching their way shorter. Such designers as Pierre Cardin in Paris, Valentino in Italy, and James Galanos in America were beginning to make their marks.

It was in the middle of the 1960s that fashion would be rocked by another revolution—the miniskirt. It was introduced by Mary Quant in London, André Courrèges in Paris, and Rudi Gernreich in America. Legs were now the focal point of the body. Pantyhose and boots were the new breakthroughs. Skirts were shorter than ever, undergarments were minimal, and hair was either blunt cut by Vidal Sassoon or piled with artificial falls. Rudi Gernreich was America's new avant-garde designer, who also gave us the first topless bathing suit.

Models of all ethnic persuasions were on the runway and in the magazines. Youth was the look. Dress codes were being broken. Pants were becoming acceptable. Until this time, the influential designers often dictated the acceptable fashion look. Designers were beginning to take their inspirations from what was happening in the streets, the discos, the movies, and the music. Young people were dressing their own way, combining the new with thrift shop finds, and making their own dress codes. Trends were coming from the street "up" rather than from the couture "down."

Twentieth-century fashion proportions

The 1970s gave us options—mini, midi, or maxi. Three silhouettes at the same time, plus the option of pants. It was in 1976 that Yves Saint Laurent designed his Gypsy Fantasy collection and the long length was the look for many years to follow. Layers and layers of soft fabrics—quite the opposite of the cookie-cutter look of the 1960s. Other prominent designers of the 1970s were Geoffrey Beene, Bill Blass, Oscar de la Renta, and Halston.

The 1980s gave us a "power dressing" silhouette—padded shoulders, big sleeves, and shorter skirts. Clothing was rich and extravagant. However, the "punk" look from London was in marked contrast to the rich look of Nancy Reagan. The punk look was defined by purple hair and safety pins, leather clothing and chains. Suddenly, rock stars were setting the fashion and Zandra Rhodes was right on target with her interpretations of this look from London where it began. Jean-Paul Gaultier, Claude Montana, Kenzo, and Karl Lagerfeld gave us fashion from Paris, Issey Miyake and Commes des Garçon's from Japan, and Ralph Lauren, Donna Karan, Calvin Klein, Perry Ellis, and Norma Kamali from America.

One of the most important contributions of the 1980s came from Milan—Giorgio Armani, whose relaxed, softly man-tailored silhouettes brought us into the 1990s.

The 1990s brings many silhouettes at the same time—short and long, opaque and sheer. Women combined combat boots with georgette skirts. Rules once again were broken. Madonna brought underwear into the streets—her bustiers, designed by Gaultier, made shock acceptable.

At the beginning of the 21st century, body perfection ruled. Whether it was spending hours with a personal trainer or actual cosmetic surgery, the human body reached toned flawlessness.

Movie stars and rock singers appeared in bias cut clinging evening gowns from Versace or Galliano, exposing more of the body than we had ever witnessed. Breasts were accentuated and the navel was exposed with low-rise pants or skirts.

Where will the next fashion revolution come from?

It will come from your world.

When you line up all the silhouettes of this century, you see that in less than one hundred years the silhouette changes to such a degree that is seems as though the body keeps reinventing itself. You also see that fashion is the relationship of the figure to the clothing. Not the body alone—not the clothes alone—both together. They are not separate.

Let's take this one step further.

Here we have the same figure divided in half—the left side represents the 1960s and the right side represents the 1970s.

It is evident that at different time periods certain parts of the body are more in focus than others. It is important in drawing the figure to remember that—even if it doesn't show—there is always a body under the clothing. Whether you can clearly see it or not, it determines how the clothing will hang. Fabric and fit are also determining factors.

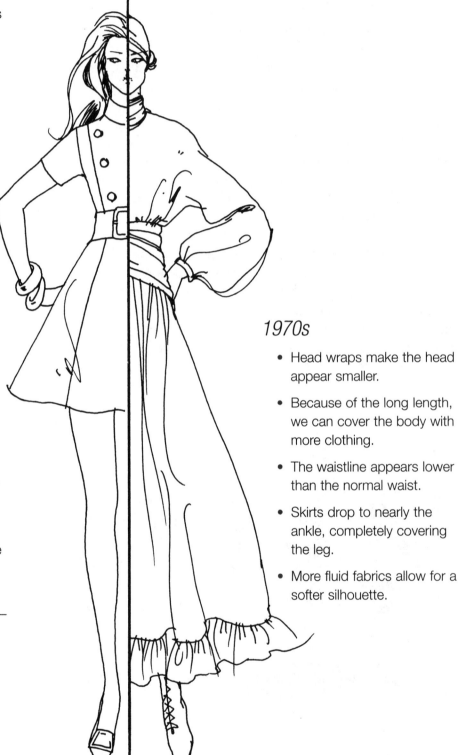

1960s

- Falls of hair cause the head to appear larger.

- Details of the dress are focused more to the top, due to the overall shortness of the dress.

- The waistline appears higher than a normal waist.

- Skirts are the shortest they have ever been. The legs are the most important part of the body.

- Dresses are very structured— fabrics are stiff.

1970s

- Head wraps make the head appear smaller.

- Because of the long length, we can cover the body with more clothing.

- The waistline appears lower than the normal waist.

- Skirts drop to nearly the ankle, completely covering the leg.

- More fluid fabrics allow for a softer silhouette.

Sometimes the body takes over. Sometimes the garment takes over. Sometimes it is more equal. When the body takes over, as in a slinky gown, the garment does not come to life until it is on the body. When the garment takes over, as in a voluminous coat, the body is merely a hanger for the clothing. But many times, it is a combination of both.

Charles Kleibacker 1969

Charles Kleibacker 1984

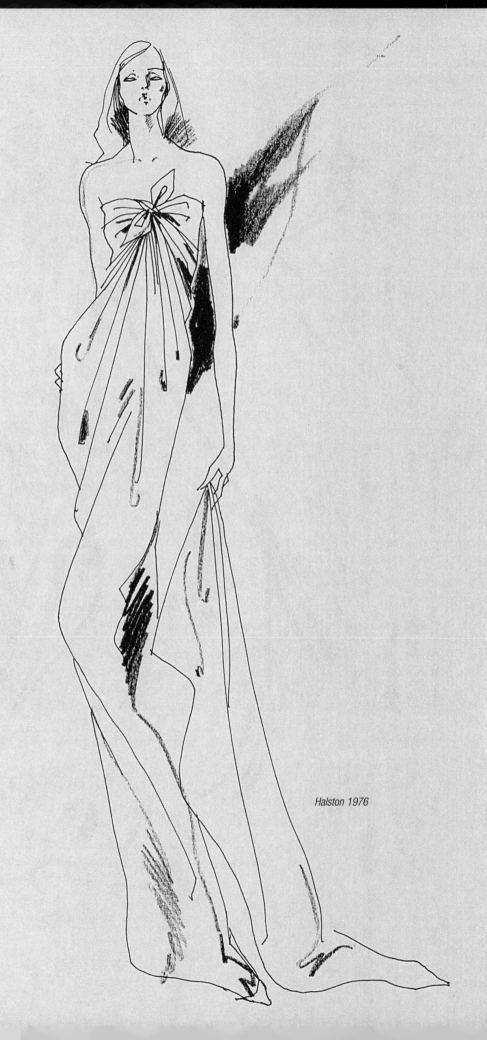

Halston 1976

2
Drawing the Fashion Figure

As discussed previously in the section on line quality in *Getting Started*, learning to draw the figure is very much like learning to write. In the beginning, you worked on lined paper, used guide lines for directions, and followed the exact rules of penmanship. The letters soon turned into words, the words into sentences, and the sentences into thoughts. After you were really confident with this process, you were able to concentrate on the content, rather than on how the letters were being written.

Learning to draw the fashion figure is a similar process. It is the way you will be able to put your ideas on paper and show the finished product of your designs. Keep in mind that a body is not an exact measurement, and as we have learned in previous chapters, there are many factors that keep changing the fashion figure from one period to another.

The figure we will study is often referred to as a *croquis* figure. A *croquis* is a working sketch. It is also a basic fashion body on which clothing can be designed and flats can be worked. It may be the take-off point for more finished art.

Following chapters will concentrate more on such specifics as balance, center front, hands, and faces.

In this chapter, we will study the factual breakdown of the fashion figure. This is the "working with lined paper" stage of figure drawing and analysis. After thoroughly understanding these principles, you will begin to slowly work your way into a simple blocking off and gestural approach to drawing the fashion figure. The ultimate goal is to understand the concept of the figure breakdown. Time and practice will give you the successful results.

Remember—everyone has their own personal growth rate and no one follows a robot-like order. There will always be one part of the fashion drawing that is easier than another. For some, the face will be easy, for others, the torso, and yet others will find rendering to be simple.

The Fashion Figure

In the beginning, there are certain rules of proportion with which you must become familiar. The figure is measured in "heads," with each head representing one inch. These heads will be used to indicate and place the different parts of the fashion figure. After some practice, all the "heads" will suddenly become a figure and after a while you will be drawing!

Blocking off a Basic Croquis Figure

We will begin by studying the breakdown of the 10-head fashion figure. First, draw a line down the paper and divide it into 10 1-inch sections. Label each line, beginning at the top with 0 and ending at the bottom with 10.

The first section will contain the head, with the chin resting at the 1-inch line.

- 1½" is the shoulder line.

- 2¼" is the apex (or high point) of the bustline.

- 3¼" is the waistline.

- 3½" is the high hip or hipbone.

- 4" is the fullest part of the hip.

- 4½" is the lowest part of the hip or the crotch. (This measurement is approximately the middle of the fashion figure.)

- 6½" is the knee.

- 9¼" is the ankle.

- 10" is the toe.

Now let's determine widths. Use the head—laid on its side—to measure the widths. This will give a guideline on how wide parts of the figure will be.

- The shoulders are approximately 1½- to 1¾-heads wide. Any particular fashion style may vary this measurement.

- The waist is approximately ¾-heads wide.

- The hips are approximately 1¼-head wide.

Now that you are aware of the sections and what they represent, you can start to block off the figure:

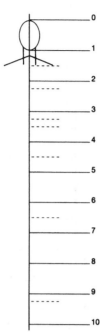

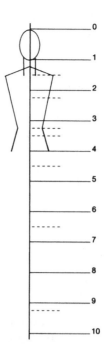

1 Draw an oval in the first section. The neck will touch the shoulder at first, but then you will have to indicate the trapezius muscles. To do this, place a shallow triangle between the chin and the shoulder. The top is ½ inch under the chin and touches the end of the shoulder.

2 To form the torso, bring a line down from the end of the shoulder to the waistline (3¼"). To indicate the hips, draw a line from the waistline to the fullest part of the hip (4").

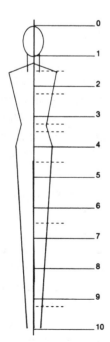

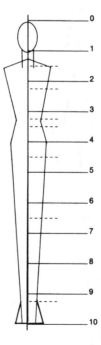

3 For the legs, draw slightly tapering straight lines from the hip to line 10. For the leg division, darken the center front line from line 10 to the crotch (4½").

4 To indicate the feet, draw a triangle on the outside of the legs. The triangle should extend from line 10 to approximately 9¼", which is the ankle.

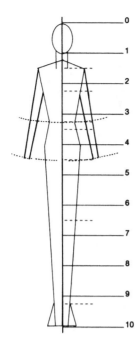

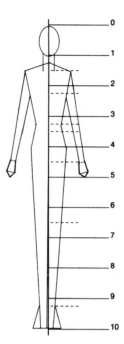

5 At the waistline and crotch, draw slightly curved lines. These lines will help in the placement of the elbow and wrist. Starting at the apex of the bustline (2¼") draw the arms with slightly tapered lines to the crotch (4½").

6 Block in the hands with rectangles and triangles. You now have a basic, blocked off fashion figure.

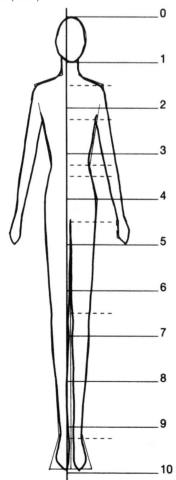

7 To round it out, place this figure under a sheet of tracing or photocopy paper and refine the oval for the head. Smooth the line from the neck over the shallow triangle. This will form the trapezius muscle and will help the neck flow into the shoulders. Round out the line from the armpit—through the breasts—to the waist.

Now, slightly round the line from the waist to the high hip and then round out the hip area. Next, draw slightly tapered lines from the crotch to the ankle. Straighten the inside of the foot, and then, for the arms, draw two slightly tapered lines from the shoulder to the wrist. Last, blend the rectangles and triangles used for the hands.

You now have a basic, rounded *croquis* figure. In Chapters 9 and 10 in which the arms, legs, and face are examined in greater detail, you will learn how to develop and refine the figure with more accurate muscle and bone structure.

The Style Lines

The style lines on the *croquis* figure should correspond to the style lines on the dress form. They are extremely important in both drawing and designing clothes. To duplicate the style lines of a dress form:

 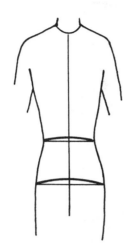

1 Indicate the base of the neck. Draw a straight line from the base of the neck to the crotch. This line represents center front.

2 Draw another horizontal line at the waist and hipline. To show the cylindrical form of the figure, make these lines slightly curved.

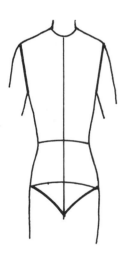 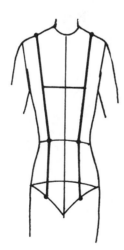

3 Draw in the armhole (or armscye) and the pantyline.

4 Dot the center of the shoulder, the apex, the waist, and the hipline. Connect these dots to form the princess seam lines and indicate the apex of the bustline with a straight line.

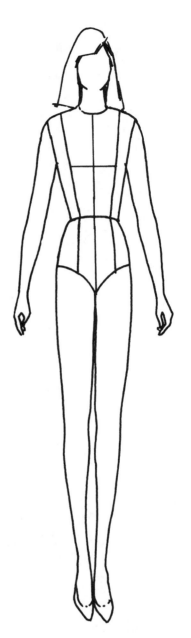

You now have duplicated the style lines of the dress form. It will be of great value to you, not only in drawing what you design, but in accurate placement of the fashion details.

Now that you have learned the "alphabet" and the "penmanship" of the fashion figure, with time and practice, you will be able to begin to develop the "content."

Your ultimate goal should be a relaxed, flowing, and luxurious figure. It should never look overworked—regardless of how much time it takes to draw. The garment and pose should be in perfect harmony with each other, and it should, above all, have your own vision and point of view.

Karl Lagerfeld/Chanel 2000

3

The Balance Line

To achieve a figure that will be "standing"—and not falling over—you must understand the "balance" line. The balance line is the imaginary straight line that drops from the pit of the neck to the ground. It never bends or goes more to one side or another—it is always absolutely straight.

As an exercise, analyze the balance lines in photographs from fashion magazines or catalogs. Gather clear photos of models in simple poses and stay away from highly distorted or exaggerated poses. With a marker, indicate the balance lines in color. Indicate the high hips and supporting legs with another color.

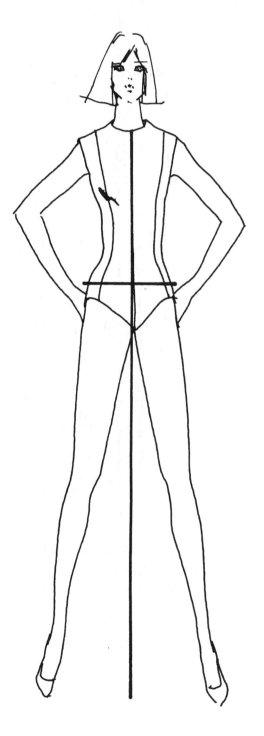

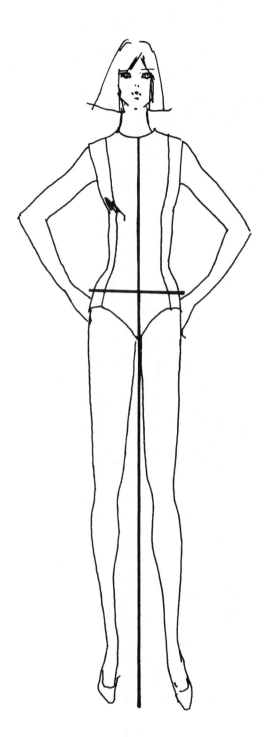
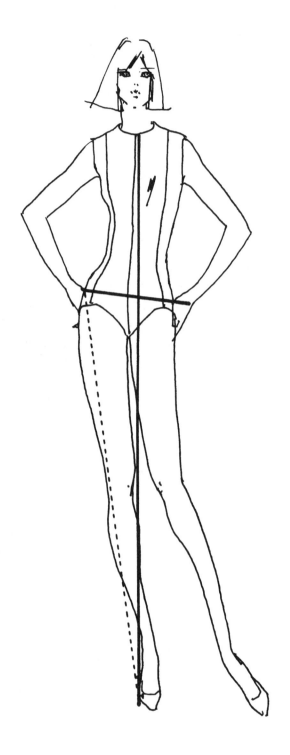

When the figure is standing with equal weight on both legs—either opened or closed—you will notice that the hips straighten out and the balance line falls between the legs.

When the figure puts more weight on one hip than the other, the high hip supports the leg that balances the figure. This supporting leg begins at the high hip and angles down to touch the balance line. The supporting leg is always at an angle—it is never straight. Also, some part of the foot should touch the balance line.

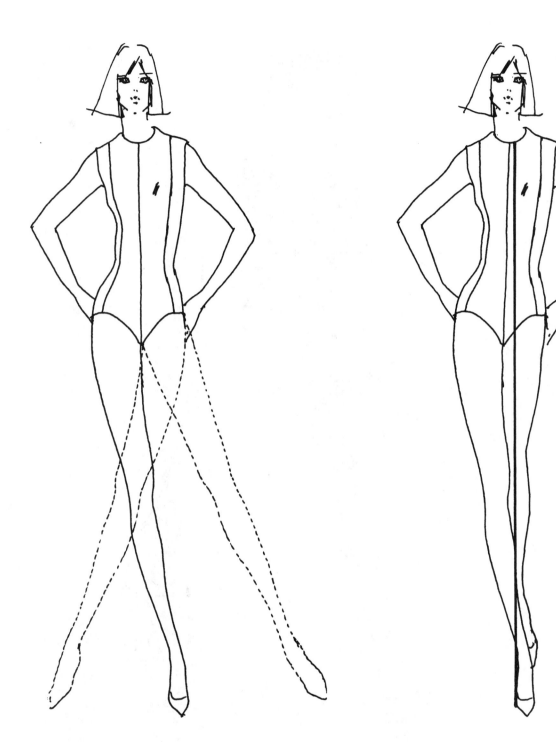

If you place the weight all on one hip, you will notice that the supporting leg is angled. Try to move it and your drawing will surely begin to topple. You can, however, move the nonsupporting leg in many different positions, and the balance will not be affected. The nonsupporting leg is completely moveable and has nothing to do with the balance of the figure. It gives the pose an attitude.

In some photographs you will notice that the balance line is slightly off. Remember that when a model is posing in front of a camera, often she is in motion and might not have settled her weight when the photo was taken. Also, in some walking poses—especially runway shots—the supporting leg might come from the low hip. However, these are exceptions. Keep in mind that each individual pose may have its own special rule.

Norell 1968

4
Center Front

Think about the way your nose relates to your face—
it divides it in half. You can look in the mirror and see
that your eyes are on either side of it. If you turn your
head, you see that the nose is no longer dividing your
face in half: more of your face is
on one side and less is on the
other. You know, however, that
your nose is and will always be
the center of your face. It is
the "center front" of your face.

The body also has a center
front. Clothing has a center
front. It is so important, that
even if it is just the slightest bit
off, every detail of the garment
will be drawn incorrectly. All
clothing is balanced from the
center front, as are all such
details as pockets and buttons.
It is the middle of every garment and the middle of every
independent part of the garment, such as the sleeves,
skirt, pant legs, and so
forth. The center front of
the body or garment moves
as the body moves. It is a
straight line from the neck
down to the feet or the hem
of the garment.

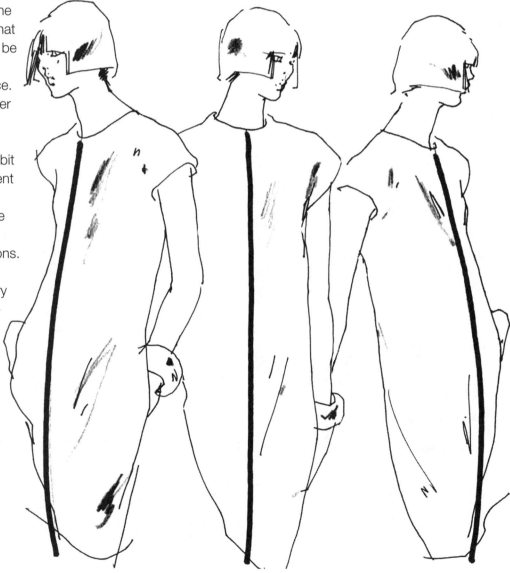

In a dress that is viewed full front, there is only one center front. When you add sleeves, you now have three centers: one on the body and one for each sleeve. When you add pants, each leg has its own center front (the crease lines might help you to see these center front lines because it is the center of each pant leg).

On a front view, the center front of each sleeve is on the outside edge of each sleeve. In a two-piece dress, the top part has a center and bottom part has a center. It might seem to you that one center front line will be enough, but for accuracy, draw it as two separate units: first, from the shoulder to the hem on the top part, and second, from the waist or hips on the bottom part.

Additionally, as the figure turns profile, the center front becomes the outside edge of the garment.

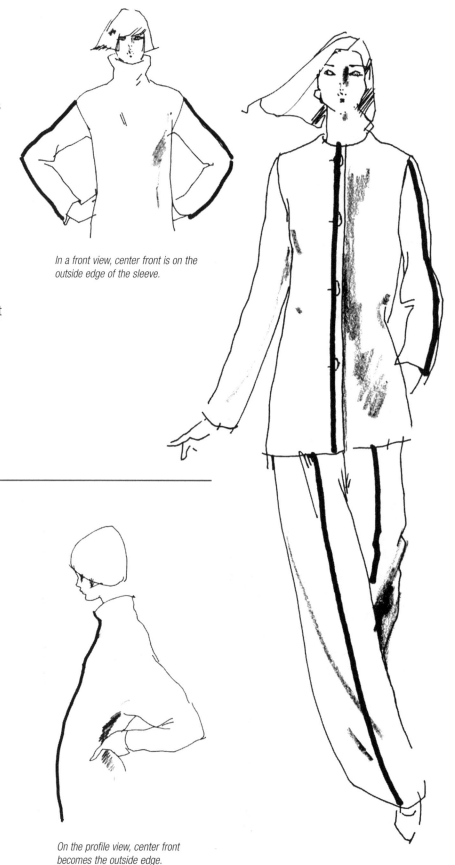

In a front view, center front is on the outside edge of the sleeve.

On the profile view, center front becomes the outside edge.

Each part has a center front.

Center Front and the "V" Neck

Center front is most evident on a dress with a "V" neck. The point of the "V" is exactly in the middle. As the figure starts to turn, the center—or "V" front—moves with it. The side that turns away from you becomes smaller. This side always shows the outline of the breast. The side that is near you becomes larger. It always has a straighter line, which is the side plane of the figure. It never shows the outline of the breast.

Karl Lagerfeld/Chanel 2001

Some garments combine single and double breasted

Center Front and the Turned Figure

In a turned figure, the center front follows this path:

- The pit of the neck or where the clavicles meet.

- The center of the breasts.

- The belly button.

- The crotch, or where the legs begin.

A helpful exercise is to take a marker and indicate the center front of each garment that you find in a magazine. In time, you will be able to eyeball it and find it easily, even in a difficult pose. Once center front is established on your underdrawing, most chances for error will be eliminated.

For clarity of this principle, let's look at a bustier. If you study the center front in a bustier, you can see:

- The underwires meet at the center.

- The boning is in the center and at each princess seam.

- The breast outline shows only on the side that is turned away.

The princess seam on the side that shows the outline of the breast is closer to the outside or far edge of the bustier. The princess seam on the side that is larger has more space before the edge. Any horizontal seam or detail also takes a slight turn to show the side of the figure.

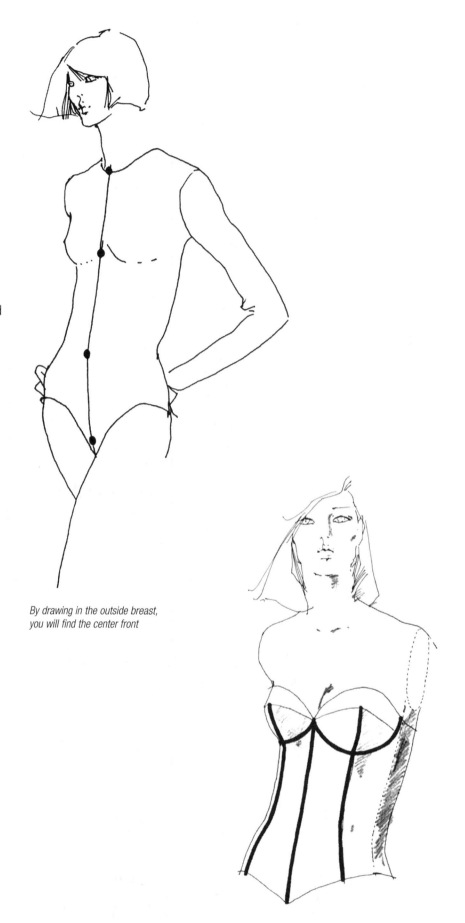

By drawing in the outside breast, you will find the center front

The side that shows the outline of the breast is always the side that is farther away from you and is always the smaller side. You will never see two profile breasts on a figure.

As the figure turns, we now begin to see the side plane of the body. To be sure of the accurate placement of the side plane, it is simpler to leave the arms off in the initial blocking stage. Draw the oval shape that the arm will fit into, and follow it down the figure. This will give you greater accuracy.

When drawing a turned figure, remember to stop drawing the center front line at the breasts, waist, and hips, even if it can be done in one line. This will help you to achieve greater accuracy. Additionally, every time that you hit a horizontal seam line, stop to check for accuracy, then continue.

For accuracy, stop at the breast, waist, and hips.

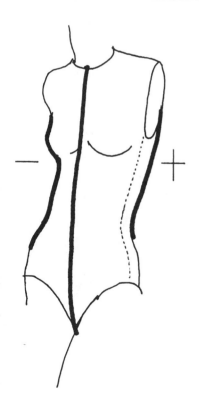 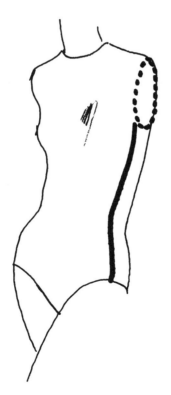 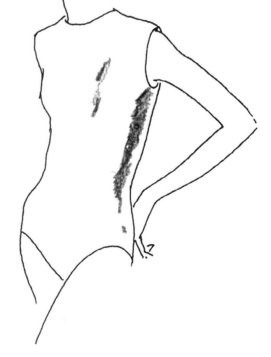

The side plane of the body.

Center Front and Garment Details

When you draw a garment detail, for example, a neckline, remember to:

- First, draw from the outside to the center.

- Then, draw from the center to the outside.

- Make sure that the line is shorter on the side away from you and is longer on the side near you.

- Check to see that the center front seams take an upward curve.

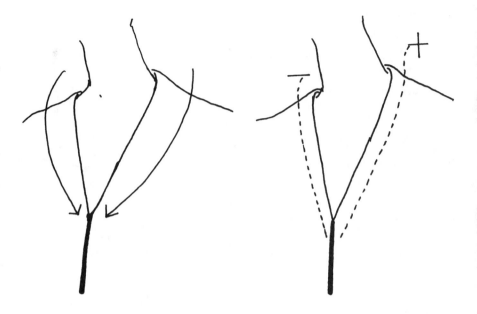

The back view has the same principles as the front, except the horizontal seams take a downward curve.

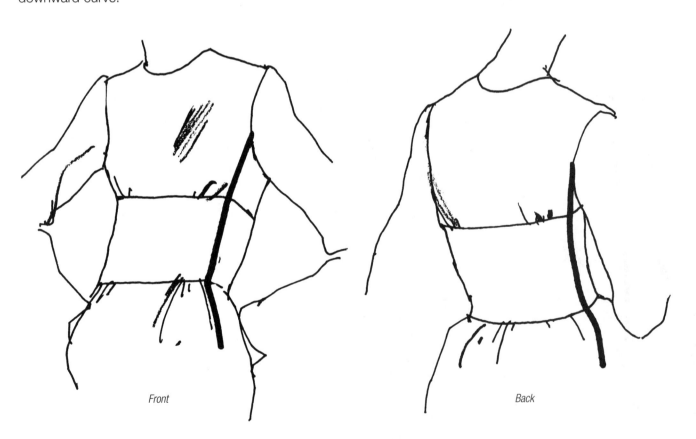

Front

Back

To apply the principle of center front when drawing clothing, let's look at buttons and closings.

In a single-breasted garment, the buttons are placed down the middle of the body, or center front. The closing goes to the side of the center front.

- The only time buttons align with center front are in:

- Buttons and loop closings.

- Zippers.

- Cardigan jackets.

- Frog or toggle closings.

Your drawing can be a shirt, a coat, or a jacket. It can have one button or a dozen. This rule never changes.

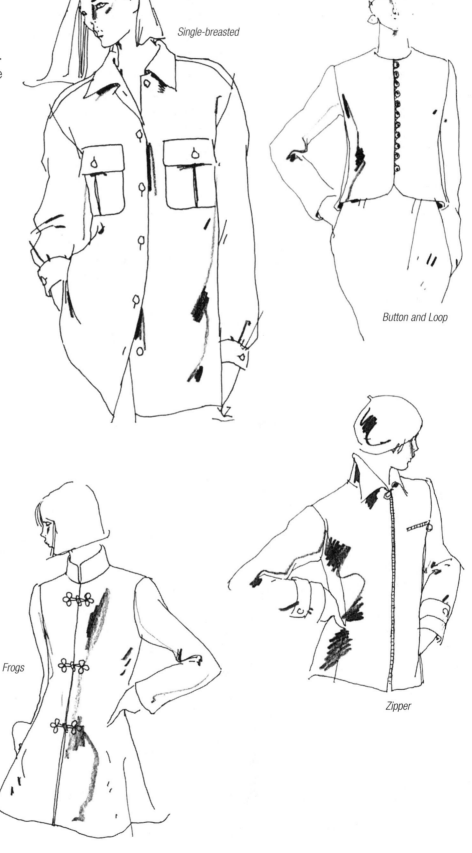

Single-breasted

Button and Loop

Cardigan

Frogs

Zipper

In a double-breasted garment, the buttons are an equal distance from the center front, regardless of how close or far apart they are. There are double-breasted garments—for example, a blazer—where there are two equal distances between the buttons.

Today, closings can be designed with many different options, but the buttons should always relate to the center front. Additionally, the double-breasted rules also apply to side closings—except the non-working buttons are left off. As the figure in the double-breasted garment turns and you sense the perspective of the body, notice that the shape of the buttons on the near side are circular and the shape of the buttons on the far side are oval. In a near-view profile of a single- or double-breasted garment, the buttons look as if they are placed on the outside edge.

Regardless of the style, the amount of buttons, or the spacing, remember that if center front is wrong—every garment detail will be wrong. In fact, if your drawing has something wrong with it and you don't know what it is, there is a good chance that the center front is incorrect.

In a double-breasted garment, the buttons are an equal distance from the center front.

Also, the center front that you find when you first begin to draw a figure may not always be correct. Keep adjusting it until it is perfect. Keep erasing on your under drawing until it is exact. Spend time practicing and working this out until you perfect your technique.

The figure as it turns

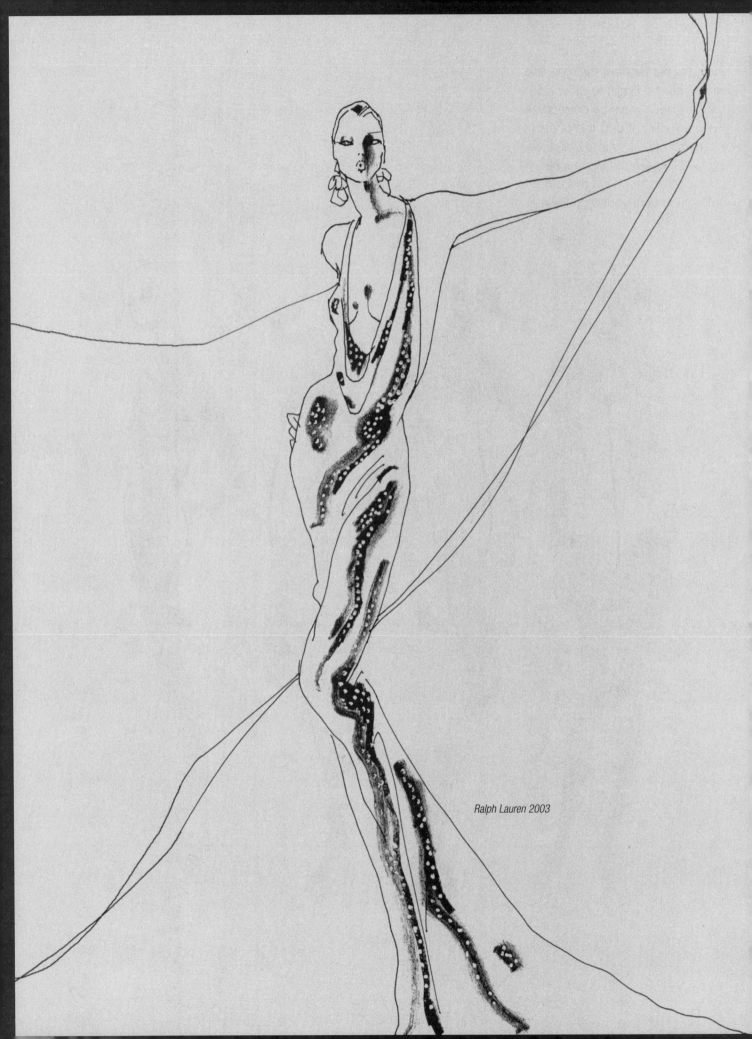

Ralph Lauren 2003

5

Gesture—
Movement or Action Lines

Ultimately, we want our fashion figure to have a wonderful flow and movement. A fashion figure should look as if she danced onto the page—as if there is no effort at all in her gestures. In this chapter, we will study the movement or gesture lines, which help to determine both the movement and the pose of the figure.

Remember, to make a fashion drawing look effortless requires a lot of effort, knowledge, and practice.

To help you understand the movement or action lines of a figure, open up a fashion magazine and start to draw flowing lines over a fashion photograph, in what you think the direction or gesture of the figure might be. What will happen is that you will begin abstractly to register how the figure could move.

Once your eyes begin to sense a
certain flow, you can begin to get
more specific and analyze the
movements. Depending on the
pose, the figure may seem:

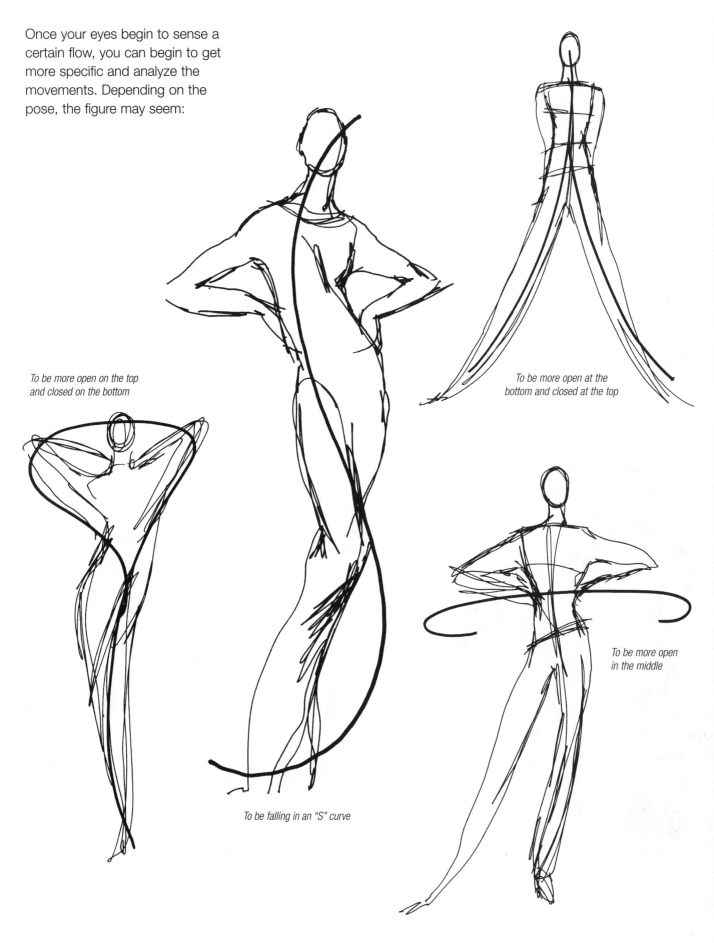

*To be more open on the top
and closed on the bottom*

*To be more open at the
bottom and closed at the top*

To be falling in an "S" curve

*To be more open
in the middle*

Next, duplicate these movements on paper by using your finger as a drawing tool. Let your fingers sense the gesture, movement, and action. Now, with a pencil or marker, duplicate these gestures on paper.

Don't even think about accuracy. This is simply an exercise and you can throw the end results away. When you begin to feel confident with this exercise, start to actually draw the gestures on paper. Start with your first reaction and keep drawing over the previous lines, almost as if you were building to the figure's gestures from scratch. Start observing the relationship of one body part to another. Aim for more and more accuracy. The following four sections are short studies of different types of figures in various gestures or movements.

The "S" Curve

This is one of the most classic and fashionable gestures or poses. It is also a very important movement—the crunch and stretch.

From the front view, the figure will have a pronounced high hip movement. The line from the head to the high hip, and from the high hip to the resting foot will form an "S" curve. Notice how the side of the figure with the high hip slightly crunches between the breasts and hips, and stretches on the opposite side.

Stretch side

Crunch side

The "S" Curve and the Turned Figure

In the turned figure, the head sits slightly forward on the neck, the torso angles toward the front, and the hips angle inward and flow into the legs.

The "S" curve movement is particularly beautiful in any slim or sleek-fitting garment. It also works well in flowing evening clothes, because it allows the fabric or any details to flow off the figure.

The Open Top and Closed Bottom (The Inverted Triangle)

In this gesture, the main emphasis is at the top of the figure, with the arms being the focal point of the pose. They can be stretched out or up. One arm might be up and the other down, or in any position in which the top of the figure occupies more space than the bottom. This movement is wonderful for silhouettes that have drama or bulk at the top of the garment, for example, a dolman or kimono sleeve.

The Open Bottom and Closed Top (The Triangle)

In this gesture, the focus is on the lower half of the figure. The legs might be in a more open or animated pose. The silhouette of the pants or skirt might be the dominant feature of the garment. This gesture works well on sportswear and more casual clothing.

The Open Middle
(The Diamond)

You will use this movement many times. It can have one or both hands on the hips. The focus of the movement or pose is in the center of the figure. This works well for most garments, because it allows a negative space on the side of the figure so the fit of the garment is clear. This gesture works with casual sportswear, as well as more formal clothes.

Remember, with practice, your figures will have an easy and flowing movement.

Gaultier 1998

The Cutting Method

The cutting method will allow you to create a "live" model on paper. Because you will be moving the body section by section, you can create simple poses and actually see how the hips, shoulders, arms, legs, and torso move. It will help train your eye to spot errors in balance or proportion, and because you will be able to correct these errors just by moving the figure parts, you will more easily understand what went wrong initially.

Once you have drawn a rounded croquis figure that you are pleased with, make several photocopies of it. You will also need scissors and a roll of clear tape.

Cut the *croquis* figure in the following places:

- The head and neck—label it 1.

- The torso—label it 2.

- Each arm from shoulder to shoulder—label both 3 and 3a.

- From elbow to hand—label both 4 and 4a.

- The hip area—label it 5.

- Each leg from hip area to knee—label both 6 and 6a.

- From knee to end of foot—label it 7 and 7a.

- The foot—label it 8 and 8a.

These labels will help you avoid confusion when you cut up the figure and move it around.

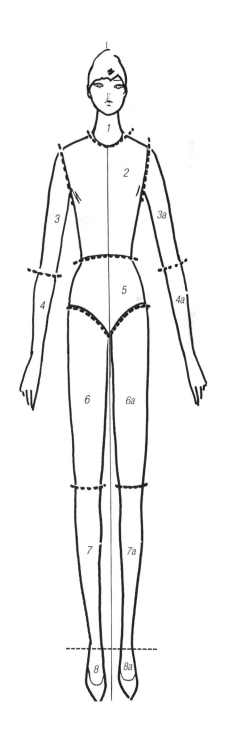

Next, on a clean sheet of paper, draw a line down the center—this will represent the balance line. Lay the pieces of the figure back on this line to look as it did before it was cut. Move the hip area to create a high hip. Connect the resting leg to touch the balance line. Lightly tape into place—the figure is beginning to "move."

Move the nonsupporting leg to different positions. Move the figure so that it shows different actions, for example, walking or running. Change this leg to create different poses. It is clear that this leg can be moved without the figure losing its balance. It will give the figure an "attitude" that is sporty, elegant, sophisticated, and so forth. Also, work the arms to different positions and blend all the open areas. After becoming familiar with this method, you can cut the hands and feet to get even more subtle positions.

When you achieve the pose you like, place a clean sheet of paper over it, redraw the figure, and make any necessary changes. Work with the other photocopies to try to duplicate simple, front-view poses from magazine photographs. This will give you a pose file for future use. If you need a smaller or larger size of the same figure, you can reduce or enlarge it when you photocopy it.

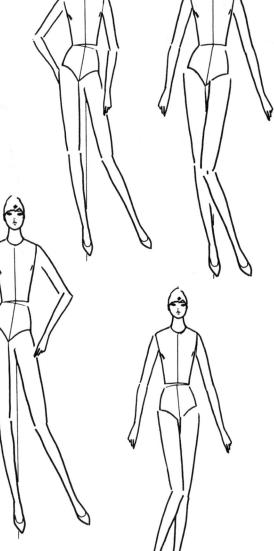

Special Exaggerations

It is important to distinguish between exaggeration and distortion. Exaggeration is enhancing the mood. It's that extra "something" that takes a drawing from ordinary to extraordinary. On the other hand, distortion is taking a single area—for example the legs—and drawing it so far out of proportion that the figure is deformed and the clothing is distorted.

As shown in previous chapters, sometimes a specific garment calls for a figure that needs a bit more length in the torso for an extravagant top, or a bit more leg for a short skirt or voluminous gown.

Using the cutting method, you can stretch the figure a bit in any area that needs this special exaggeration. In reality, what you are doing is choosing a model who will have a longer waist, a longer leg, or whatever is needed to "wear" that particular garment perfectly.

The cutting method can help you to see how a figure can be exaggerated, without the use of a live model. It allows you to see mistakes and correct them, as well as to keep the proportion accurate while emphasizing that area of the garment that has special focus.

Distorted

Exaggerated

Keep in mind that there is never one exact way or method of drawing. You should be open and flexible to determine what works for you and how you can use an exercise (such as this one) as a taking-off point to further develop your skills and abilities. Also, this method makes combining several figures easier, as you are able to easily manipulate the arms and legs to make the composition work better.

The cutting method helps when combining figures in a layout.

Cardin 1970

7

The Tracing Method

I both use and teach the tracing method. It produces very good results, because there is always an under-drawing from which to work. You are actually doing a direct drawing, but because there is a guide underneath to help you, there is a greater chance of doing a better, more accurate drawing.

Direct drawings often present problems. When the head is correct, the arms might be too long. When the arms are right, the waistline might be too high, and so forth. The tracing method helps eliminate these kinds of problems. In the beginning, it will enable you to make corrections in proportion, details, line, and so forth. At the more advanced levels, it allows a refining of the figure or pose.

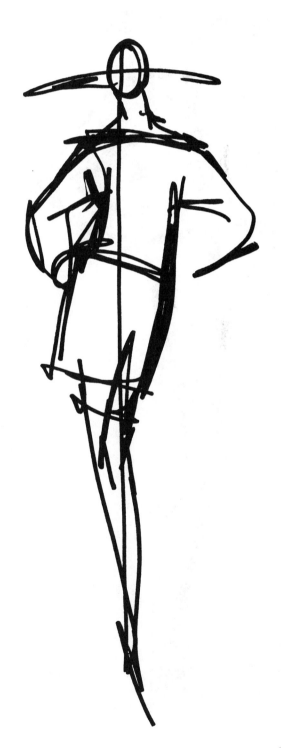

Begin by blocking a figure. Using this figure as a guide, slip it under a piece of tracing paper or all-purpose paper. You should be able to see through the paper slightly. If it is too transparent, slip it under two or more sheets. Draw as if it was a direct drawing, except you have a guide. Do not think of it as tracing.

If you are not pleased with the results, make corrections. Keep repeating this until you have a finished sketch that is correct enough to render.

Because you are always working with an underdrawing, you can allow yourself to feel secure and relaxed and consequently the art will look fresh and spontaneous. This method is also helpful in correctly placing plaids, stripes, prints, or construction details on the clothing.

Please note that if the paper is not transparent enough, you will need to use a light box.

Donna Karan 1999

8
Simple Blocking of the Figure

To learn how to draw a fashion figure, you begin by following established rules, which are guidelines for learning. Rules, however, are different than facts. Facts give you knowledge and accuracy, and while rules are helpful in the beginning, later on they can be unproductive. If too many rules control your art, your own reactions, points of view, and creativity are being repressed, which can lead you to produce rigid pieces of art. The ten-head figure, the cutting and tracing methods are all ways to help you along, but one day it is time to just "draw."

When you baked your first cake, you were careful that each ingredient and measurement was exactly as the recipe dictates. As you became more familiar with the entire process, you began to alter the ingredients to your own taste, and after a while, the cake became more yours than the original recipe.

A beautiful piece of art must have your own personal qualities as well. It should look effortless—regardless of the amount of work. It should be joyous—not uptight. At first, it is frightening to put aside the rules, especially if you have used them for a long time. To make it easier, ease up on the rules gradually.

Blocking off the figure is a very natural way to draw, but there is always the problem of proportion errors. I have developed an almost mistake-proof method to help solve this problem, and have found this technique to work very well.

We will start with the assumption that regardless of the height of a person, the hips are basically the middle of the body. Because a fashion figure needs extra length, we will add one head to the bottom half of the figure. This will produce a very nicely proportioned fashion figure to work with.

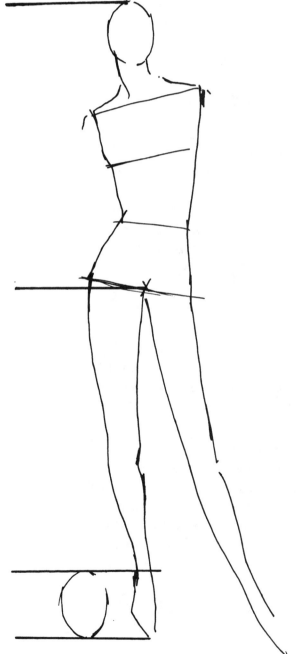

Add one head to the bottom half of the figure.

Simple Blocking of the Figure with Skirt or Dress

Now that we are familiar with the proportions of the croquis figure, we will want to give the figure some movement.

The classic fashion figure has opposing movement between the shoulders and the hips. When the shoulders move in one direction, the hips move in the opposite one. This will form an "S" curve, which gives us an agile and flowing movement.

When we study the proportions of the fashion figure, we find that the bottom half is longer than the top half. If we take a photograph of a front view action figure and fold it horizontally at the bathing suit line, we notice that the feet fall above the head.

Logically we can conclude that the figure will not be half and half, but half, half, and more at the bottom. If we add one head to the bottom half, our figure becomes half/half/ plus one head.

To block off the top half of the figure:

1 Draw in an oval for the head. It should be a bit smaller than one inch. Drop the balance line to the bottom of the page.

2 Block in the shoulder direction and the breast direction. The shoulders and breasts always go in the same direction. The distance from the neck to the shoulder will be the head measurement turned sideways.

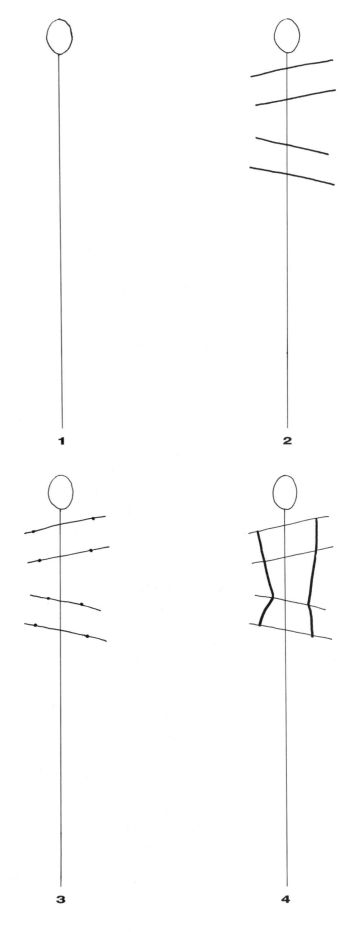

Block in the waistline and hips in the opposite direction. The waistline and hips always go in the same direction.

Notice that the shoulders and breasts are about equal in size to the waistline and hip. The area from the breasts to the waist is a bit larger.

The largest horizontal measurements are the shoulders, followed by the hips, the breasts and the waistline, which is the smallest. We will now block out the torso:

3 Dot the measurement of the head on each side of the balance line. This will give us the shoulder measurement.

- Dot in a bit smaller than the shoulder measurement for the hips.
- Dot in a bit smaller than the hip measurement for the breasts.
- Dot in a bit smaller than the breast measurement for the waistline.

4 Connect the lines. You will notice that there is a crunch on the side of the high hip and a stretch on the opposite side.

5-5a Now add a bikini bottom and neck.

This completes the top half.

6 Place one finger on the top of the head and the other at the bottom of the bikini. Repeat this measurement for the bottom half. Add the head measurement to the bottom to give us the measurement of half/half plus one head

7 Join the high hip to the balance line. This becomes the supporting leg. The supporting leg will become the back leg and the nonsupporting leg will become the front leg.

5a

5

6

7

8-8a To lengthen the figure even more, draw diagonal lines at the knee, ankle, and bottom of the foot. Draw in the nonsupporting leg between these lines. Your basic action figure should not be blocked off with the nonsupporting leg or the arms. The garment and the attitude determine the non-supporting leg and the arms.

9 Notice how by bringing in the non-supporting leg and dropping the arms, we have the basis of a very slinky figure that might work very well for a bias cut slip dress.

10 If we move out the non-supporting leg and put the hands on the hips, we have a very casual sportswear figure.

* After this proportion is established, it is possible to add 1½ heads for further exaggeration.

The possibilities are endless.

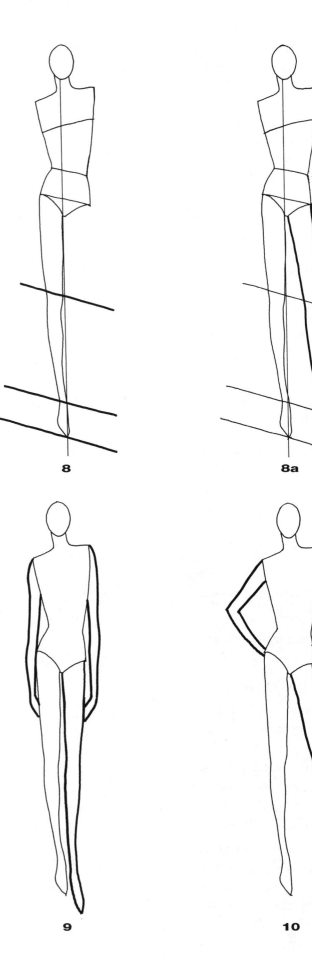

8

8a

9

10

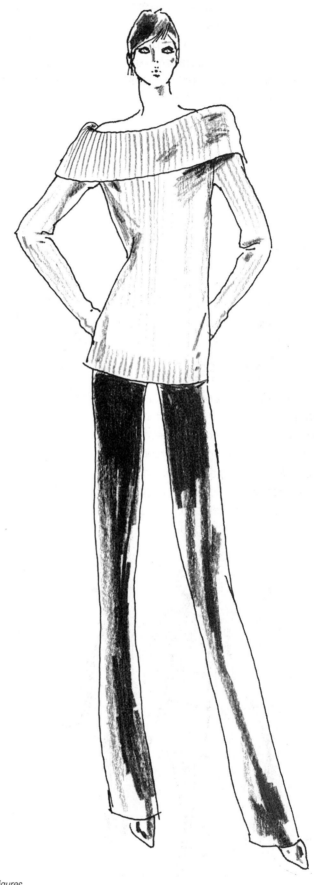

Completed figures

As an exercise, try taking a simple, realistic pose from a magazine. If you like, it can be a runway pose. Put a piece of tracing paper over the photograph and analyze what the figure is doing. Look for:

- Balance.
- Center front.
- Shoulders, waist, and hip movement.
- Supporting leg.
- Nonsupporting leg.
- Arm.

Next, go through fashion magazines and analyze the movements in the photographs directly with a magic marker. Always choose photographs that seem as though the model is directly in front of you, taking a natural pose. Avoid extreme, trendy, or artsy poses that have distorted positions or proportions. Also, don't use photos in which the photographer has created a highly personal mood. Remember, you want to create the mood.

Combining More Than One Figure

By combining the "simple blocking method" with the "tracing method," you can use single figures to create groups. It is possible to work each figure to a finish and combine them, or combine them and work them to a finish as a group.

Work with the figures individually until you achieve a pleasing composition. Cut the figures out, leaving at least one-quarter inch all the way around each figure. Tape each one in place with the others. Start developing them, and rather than thinking of a finished drawing, let each step bring them more to life. At times, this can be done with two or three steps, and at times it will take many more. This all depends on the intricacy of the fashion, the rendering, or the figure itself. However, the "finish" should take place as naturally as possible.

Simple Blocking of the Figure

63

Carolina Herrera 2003

The Turned and Profile Figures

Imagine the front view figure as 100 percent, with each side of the center front being equal. In the turned figure, the side that turns away from the center front becomes smaller. In the profile figure, the center front becomes the outline of the front of the figure.

In the front view, we do not see any outline of the breasts because the sides of the figure are the ribcage. As the figure turns, we begin to see the breast on the side that is turning away. We can also note that the side with the outline of the breast is the smaller side.

On the larger side of the center front, we are now beginning to see the armhole and the side plane of the body. Since the figure is turned, the armhole, which is round, becomes an oval shape. The supporting leg still follows the rules of the front view and the nonsupporting leg can be manipulated into various positions. When resting on the hip, the arm on the turned away side becomes slightly foreshortened.

Karl Lagerfeld/Chanel 2004

Drawing the Turned Figure

1 Begin by blocking off a front view figure, with the shoulders and hips going in opposite directions.

2 To convert this into a turned figure, we only need to concern ourselves with the top half of the figure. Indicate a line that would remove approximately one-quarter of the figure on the side of the high hip. We have already divided the center front into unequal parts.

3 Tilt the neck toward the side opposite the high hip.

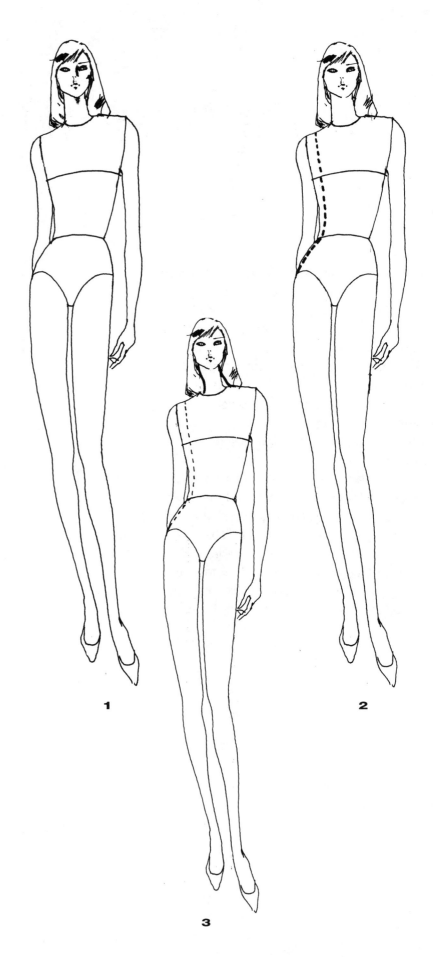

1

2

3

4 Indicate the outline of the shoulder.

5 Indicate the outline of the breast.

6 Draw down the ribcage, past the waistline and blend into the hips.

7 Completed figure thus far.

4

5

6

7

Center Front and Side Plane

To indicate the new center front:

1 Draw in the breast that is on the outer edge.

2 Bring down a line that is parallel to the outside edge and blend into the bottom of the bodysuit.

3 The second breast is drawn in between the center front and side plane.

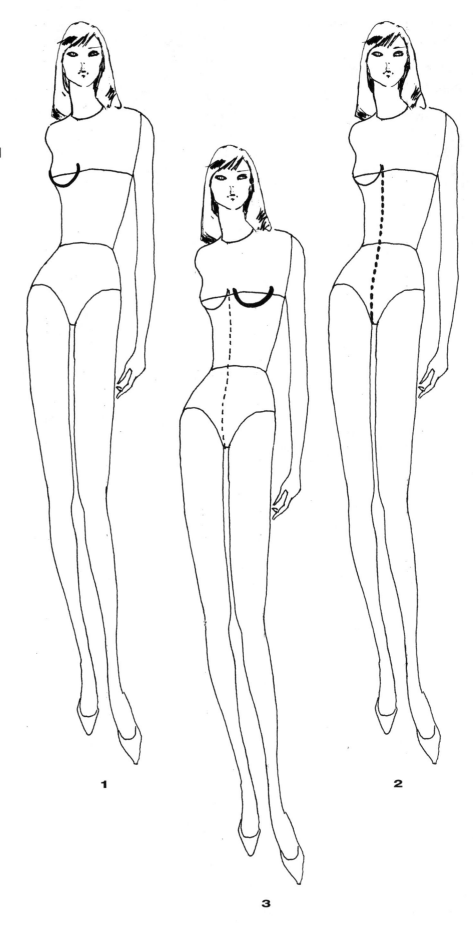

1

2

3

To indicate the side plane:

4 Indicate the placement of the side plane by drawing an oval for the armhole a bit past the existing armhole.

5 Bring down a line parallel to the outside edge to indicate the side plane.

6 Blend along the outside edge past the waist to the hip.

7 The side plane will generally be in shadow, because the arms cover the side of the body. A slight shadow will appear under the breasts in a fitted garment. The torso will be behind the arms.

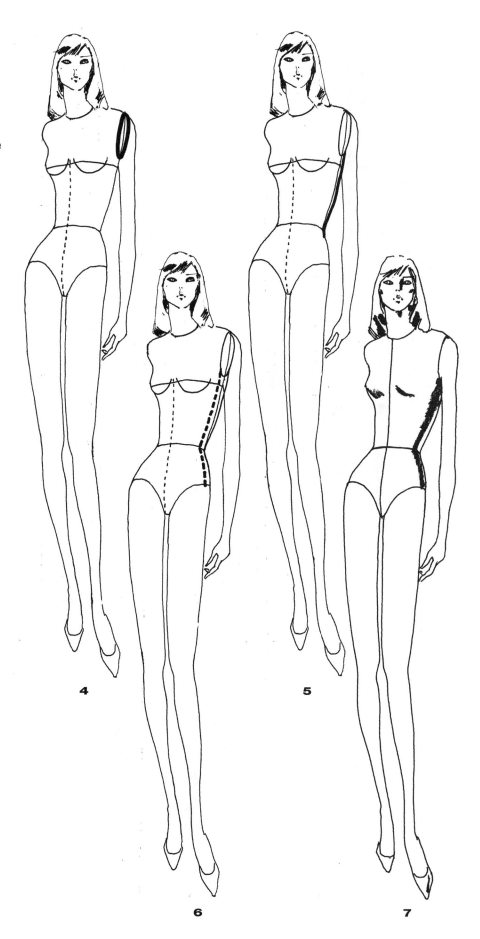

4

5

6

7

A variety of poses can be achieved by manipulating the arms and nonsupporting leg.

Drawing the Profile Figure

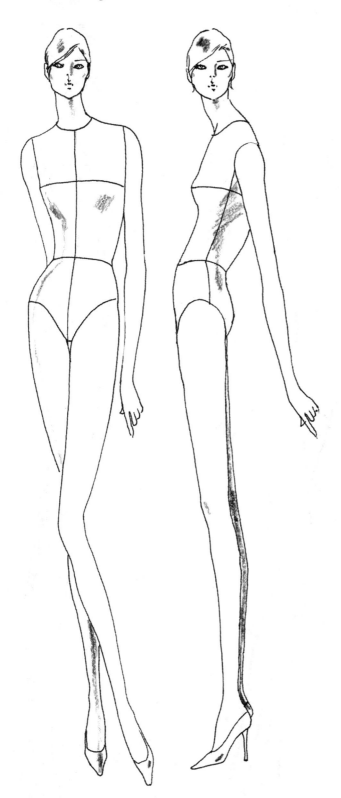

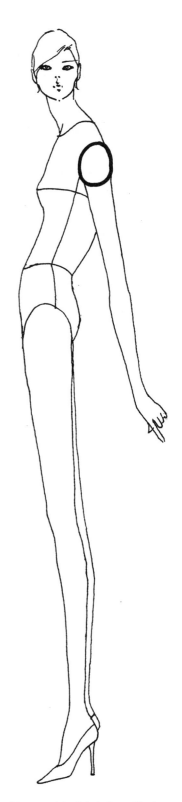

Comparison of front view and profiles figures.

The armhole turns into a complete circle in the profile view.

Drawing the Profile Figure

When the body turns completely to the side we see it in profile. The greatest portion of this figure becomes the side plane and the armhole turns into a complete circle. The neck takes on a forward angle and the hip area moves slightly forward.

1 Begin by lightly blocking off a front view figure with the shoulders and hips going in the same direction. Draw profile figure next to it. All horizontal measurements (shoulders, breasts, waist, and hips) remain on the same level.

2 The oval shape of the head remains the same. Tilt the neck towards the back.

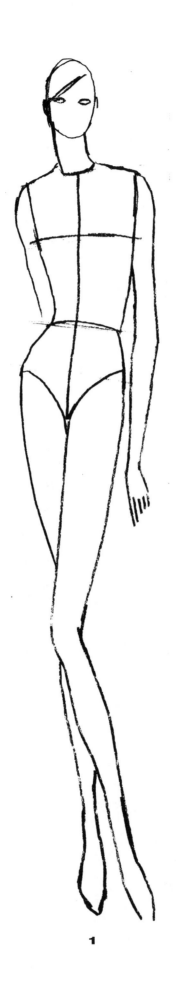

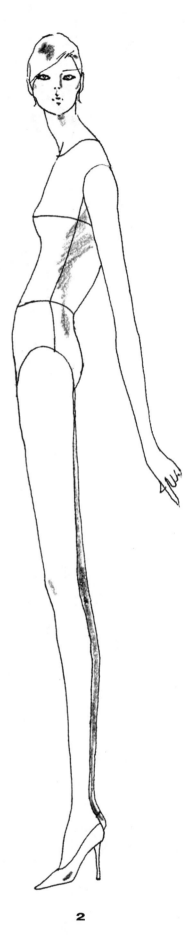

1

2

3 Draw in the breast outline at the bustline and continue to the waist.

4 Tilt the hip slightly forward.

5 Bring the leg down until it touches the balance line.

The nonsupporting leg can be manipulated into various positions, allowing for a variety of poses. To create various poses, manipulate the arms and nonsupporting leg as with the front view.

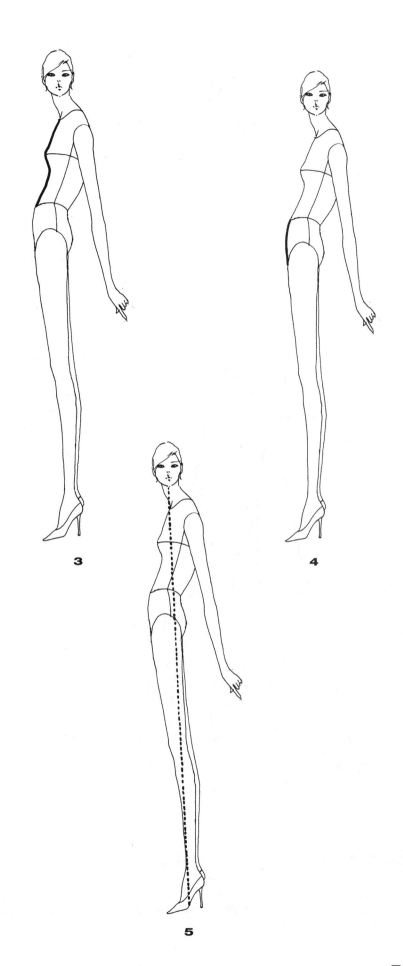

3

4

5

Poses and attitudes can be changed by manipulating the nonsupporting leg and arms.

10
The Fashion Face

When you look around, you will notice how different your face looks from any other. Yet, when you stop to analyze it, you can see that the face is composed of four basic parts: two eyes, a nose, and a mouth. Unlike clothing, which has such added details as collars, sleeves, and belts, the face is a series of shadows and openings.

The head represents about one-tenth of the body and is completely self-contained. You cannot move your nose the way you move your arms and legs. If you bend your head down, all the features stay in place.

No one is accustomed to seeing a still face. People talk, open and close their eyes, and constantly change their expressions. The hair sometimes might cover parts of the face, but at other times it frames the face, leaving it completely exposed.

The different combinations—full lips, thin lips; prominent nose, flat nose; high cheekbones, round cheeks; dark skin, light skin; frizzy hair or sleek hair— are mind boggling. And by slightly turning the head from the front to the profile, all the features seem to change.

The fashion face differs from a real face because different styles of makeup can focus on certain features and make others less important. These styles change from decade to decade and sometimes even from year to year. When drawing the face, it is extremely important to keep this focus in mind.

The fashion face is the ideal of what is beautiful at a given time. It is not a single woman, but rather a blending of all races and types, with each contributing special qualities that give us the look of the moment. Popular personalities, fashion, and the state of the world also contribute. Fashion models are chosen because they best represent that ideal.

Let's go back several decades and study how hair and makeup have changed the fashion face. Study the focus of each decade, so that you learn to give your artwork the look you wish to achieve.

1920s

The 1920s was the age of the flapper. Women were much more emancipated than they were at the turn of the century. Makeup had a painted doll look to it with Clara Bow and Gloria Swanson setting the style. There was an equal balance between the eyes and the lips, which were often cupid-bow-shaped and red. The eyes were shadowed and the brows rather thin. The cheeks were rouged, and at times a beauty mark was placed near the chin. The hair was sleek and bobbed, giving the head a very small look.

Gloria Swanson 1920s

Jean Harlow 1930s

Greta Garbo 1930s

1930s

The look was very glamorous. Hollywood ruled, and women wanted to look like movie stars. Jean Harlow was the ultimate sex goddess. She was one of the first platinum blondes to become a movie star. Her hair, in waves against her face, appeared almost white on the screen. Eyebrows were very thin, almost a line. Lips were shiny and very red. The look was completely glamorous and artificial.

Along with all this glamour, there was also the ultrasophisticated look of Greta Garbo. Very low-key and never flashy, her deep lids were very exaggerated and her sultry eyes very defined. Her lips were pointed and her hair was naturally styled and sleek.

1940s

Due to the restrictions on makeup and clothing during World War II, "Rosie the Riveter" was often the image of women working in the factories during the early 1940s. Even with these restrictions, however, women still imitated movie stars. One example is that women wanted to wear their hair like Veronica Lake did—draped in front of one of the eyes. As this was a dangerous way for factory workers to wear their hair, the U.S. government asked Veronica to cut her famous eye-hiding hair, and she complied.

However, after the war and Dior's New Look, women once again wanted to return to the glamour they once had. The fashion face of the forties had strong focus on the lips. They were very dark, often exaggerated about the natural lip line. Eyebrows were natural and the lashes mascaraed. Hair was shoulder-length and wavy or upswept at the back. Joan Crawford and Ava Gardener were the Hollywood stars who most exemplified that look.

Joan Crawford 1940s

1950s

Technicolor in the movies and Max Factor makeup were strong influences in the fifties. Hair was dyed yellow-blonde or carrot-red. Eyebrows were heavily penciled and dark eyeliner was turned up at the ends of the eyelid. Hairstyles ranged from jaw-length and wavy, to the short, Italian cut. Elizabeth Taylor, Marilyn Monroe, and Sophia Loren were excellent examples of these looks. Fashion models were aloof and artificial. They represented, along with movie stars, an untouchable ideal that women hoped to duplicate.

1960s

During the first half of the sixties, the look was elegant, lady-like, sophisticated, and polished. Jacqueline Kennedy and Audrey Hepburn best represented this look. Makeup was more natural and the emphasis was on the eyes. Brows were penciled, lips medium-colored, and the hair was styled in a bouffant or a French twist.

The youth quake in London, Biba makeup, and Vidal Sassoon haircuts were major influences in the second half of the 1960s. Eyes took over the face, with false lashes and heavily shadowed lids. Lips were pale, often a white color. Hair was cut geometrically or piled high with hairpieces called falls. Twiggy, the London fashion model, best represented this look, with her false lashes—on both the top and bottom lids—very pale lips, and short, cropped hair. Models of all ethnic backgrounds began to bring their own unique looks to the runways and magazines.

Elizabeth Taylor 1950s

Hioko 1960s

Audrey Hepburn 1960s

Twiggy 1960s

The Fashion Face

1970s

The fashion face of the seventies brought a realism and sensibility. The look was completely natural. More emphasis was placed on skin care and health. The eyes and lips shared an equal focus, and earth-toned makeup colors were used to shadow and enhance the face. The hair was simply cut and styled or permed. Models no longer were intimidating, but looked real and believable. Lauren Hutton became one of the top models of the decade and was one of the highest paid models in history. Women seriously entered the work force and were no longer painted goddesses of the past.

1980s

Depending on who you were, the eighties were either about power makeup or punk rock. On one side, the face had to compete with the padded shoulders of the clothing. Such primetime "soap" stars as Joan Collins and Linda Evans gave rich, bold makeup a new personality. Brooke Shields became one of the first supermodels. She did runway, photography, and television work and was the "image" for Calvin Klein jeans. Lips were red, eyes were shadowed, brows full, and blush defined the cheeks. The face had an even balance and hair was very voluminous or short.

At the other end were the "punks," who were in direct contrast to the rich, "establishment" look. Hair was shaved, sculpted, and held in sometimes weird shapes by mousse and gel. The makeup was made to shock, and studs and hoops were pierced through noses and lips as well as ears. Such rock stars as Madonna set the style.

Lauren Hutton 1970s

Brooke Shields 1980s

1990s and on

The fashion face of the nineties was about individuality. It had a healthy, clean, and natural look or the shock value of a rock star. Often, retro clothing determined the makeup. Fashion models were becoming the superstar faces and their makeup ranged from the waif-like innocence of Kate Moss to the sultry sexiness of Naomi Campbell. Hair was short, long, or anywhere in between. Women set their own style.

The fashion face from the end of the 1990s to the middle of the 2000s was one of opposition and contrast, and no one makeup look was dominant. There was the polished blonde of the Upper Eastside sharing the spotlight with inner city Hip-Hop, downtown Punk, and Goth looks. Tattoos and body piercing became as acceptable as cosmetics.

Celebrities such as Madonna and Nicole Kidman changed the look of their makeup and the color of their hair as often as they wanted to. The quest for perfection and the desire to remain young looking made cosmetic surgery and botox injections commonplace.

From this overview, we can see that the ideal face of one decade is very different from ones that came in the decades before or after. When drawing a fashion face, you must be aware of the structure of the face under the makeup and blend these elements into one. We are in a world where every race and ethnic group has its own identity and beauty, and consequently the possibilities of what is beautiful become even greater.

Naomi Campell 1990s

Madonna 1990s–2000s

Kate Moss 1990s

Drawing the Fashion Face

In this chapter, we are studying the face as an isolated unit. When it is drawn as part of the complete figure, however, it is much more simplified. First we will study and draw the front-view face.

Generally, the best shape to begin with is oval. Remember, the face is not round. The rounder the face, the younger the look. Babies have the roundest shaped face.

1 Block in the oval for the face. Divide the face in half, in both the length and width.

2 Think of the eyes as almond shaped and place them on the horizontal line. There is usually one eye between the eyes. There is also one-half of an eye at the end of each eye. Block it in first so that the eyes will not be too close or too far apart and will be positioned correctly.

3 Draw two lines, from the center of the oval to the outside end of the eyes.

4 Divide the lower portion of the oval (face) in half.

5 Place the mouth opening under this line, with the sides of the mouth touching the diagonal lines.

6 Draw the lips pointed for accuracy in placement. (Later, you will find it easier to round out the points.) The top lips have the points coming from the center and extending to each side of the center front lines. The bottom lip is a curved line that stretches from one end of the diagonal to the other.

7 Place a dot on each side of the center front to indicate the nostrils. These dots should be fairly close to the mouth.

8 The diagonals will give you accurate placement guides for the eyebrows and cheekbones. Draw in a slightly hooked-shaped line on the outside from the bottom of the eyes to the bottom of the nose to indicate the cheekbones. The ears are placed at the sides of the oval starting at the eyes and ending at the top of the lips.

You now have a blocked off head. Erase, correct, and refine it until the proportions look accurate.

Place this blocked off head under a sheet of photocopy or tracing paper. Make sure that you can just see through it. (Sometimes it is better to place the basic drawing under two or three sheets of tracing paper, so that it does not show through as much.) We will now study each feature separately and draw them over the underdrawing.

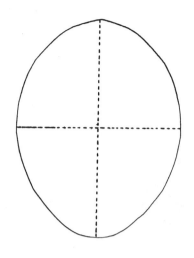

1

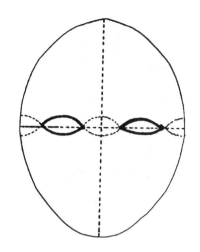

2

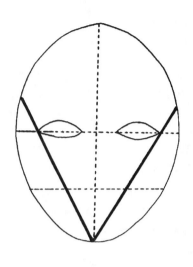

3

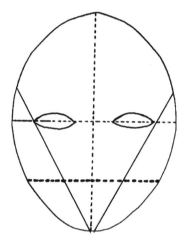

4

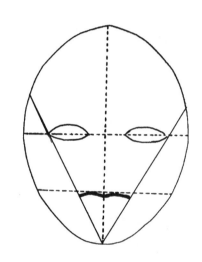

5

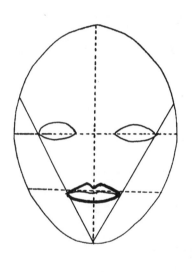

6

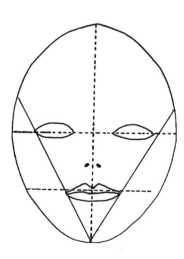

7

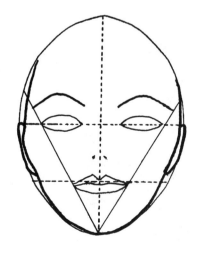

8

The Eyes

1 Refine the almond shape. Indicate a slight tear duct. The eyeball extends past the top of the eye. Never draw the full circle of the eye inside the eyelid. The pupil, which is a dark dot in the center of the eye, is at the center of the full circle of the iris.

2 The eyelid follows the general shape of the eye. It can just barely show or be very deep.

3 To give the lid depth, concentrate the darks at each end of the eye and keep the center lighter.

4 Draw lashes as a mass, rather than individual hairs. Draw the brow by feathering in the strokes.

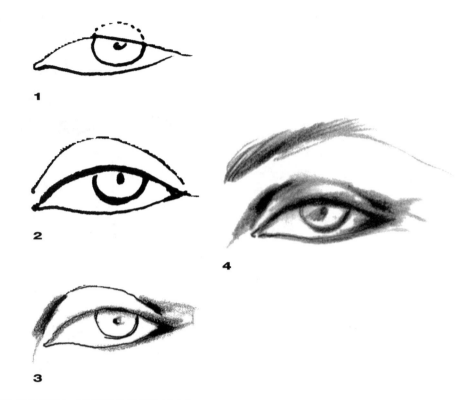

The Mouth

1 Draw the center of the mouth first as a very stretched out "M" shape. To give it depth, concentrate the darks at each end and in the very center.

2 Draw one-half of the top lip and then the other. The center of the top lip is on the center front line.

3 Draw the bottom lip. It is a bit fuller than the top. Place a shadow under the center of the bottom lip.

4 To draw a mouth that is slightly open, fill in the top half of the "M" shape. This can give the mouth more life and expression. Never draw the individual teeth.

5 When refining the lips, keep in mind that an outline will look fake. Try to shade the lip color instead.

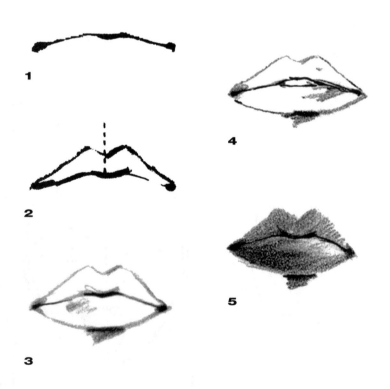

86

The Nose

The nose is a bit more difficult because it is more shadow than line. The less done on the nose the better—keep it as simple as possible.

1 The bottom of the nose is made up of three circles. The center is the largest, the sides are smaller and evenly sized. The nostrils are oval-shaped. To give the nostrils a dimensional quality, do not close the entire line.

2 One way to draw the nose is to think of it as having a shadow that is on only one side. Feather strokes at an angle to show the depth.

3 Another way is to do it as a line drawing. If you draw it in line, keep it lighter than the other lines on the face.

4 Watch the relationship between the nose and the eyes. There should be a slight space between them.

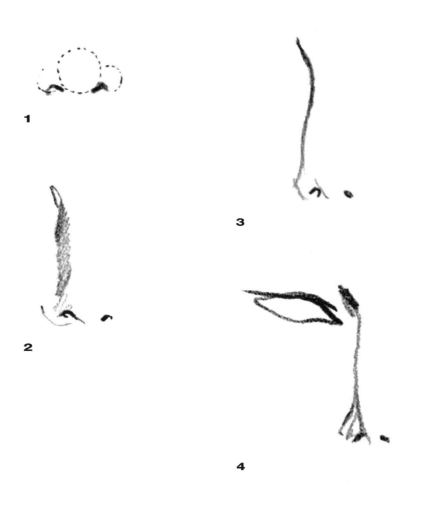

The Ears

Perhaps no other part of the body has so much going on in so little a space as the ear. Again, the less the better.

1 The ears make question-mark shapes on each side of the face.

2 From any view, indicate a light, graceful line for the inside.

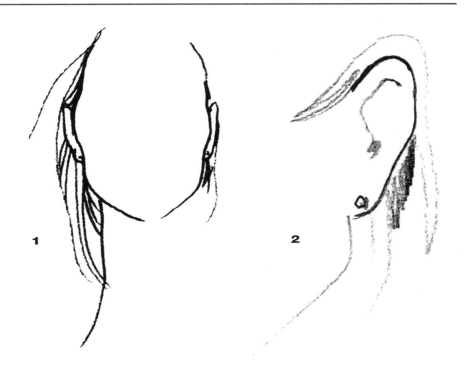

Refining the Outside Shape

This is a very subtle part of the face. It is also very individual. Some of you will want a smaller chin, a rounder shape, a squarer shape, higher cheekbones, and so forth.

The most beautiful way to finish off the fashion head is with a long, graceful neck.

1 The neck blends into the trapezius muscle before reaching the shoulders. It is indicated with a triangular shape. It does not flow directly into the shoulders.

2 Do not continue the neck directly from the jaw line.

3 Allow some space inside the jaw. Do not extend the neck from the jaw.

4 Be careful to leave enough space around the features. Otherwise, they will appear too large for the face.

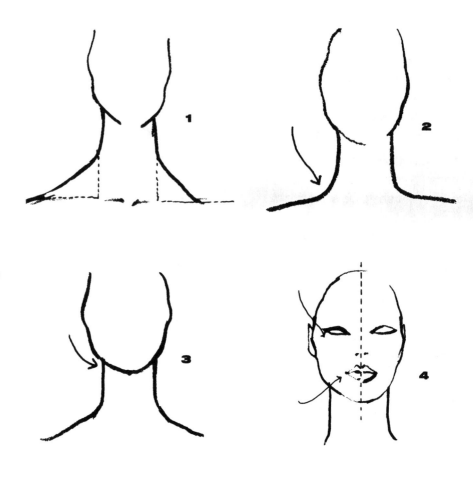

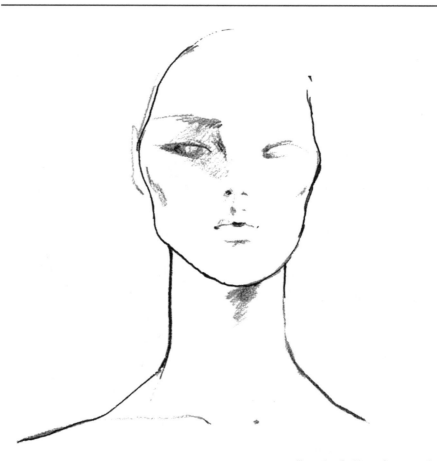

The Hair

The hairline begins approximately one-third down from the top half of the face. Establish the relationship between the style and the amount of hair to the face. Is it fluffy, frizzy, sleek, or geometric? Long, medium, or short? How does it grow from the head? Where is the part?

Generally, the darkest shadows in the hair are those closest to the face. The top and outside are the lightest. To see this clearly, study photos of blonde hair because it is easier to see these shadows.

Rather than drawing a rigid outline, think of "combing" the hair with the pencil. What are the movements you would do with a comb? Bring these movements to the paper with the pencil. This will give you the flow of the hairstyle.

Think of "combing" the hair with the pencil.

The darkest shadows are closest to the face.

Hair should not look rigid.

For smooth or wavy hair, you might start at the part and use downward movements. For permed hair, duplicate the movements that your fingers would do to bring out the frizz. Geometric cuts have an exact, definite shape. They are cut to fall into place and should be drawn with a linear, geometric outline. Hair worn piled up on the head should have a nice flow and rhythm to its line. Keep tendrils and bang wisps very light.

Never draw hair with a stiff outline. Block in the mass and volume of hair around the facial area and anywhere else that the particular style dictates. Keep in mind that the hair goes around the head. Make sure that the shadow touches the face and does not stand away from it.

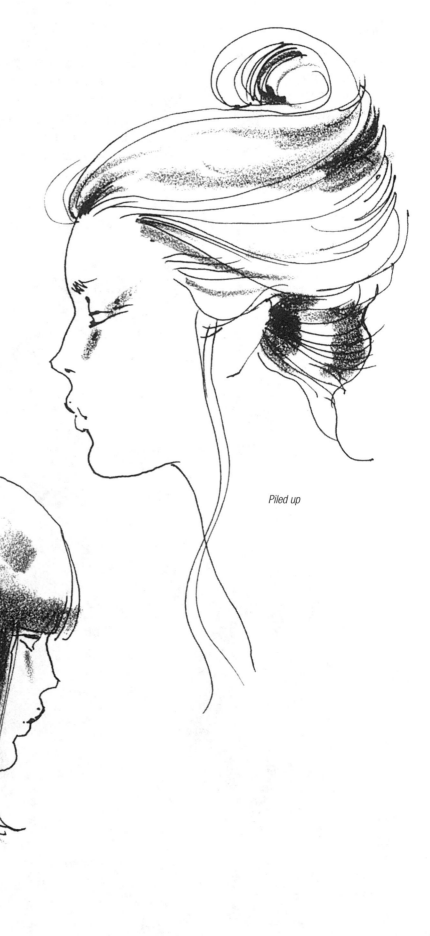

Piled up

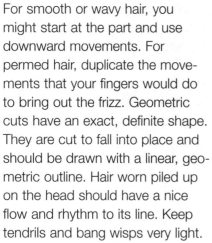

Blunt cut

Smooth or wavy

Curly

The Turned and Profile Heads

The center front line divides the front view face in half. As the head turns, so does this line. By the time the head turns profile, the center front line will be the outline of the face.

To understand the features of the turned and profile heads, let's think of these principles: as the head turns away from the front view, we begin to lose a certain amount of the front view features. When the head is turned completely profile, we lose half of the features. Therefore, the front view will represent the entire eye or mouth. In the turned, or ¾ head, we will be cutting off one-quarter of the features.

The larger portion will be placed on the side of the drawing nearer to you. The smaller portion will be placed on the side farther away. The side that shows the outline of the cheekbone is always on the side of the drawing that is farther away. With the ¾ nose, we lose the two planes, and see just one side.

Creating the turned or ¾ features

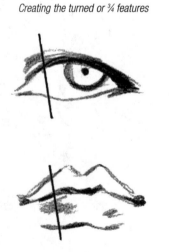

In the profile head, we cut off one-half of the eye and mouth. And we see only one plane of the nose.

You may have noticed a strong diagonal \\\\\ direction taking place in the turned head. In profile, it becomes completely diagonal \\\\\.

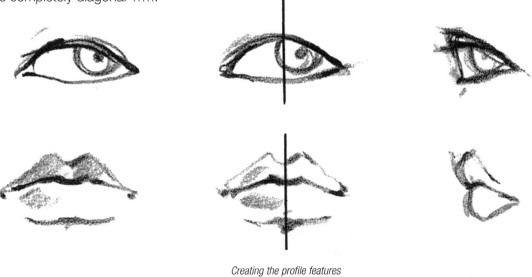

Creating the profile features

Drawing the Turned or ¾ Head

1 Draw an oval. Block off the head with the same oval as the front view, but round the guide lines. Block off the two horizontals, rounding them to show the side plane.

2 Indicate the eyes. (Remember to leave a ¾-eye between them.) Place the diagonal lines and draw the mouth. Place the larger features on the side of the drawing closest to you. Place the smaller features on the far side.

3 Indicate the nose. The bottom touches the center front and the nostril is on the other side of it. Indicate the eyebrows. Do not let the eye or mouth touch the outline. Always leave a bit of space.

4 The skull is one-half of the head turned on its side. Make sure it touches the center front line on the top of the head.

5 I find it easier to draw the outline of the face after the features are placed. The forehead hooks into the eye. The cheekbone extends from approximately under the eye to the top of the mouth and there is a small swelling in the mouth area and the chin.

6 In a turned view, the outside line of the neck stretches into the trapezius. The inside line is shorter and flows in front of the shoulder line. Notice how the neck is lower in the front than the back. Place the ear. Erase and refine until your drawing looks correct and then put it under a clean sheet of paper and redraw.

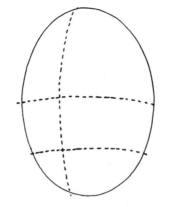

1

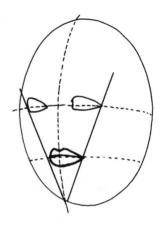

2

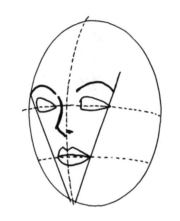

3

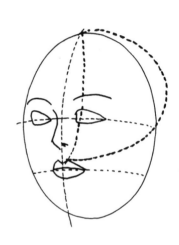

4

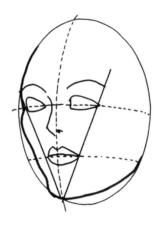

5

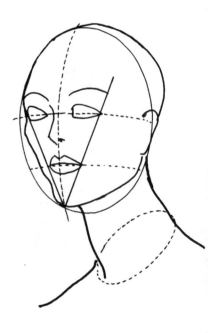

6

94

Drawing the Profile Head

1 Draw an oval. Block in the face the same as the front view.

2 Place the one-half eye slightly above the top line. The eye should be a bit less than an eye in from the edge. Indicate the nose.

3 If you draw an imaginary straight line in front of the oval:

- The forehead will touch it.

- The nose will pass it.

- The top lip will touch it.

- The bottom lip pulls away slightly from it.

- The chin is also slightly in back of the line.

4 The width of the skull is one-half the length of the head.

5 Keep a light touch when drawing the jaw. Place the ear in the area between the eye and the top lip—a bit away from the center line. On a profile view, keep the neck slightly straight as it descends from the skull. There is a slight curve to the front of the neck. The front of the neck is lower than the back. Now, add the hair as you did previously. Refine and place under a clean piece of paper and redraw.

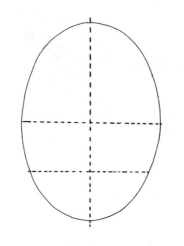

1

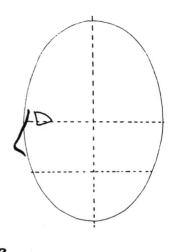

2

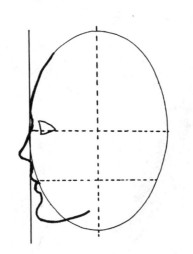

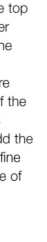

3

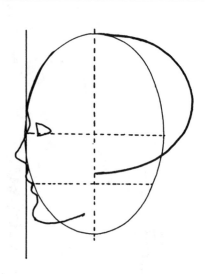

4

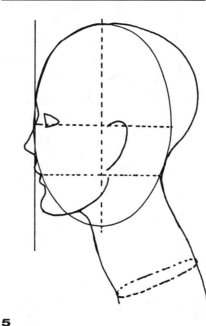

5

The Fashion Face

Tilted Heads

When the head tilts in an up or down direction, the guide lines have a more extreme curve. In a down view, the guide lines take a "arc" shape.

After you begin to draw the face with more confidence, you can practice different expressions and attitudes.

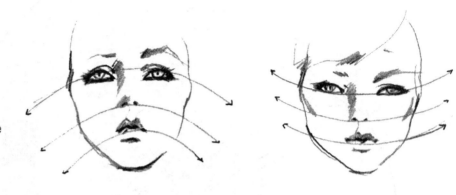

Expressions and attitudes

Ethnic Faces

As we talked about earlier, beauty does not have one standard face. Every race has different ideals for what is considered beautiful. Fashion models come from all parts of the world and represent all people. Study and observe different types of beautiful women and learn what it is that makes their faces special and unique.

Whenever possible, draw faces from life to learn structure. Study fashion faces from clear, well-lit photographs. You will probably not find everything perfect in just one photograph. Learn to work with different ones for specific features and hairstyles.

11

Arms, Legs, Hands, and Feet

Other than the realistic functions of the arms and legs that include balance, movement, and action, the arms, legs, hands, and feet give the fashion figure an attitude. Changing their positions can turn a pose from sporty to sophisticated.

Think of a figure in active sportswear, a tailored suit, an evening dress, or even a bridal gown. The positions of the arms and legs allow the pose to be perfectly suited for the garment. Yet most students think of the arms and legs as appendages that are stuck on to the torso. It is important to remember that they are attached to the torso and all the units work with each other. Both the arms and legs are broken down into similar divisions, which are upper, lower, and either foot or hand. Each unit is connected by joints and is capable of its own movement.

The muscles and bones are very similar in both the arms and legs. A long bone at the top half, two bones at the lower half, and muscles that give the outside shape a similar definition. Each is a graceful series of round and straight lines.

Arms

The arm does not hang straight. In a natural position, it has a slight curve to it. When establishing the arm, think of it as starting from the shoulder and having four divisions:

- The upper arm.
- The elbow.
- The lower arm.
- The hand.

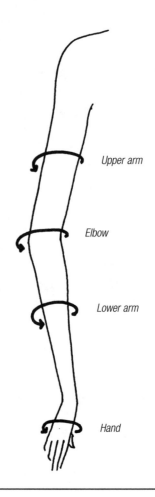

Upper arm

Elbow

Lower arm

Hand

Drawing Arms

To draw the arms, you must keep in mind that:

1 The shoulder muscle has a gentle roundness to it.

2 The upper arm will appear almost parallel.

3 The outside muscle of the lower arm makes a gentle, smooth shape.

4 The inside of the arm divides in half. The upper half is rounder, while the lower half straightens into the wrist.

5 The wrist should be narrow, blending into the palm.

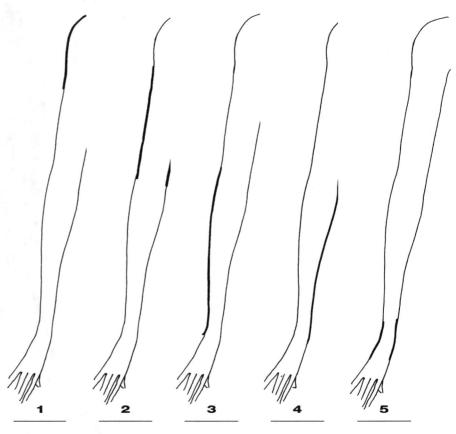

1   2   3   4   5

102

Notice, when the hand is resting on the hip, or if there is any fore-shortening, there is a roundness to the inside muscle of the lower arm and a flatness to the outside.

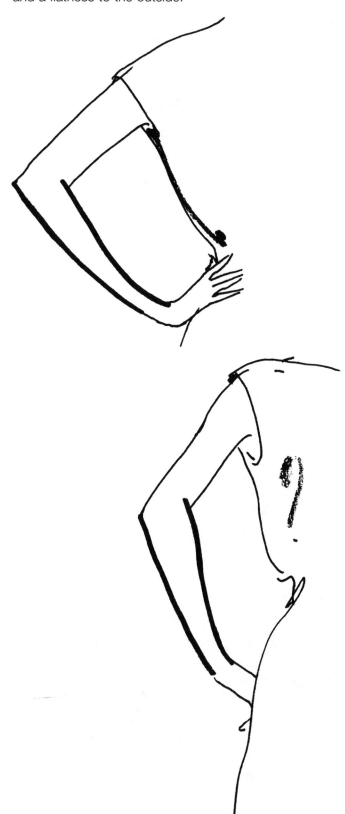

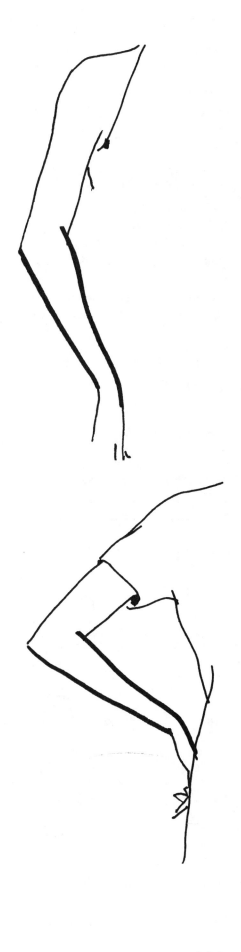

Hands

The hand consists of two equal parts, which are the palm and the fingers. It is approximately the size of the face, from the chin to the hairline.

Hands can offer the fashion figure a range of actions and emotions. Unlike the face or torso, a hand can be placed in countless positions, therefore making it confusing and difficult for the student to draw.

Rather than imagining the hand as a single unit, think of it as these independent parts:

- The palm (or the back of the hand).

- The four fingers.

- The thumb.

Because they are independent, each of these parts is able to move on its own, within the whole unit.

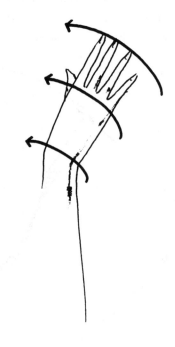

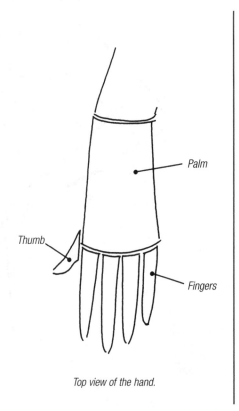

Top view of the hand.

Palm

Thumb

Fingers

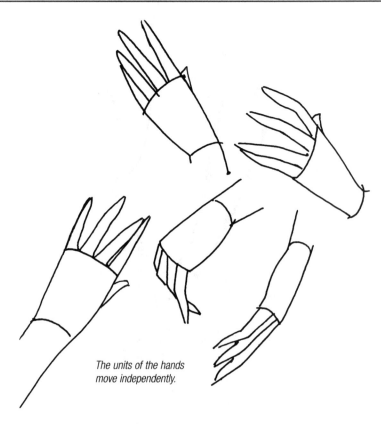

The units of the hands move independently.

104

A fashion hand is more simplified than an average hand. The knuckles and wrinkles should be treated lightly. Think of a ball separating the wrist and palm. The palm should be long and graceful. Imagine it having the same relationship to the hand as the neck to the head—a graceful connector.

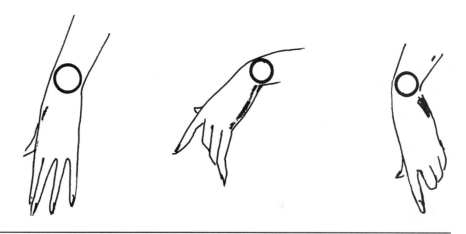

Block off the finger line with a subtle curve. Add the fingers, one at a time, being careful to keep them tapered with oval-shaped nails. When placed correctly on the hand, the fingers give a rounded shape to the back of the hand. Because it is attached to the wrist and moves independently of the other fingers, I find it is easier to place the thumb correctly after drawing the fingers. Also, be aware of the side plane of the hand.

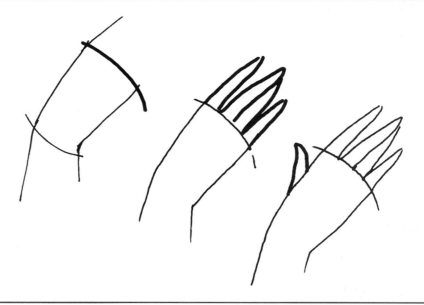

Be aware of the side plane of the hand.

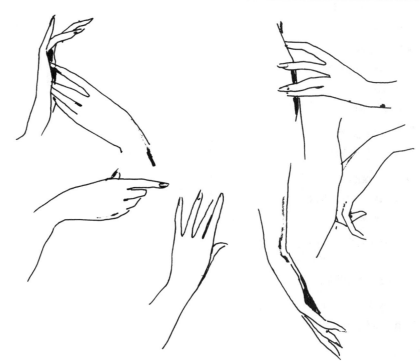

Legs

The leg—or how much of it shows—will always continue to be an issue in fashion. In a short garment, the legs become a major part of the fashion figure. As with the arm, the leg can be divided in four parts:

- The upper leg or thigh.
- The knee.
- The lower leg or calf.
- The foot.

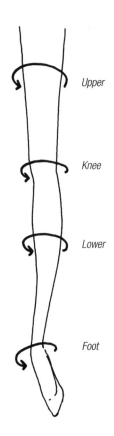

When you look at the leg in terms of placement and proportion, you will notice:

- The knee to mid-calf length is equal to the mid-calf to ankle length.
- The top part of the leg is wider than the bottom. In a fashion leg, there is a gentle tapering to the knee.
- The knee should appear to be slightly in front of the lower leg.
- The muscles of the lower leg form a smooth shape on the outside.
- The inside divides in half where the calf muscle blends into the ankle.
- The thinnest part of the leg is above the ankles.

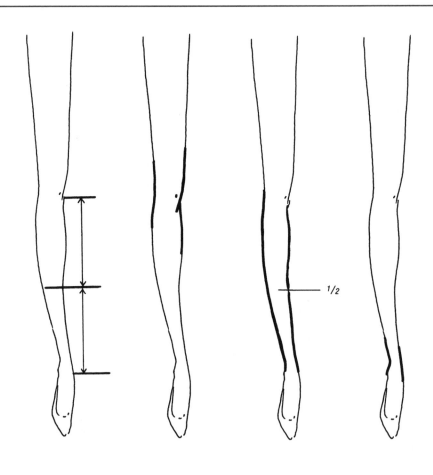

106

Drawing the Leg

1 First block off the four divisions.

2 Keep the outside muscle long. Treat the knee very simply.

3 Divide the inside muscle in half and blend the line.

4 Keep the foot area long and thin.

5 The fashion leg should have a graceful and elegant shape. It gives balance to the garment and an attitude to the figure. Keep it long, but not so long that it distorts the figure. The muscles should look toned, but should not be overly exaggerated. Additionally, the shoe, stocking, or boot should become a harmonious part of the leg and enhance rather than overpower the figure.

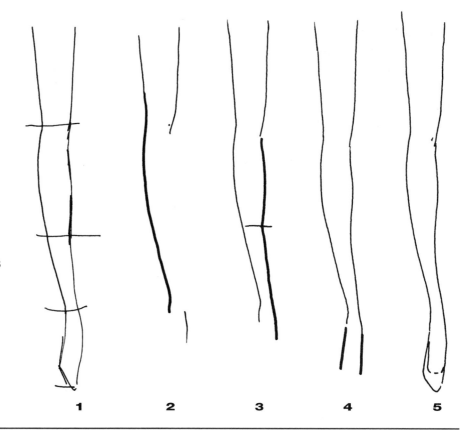

1   2   3   4   5

Feet

Like the hand, the fashion foot should be long and narrow. Also, the fashion foot is rarely, if ever, drawn without a shoe. However, when you are first learning to draw, you should practice sketching bare feet. This will help you with placement and perspective.

When drawing either a full front foot or a turned foot, notice how the perspective changes. Make sure that the ankle and arch flow in front of the heel. Keep the toes and nails simple.

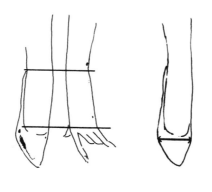

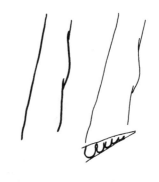

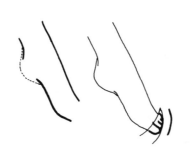

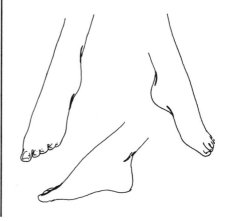

In fashion drawing, however, you will almost always draw the foot with a shoe. When drawing the foot in a shoe, think of a right triangle. The inside is straighter, while the outside has a curve to it. Keep in mind that the inside of the sole is smaller than the outside. Also, from a profile view, the arch keeps the foot from being perfectly flat on the floor.

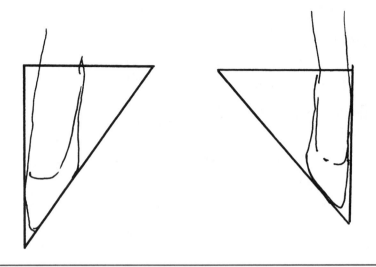

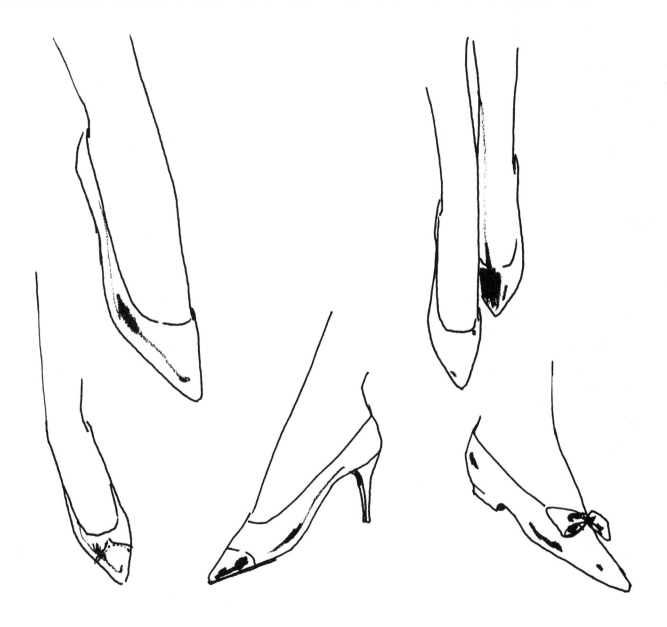

With practice, you will discover
that the arms and legs can give
the figure great drama and attitude.

Calvin Klein 2003

12
Shaping the Body

The human body is three dimensional—front, back, and sides. The female body has curves that go out, in, and out. Fabric on the other hand is one-dimensional. When we choose to cover the female body with fabric we shape it with seams and darts. Other details such as gathers, pleats, draping, and ease may be employed.

Often, students ask about the correct seams and darts for shaping, and the answer to this question is—an infinite amount. The many selections that a designer makes are often based on the desired look.

If we study construction through the years we can conclude that seams and darts are often based on the particular silhouette of the time.

If we study the bias cut dresses of the 1930s, especially those of Madeleine Vionnet, we can observe sinuous bias seaming curving around the body to exaggerate the female form.

In the 1950s, there was emphasis on a fitted silhouette with a very small waistline. By studying major designers of that decade such as Chistian Dior, Jacques Fath and Charles James, we see that there were many seams and darts that allowed the fabric to go from the bust to the waist, and often out again over the hips. Keep in mind that there were waist cinchers to allow the waistline to become smaller than it would naturally be, and petticoats to hold the extreme shape of the skirt. Fabric was generally underlined to further accentuate the silhouette.

In the 1960s, the silhouette of clothing became more architectural. Seams and darts were not only used to keep this shape, but were often decorative as well. Seams were top stitched on the outside to further define the shape. Designers such as Balenciaga, Givenchy, Courreges and Ungaro offered countless possibilities.

As we approached the end of the 1990s and entered the new century, the bustier and corset became an extremely fashionable silhouette. Not only are seams used to shape the bustline and hips, but boning is inserted into the seams to keep the shape crisp and exaggerated. Countless designers have experimented with the bustier and corset, which were once meant to be worn under clothing not on the outside. Jean Paul Gaultier and his pioneering designs for the singer Madonna were the start of this craze. Christian Lacroix, Azzedine Alaia, Versace, Tom Ford for Gucci, and Dolce and Gabanna have used the bustier or corset look in many of their collections.

By constantly going to the stores and studying clothing and by researching magazines, books and museum exhibitions, one will acquire a great knowledge of seams and darts. Designers such as Karl Lagerfeld for Chanel, Valentino, John Galliano, Alexander McQueen, Marc Jacobs, and Prada are often using construction ideas from the past and translating into the present.

Shaping the Body— Seams and Darts

1 Notice the planes of the female body—out over the breasts, in underneath them, going in at the waistline, and rounding out over the hips. You can observe how shadows form under the areas that curve in and disappear on the areas that extend out.

2 There will often be a shadow along the side plane.

3 Princess seams can begin at the shoulders or the bustline. Their sections allow the fabric to be fitted over and under the breasts and into the waist, sometimes down to the hem.

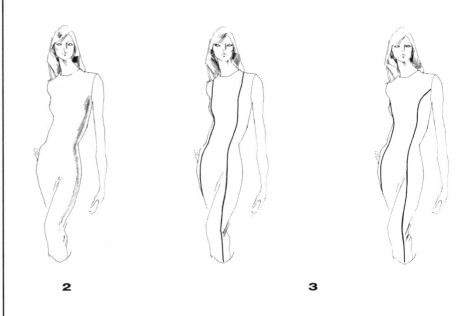

2   3

4 A dart brings together the fabric at the most exaggerated section and tapers to nothing.

5 A seam attaches two pieces of fabric.

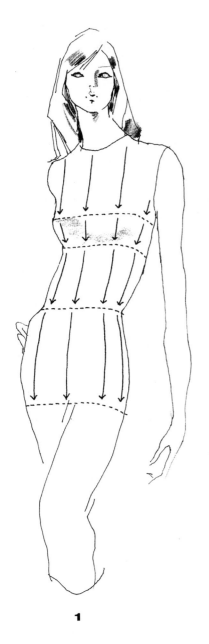

1

4   5

Vionnet, 1932

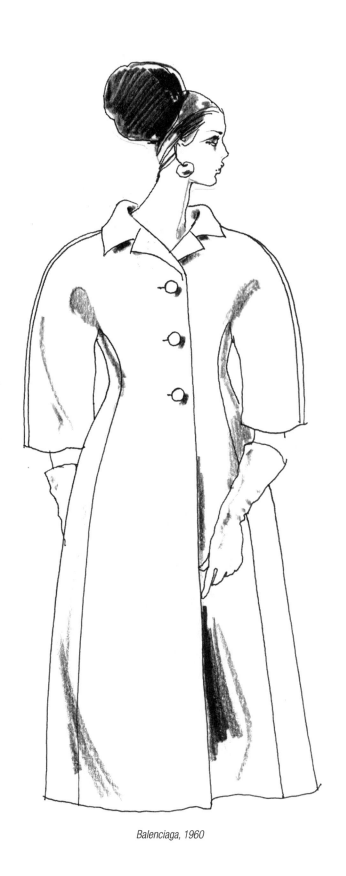

Balenciaga, 1960

Charles James, 1952

Givenchy, 1962

Azzedine Alaïa, 1987

Norell, 1968

Valentino, 1999

Chanel, 2000

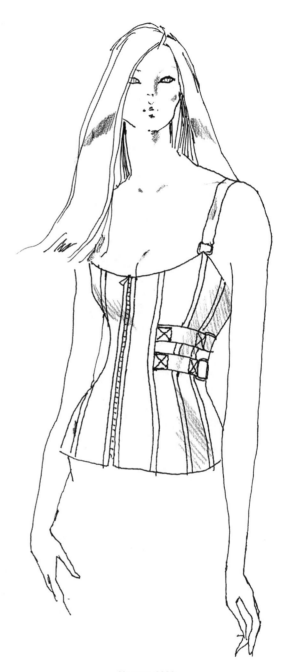

Versace, 2003

1960's seaming become the inspiration for a contemporary design

Marc Jacobs, 2003

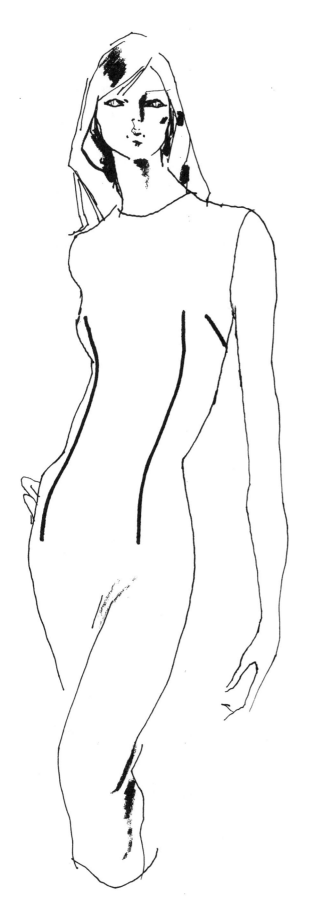

Classic darts used for fit

Dart manipulation can create countless variations

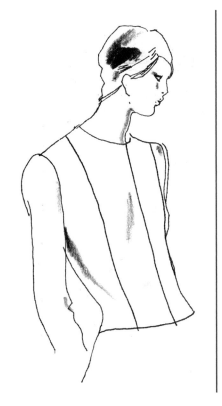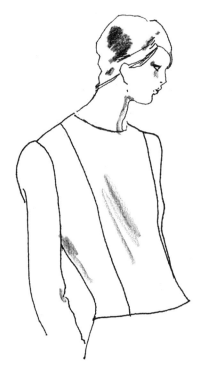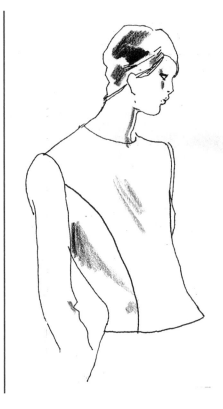

Princess seam variations

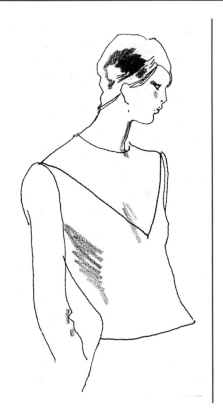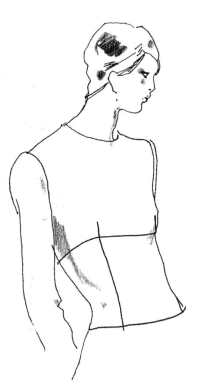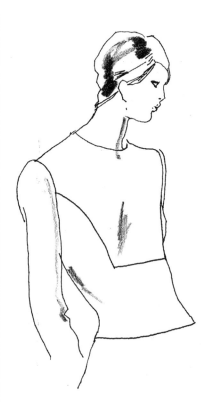

Seam variations

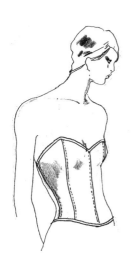

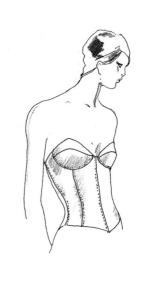

Bustier Variations

Drawing Seams and Darts

The most important thing to remember is that there are no straight lines. The body is round and goes in and out. Be sure all lines are slightly curved. We always begin from the center front, not the sides. In a front view figure, assume that the measurement will be identical on both sides. As the figure turns, we lose the detail on the side that is turning away.

1 Begin at the outside and place seams, darts, or any design details. Measure on a scrap paper the distance of each detail from center front.

1

2 Move this measurement towards the side that is turning away. You will now have the exact placement of the seam, dart, or garment details such as pockets. Be aware that you will lose some of the detail on the side turning away. Proceed with the rest of the drawing.

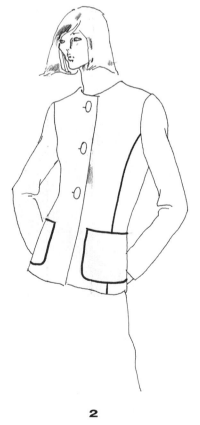

2

Nicolas Ghesquière/Balenciaga, 2003

Interesting seaming can create beautiful shapes.

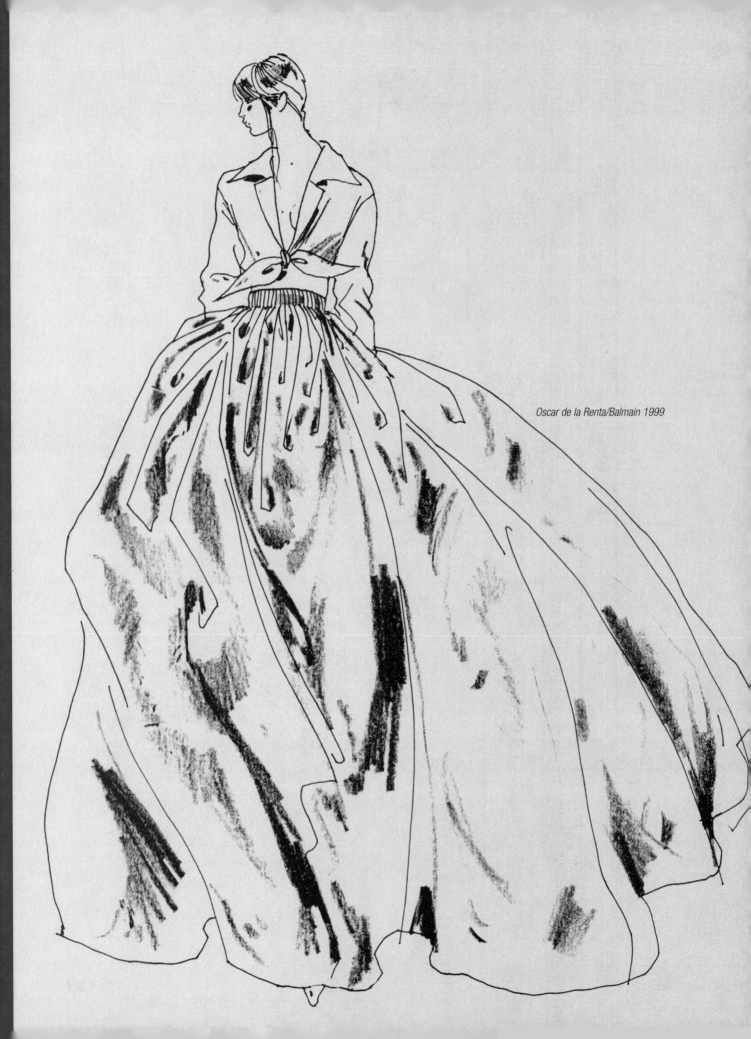

Oscar de la Renta/Balmain 1999

13

How to See and Plan the Figure

Designers and all the assistants and experts that work with them spend months of preparation and hard work before collections are shown. As an artist and designer, your artwork, projects, and portfolio become your collection, therefore all the same thought processes must go into each drawing. Very often, more time goes into planning a drawing than actually doing it. But by planning, the drawing will be more successful. If you think about it, it only takes the model minutes to walk down a runway, but the work behind the designs takes months. The most dangerous thing you can do is to sit down and attack the paper without any preparation and planning. The more you plan, the more successful your drawing will be.

As an artist, you really can only rely on your own taste, knowledge, and abilities. Therefore, it is most important that you constantly look at and study the best examples of clothing possible. Be most careful not to put your personal feelings into this—be objective. Remember, you do not have to wear these clothes, but you must understand how and why they are created, and where they fit into the world.

Go to the best stores that you can find and study designer clothing. It is important that you look at the finest clothing available, because the "look" gets filtered down as the price is decreased. After observing the best, you will begin to see how the "look" trickles down to the different price levels—what is kept and what is changed. See any historical costume exhibits you can, and read old and new fashion publications. There are many beautiful books on designers available—read and study them. Make yourself as fashion literate as possible. It will make your art that much more special.

A fashion drawing represents not only a garment, but also a specific woman in a specific place and time. Therefore, when you become more skilled at drawing the fashion figure, you will want to make this general figure into a more specific person.

Imagine that as a designer or illustrator, you have access to all the different headsheets of the model agencies. Who will you choose? Why? Will she have short, sleek, dark hair or masses of curly blonde hair? What will be the focus of the makeup—dark eyes and pale lips, pale eyes and dark lips, or a natural look? What skin color would be best for the garments? What part of the model's body is the most important and necessary to successfully pull off the design? Should she have long legs to wear a very short skirt or perhaps a longer neck to carry off an oversized cowl neckline?

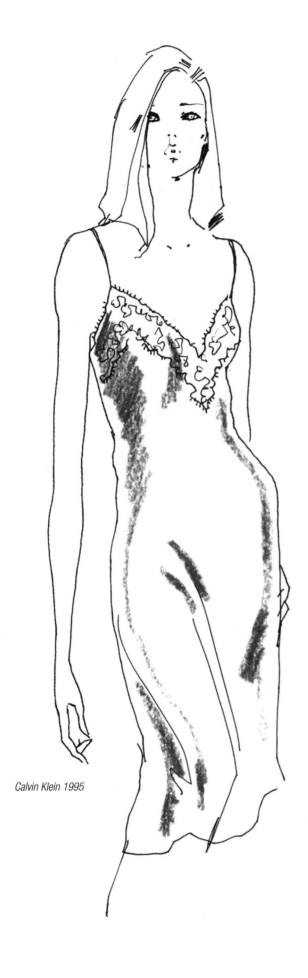

Calvin Klein 1995

Before beginning to draw any piece of clothing, it is extremely important to study and analyze:

- Who will wear it?

- Where will it be worn?

- What will be the attitude of the pose?

- What will be the expression of the face?

- What media will show the design and fabric in the best way?

Now, go through your swipe files and pull out all the photos of heads and poses that you think you will need. Find examples of the fabrics—both real and from photos—so that you will be able to render them accurately. Keep photos on hand of designs and personalities that inspire you.

Try to describe the garment with your hands. Pay close attention to the movements because often they will dictate the line quality. Here are a few examples. If you have a satin pouf skirt, your movements will be slow and round. If you have the same skirt in taffeta, your movements will be a little faster and sharper. A clingy bias-cut gown will bring your hands closer to your body, indicating that the body is defining the clothing. Slow movements will indicate a sensuous fabric, such as crepe de chine. A ruffled gypsy dress in a brightly colored and patterned cotton will cause faster and more lively movements, again indicating the appropriate line quality.

Next, make a list of the most important parts of the design you are about to draw. Number one should be the absolute single most

Attitude sketches

The next numbers should be the secondary parts of the design—these are important, but not critical. They do not get the most focus. Perhaps the dress has been made in shades of ivory satin.

Because the fabric is subtle, it becomes less important. Would the dress look that different in any other pale-colored evening fabric? Not really. However, if the gown was made in a vibrant color or a large print, this would definitely change the focus.

The last numbers should be the least important parts of the design. These are parts, which if they were eliminated, it would hardly matter at all. These elements include the shoulder straps and certain accessories. Remember, a drawing must have focus. When everything is treated equally, often we get nothing.

The next step is to do little gesture or "attitude" sketches of what you want the pose to look like. How will the movement flow? What is the best angle to show off the clothing?

After you have done some attitude scribbles and made some notes, the next things to do are some little color sketches of different faces. This will help you to find the look you want.

important thing—be it the shape, the color, the fabric, or a very major design element or detail. This should be the one element—that if taken away—would change the garment in the most dramatic way. When you look at the Calvin Klein slip dress on page 126, it is not that difficult because there is only one major element—the shape of the dress and how it clings over the body. The lace becomes number two, because even if it weren't there, the dress would not really lose its look. When you look at the Christian Lacroix design on page 128, you can see that there are many important elements. The shape of the gown itself—fitted to the body through the bodice and then opening up to tremendous volume at the skirt. The many design details—the finely draped bodice, the loosely draped fabric at the hip, and the huge poufs that

fall from it. Write all the elements down in the order of the importance you want to focus on. Often there are many possibilities. If the bodice is primary, you might want to lengthen it a bit. If the hip detail is most important to you, the waist and hip areas could be lengthened. If the sweeping, voluminous skirt is the major focus, you could elongate the legs.

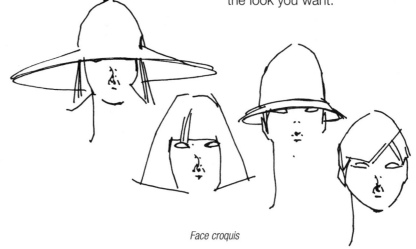

Face croquis

If there is more than one figure, imagine a group of models walking down the runway. How do they relate to each other? Are the colors and fabric stories working well together? Is everything balanced? Fashion designers hire the best hair and makeup people, the best choreographers and lighting designers, the top stylists, and certainly the best models on which to show the clothing.

With access to so many fashion shows on television or Internet and videos of different collections at department stores or cosmetics counters, now you can actually see models as they walk down the runway. Notice how they have a specific look, style, and attitude that the designer wishes to convey. Pay careful attention to the way the clothing moves as they walk. Keep this motion in mind as you draw. Any part of the garment that moves on the runway can have the same life in your work.

As the artist, it is most important that you put the same considerations into your artwork before you begin to draw because you want to draw the woman that is most perfectly suited for the garment. For example, in a bathing suit, your figure should have the most toned body. Perfectly defined arms and legs—tight, long torso, and a very easy, casual attitude. In a coat or suit, she should have a sleek and confident look—with a perfectly poised expression. A cocktail dress demands a worldly and sophisticated woman, while an organza evening gown becomes a heroine out of a romantic novel.

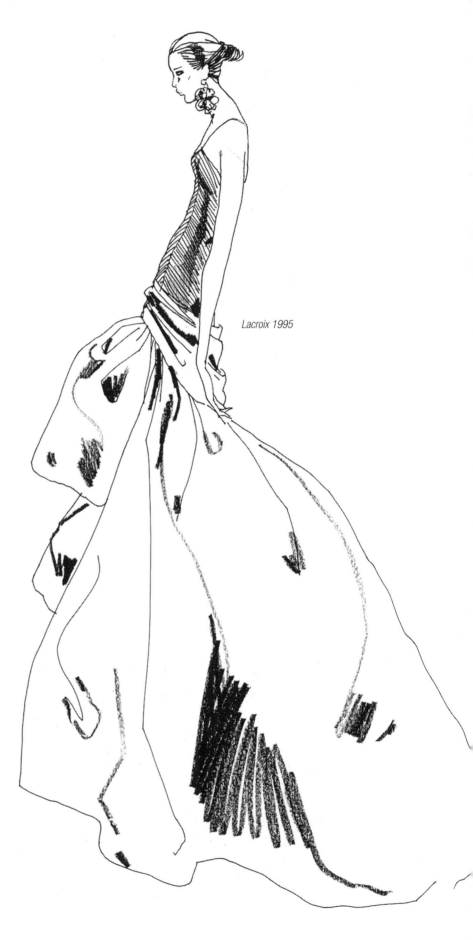

Lacroix 1995

Kenzo 1971

St. Laurent 1999

14
Figure Types

As we have already learned, our goal is to create the most perfect woman for the garment we are drawing. To do this, we have to understand the different "types" of fashion figures and what their looks, gestures, poses, and attitudes are.

Think of a fashion figure as a type of person who falls into one of the following categories:

- Misses
- Junior
- Sophisticated
- Active
- Career
- High-fashion
- Eccentric

Within these categories, there will be subdivisions:

- Natural
- Dramatic
- Animated
- Sleek
- Romantic
- Casual

Misses

Active

Junior

Sophisticated

Career

High Fashion

Eccentric

There will also be the different categories of clothing these figures will wear:

- Couture
- Sportswear
- Tailored Clothing (coats or suits)
- Activewear
- Lingerie
- Eveningwear
- Bridal

Because of all these elements, there can be unlimited possibilities. A sportswear look can be for a working woman or a very sophisticated woman on a yacht. Evening clothes can be for an eccentric younger woman at a club or the most high fashion sophisticate at a gala ball. Activewear can be a sweatsuit, jogging suit, or swimsuit. A coat can be a casual, camel hair wrap worn to a football game or a dramatic black coat trimmed with fur.

As part of maintaining your fashion swipe file, you should constantly clip photos of these different types from fashion magazines. Keep them in separate, labeled folders. When you need them, they will be easily accessible.

In order for the figure to become a "real" person, you can use one photo or swipe—or several different ones for the same piece of artwork. One can be used for the pose, another for the face, and even another for the hairstyle. Rarely will one swipe be perfect. At the beginning, work with only one or two swipes. As your art abilities become more advanced, it will be possible to work with many more. Do not begin until you can actually envision a "real" person. Remember, just as the designer picks the most perfect woman, so should you.

To understand them a little better, let's study the different types of figures.

A misses figure wears the typical fashion garment and silhouette of the moment, cut for a well-proportioned body between 5'5" to 5'6". Generally, the garments are even-number sized from 6 to 18, but often including 2 and 4. She is the classic fashion figure. Her hair and makeup is contemporary and fashionable. You probably would choose more typical fashion-type poses—perhaps the classic high hip and opposite high shoulder with one arm bent and the other arm down. She would represent the fashionable look of the moment.

A plus-size figure is a larger type than one in the misses range. These sizes range upward from 18. This figure can be very fashionable, but is drawn to look heavier than a misses size. Choose a pose that is slightly less animated, with emphasis on flattering hair styles and makeup.

A junior figure is an adult figure that is 5'5" and under and is shorter waisted. These sizes range between 5 and 15 and frequently include 3. This figure often is younger and the clothes not as high-fashion. Perhaps your poses will be less serious and more animated.

Again, because a size does not always determine age, the possibilities are endless. The younger the figure, the more round the face and eyes. The youngest, a baby, has the roundest face and eyes. As the figure gets older—child, teenager, young adult—the face takes on a more sophisticated bone structure. Keep the hair free and moving and the figure more animated.

Plus size, misses, and junior figures

The more sophisticated the figure, the more dramatic and studied the pose can be. The expression is more controlled and has more attitude. The more high-fashion the figure, the most exaggeration it can have. This is a figure of the moment and should have the most fantasy to it. A high-fashion garment, however, can be young and outrageous—as with Jean Paul Gaultier or Betsy Johnson—or as polished and haughty as Valentino or Givenchy.

Valentino 1995

Betsy Johnson 1984

A lingerie figure should not have a feeling of being overly styled. There should be minimal makeup and hair should never look "done." Imagine the most sensually posed figure with masses of hair. She should be very relaxed and dream-like.

Activewear often has a pose typical of the garment's use—tennis, swimming, skiing, or jogging.

Collect poses from appropriate magazines or swipes so that your drawings are accurate. Keep in mind that the figure's pose not only shows the garment, but creates a mood. The pose should sense the front, the back, and the sides, regardless of the view.

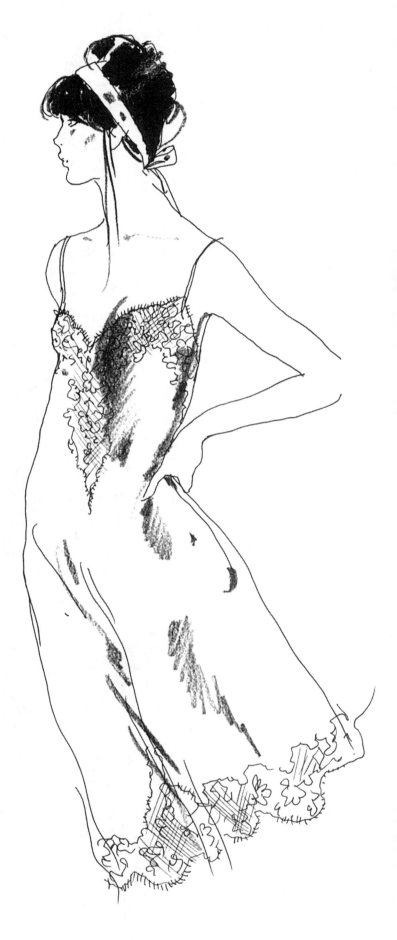

A sportswear figure has no set age—she can be junior and lively or polished and sophisticated. It is important when selecting a pose, to remember that sportswear generally has many pieces to it. A coat may have to be opened to show a vest and blouse. Be sure to avoid a pose that would cover any important details.

Imagine the fashion figure as a ballet dancer in mid-air. We see her in motion, before she touches the ground. Once she touches the ground, the pose is final and it becomes reality. It is a moment stopped in time.

A drawing should always maintain some of that "in-motion" quality. One way to achieve this is to "move" any part of the drawing of the garment or figure that the wind or a fan might move. This includes hair, streamers of a bow, billowing sleeves, circular skirts, or yards of such fabrics as chiffon or georgette. This movement gives the figure life.

An evening gown can have a very dramatic and gestured pose. It can have yards and yards of fabric and be very soft and romantic. It can have the opposite look as well—sleek, body conscious, and stark. Select a pose that best shows off the garment. Makeup and hair can be most exaggerated. Let your fantasy and dreams be the most extreme!

Galanos 1972

St. Laurent 1968

Part 2

The Fashion Details

Balenciaga 1956

We have discussed that fashion art is the combination of clothing—which has its own life and the figure, with its own life—becoming one. After they become one unit, one of two things can happen:

1 The figure can take precedence over the garment.

2 The garment can take precedence over the figure.

Let's imagine for a moment a beautiful bias-cut gown designed by Vionnet in the 1930s. Notice how it falls on the body as if there is nothing underneath to interfere with the figure and the gown. If we take this gown and drop it on the floor, it would fall into a puddle of fabric. All of the construction and details were designed to enhance the way the dress fits and falls on the body without any understructure. We can then say that the body is dictating the way this dress looks or that the body is taking precedence over the garment.

Now let's imagine this Balenciaga ball gown—from its high waistline, the dress lifts completely away from the body and falls to the floor. The design, fabric, cut, and understructure are dictating this dress. We can then assume that the body is merely a hanger from which this dress falls. The dress is creating its own shape. We can say that this garment is taking precedence over the body.

These evening gowns from Vionnet and Balenciaga represent two completely different points of view—each designer has taken a different approach to what they believe is beautiful. They do not view the body or clothing the same way, but each one of them ends up with a magnificent result.

I am not implying that the figure is of no importance to the Balenciaga gown and therefore it should be ignored. On the contrary, it becomes even more important because we lose sight of it under the garment. Therefore the knowledge of anatomy becomes even more crucial. You have to begin to make decisions of the relationship about the garment and the body. This is one of the most difficult parts of fashion art, and it takes time, knowledge, and practice before it can be done well.

Balenciaga 1958

Vionnet 1935

Sometimes, the figure and the garment are more balanced. Let's imagine a cowl neck sweater and a pair of pants. If you analyze this combination, you will find that the figure is taking over, as much as the garment. Most contemporary clothing—especially sportswear—has this balance. Part of the body conforms to the sweater, with the bulk of the sweater covering and hiding some of the body. Dressing a figure is fine at the beginning, but as you become more confident about your drawing skills, try to think of the figure and the garment as one unit. This will help you as you advance into more difficult silhouettes.

A fashion silhouette is how we refer to the outline or outside shape of a garment. However, nothing can happen on the outside without some construction (for example, seams, gathers, darts) on the inside. It is also important to remember that every silhouette can have endless variations and possibilities, as you can see in the flats of the princess silhouette on this page.

The designer and the look of the moment dictate the actual fit of the silhouette at any particular time. In the next few pages, we will look at some of the major fashion silhouettes.

Princess Line Variations

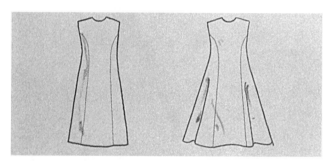

A princess line can be fairly close to the body or quite full at the hem.

The fit can be higher than the waist or directly at the waist.

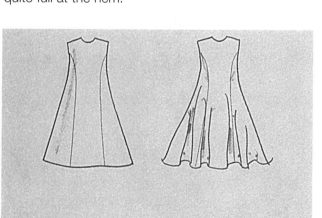

It can have an underlining and appear quite stiff or can be flowing in a sheer fabric.

It can be mini-length or floor-length—even a tunic.

Chemise

This silhouette hangs straight from the shoulder. At the end of the 1950s, Balenciaga and Givenchy were greatly responsible for introducing this silhouette.

Norell 1966

Belenciaga 1966

Givenchy 1956

Wedge Chemise

This silhouette is a chemise shape
that tapers towards the hem.

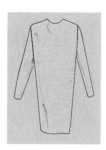

Givenchy 1957

Sack or Barrel

This silhouette has a line that is loose and unfitted at the waist and touches the body at the hem. A very major silhouette developed by Balenciaga.

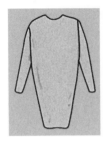

Balenciaga 1955

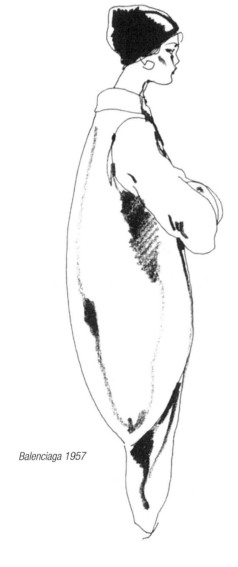

Balenciaga 1957

Trapeze

This is a silhouette that stands out at the hem without any fit through the body. Yves Saint Laurent is greatly associated with this shape.

Saint Laurent 1958

Saint Laurent 1958

Tent

This is a silhouette that generally is fuller and softer than a trapeze, and also is more fluid. This shape was attributed to Claire McCardell. In 1938, a dress manufacturer referred to this shape as "a dress with no back, no front, no waist-line, and my God, no bust darts!"

Madame Grès 1977

Claire McCardell 1938

A-line

This is a popular name given to a dress shape that falls from the shoulders and stands away at the hemline. Dior named this silhouette in 1955.

Ungaro 1966

Dior 1955

Sheath

This is a silhouette that is fitted by darts or seams so that it conforms to the body. A very popular style in the 1950s.

Sheath 1950s

Empire

This is a silhouette that is seamed under the bustline. We can trace this shape as far back as Empress Josephine in the early 1800s. It is sometimes referred to as "high-waisted."

Norell 1963

Valentino 1965

Madame Grès 1968

Dropped Waistline

This silhouette has a waistline seam that falls either at or below the hips. This was a very fashionable look in the 1920s.

Norell 1963

Saint Laurent 1981

Princess Line

This is a silhouette in which the shape is controlled by a seam that curves from the bustline or shoulder and continues down toward the hem. It may also have a seamline that starts at mid-shoulder and descends straight down to the hem. It can shape the body anywhere between the bust and waist, and can have any degree of fullness at the hemline.

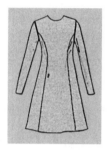

Saint Laurent 1964

Bubble or Harem

This is a shape in which the hemline is gathered to an under-structure. This silhouette can be used in pants as well as dresses and eveningwear. Balenciaga, Givenchy, and Norell made this popular in the late 1950s. Variations of this silhouette include Poiret's hobble skirt at the turn of the century, all the way up to the Lacroix pouf skirt in the late 1980s.

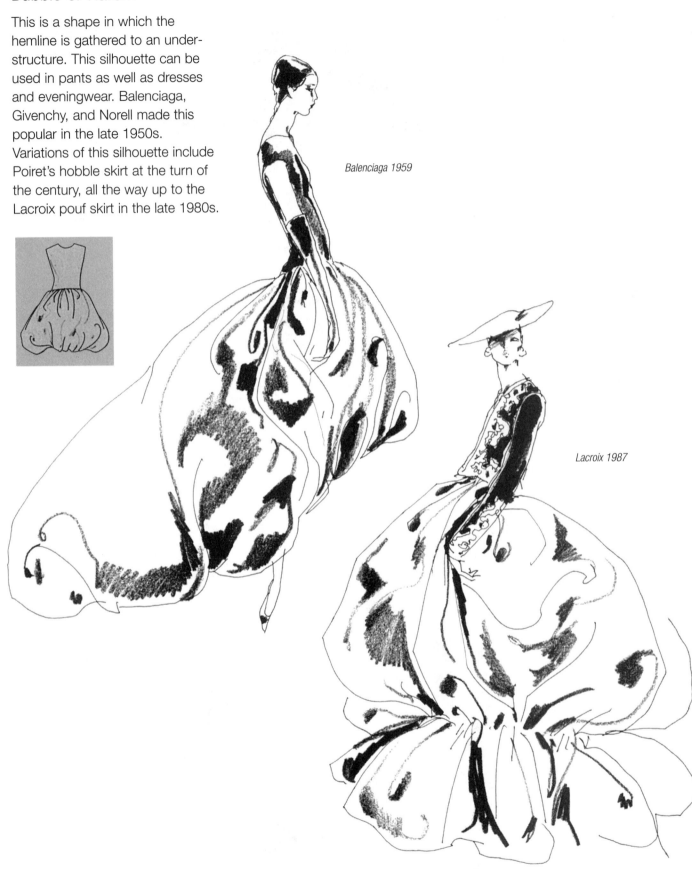

Balenciaga 1959

Lacroix 1987

Blouson

This is a silhouette in which the excess fabric blouses over a skirt or band. In a dress, this can be achieved by attaching, easing, gathering, or pleating the excess fabric to a shorter understructure. In a two-piece blouson garment, this may be achieved by the use of elastic or a drawstring. It can also be gathered or pleated onto a separate or attached band.

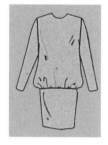

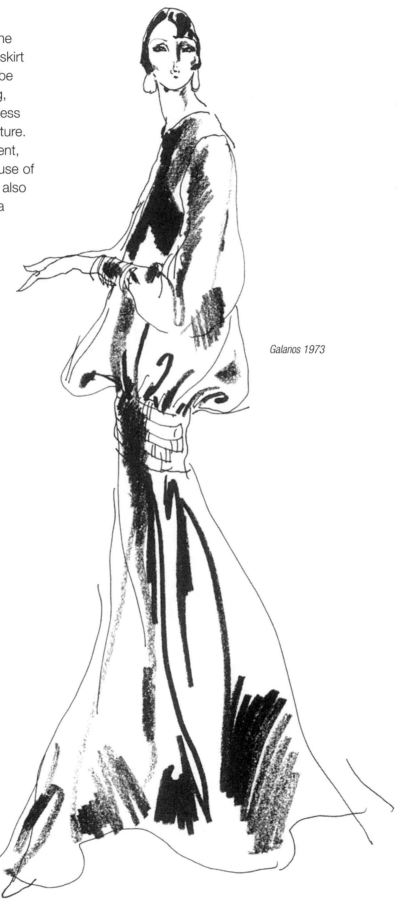

Galanos 1973

Shirtwaist

This is a dress styled with shirt details. It may button anywhere from above the waist to the hem. It can be slim or full, with or without a waistline seam. The Gibson girl image popularized this style in the 1890s.

Halston 1973

Tunic

This is a two-piece silhouette. The top may fall anywhere from the hip area to just above the hem.

Saint Laurent 1962

Saint Laurent 1976

Peplum

This silhouette has a flared section joined to the waistline of a garment. In 1948, Dior's New Look gave this silhouette great impact.

Dior 1950

Caftan

This silhouette is a full, floor-length robe that is slit at the neckline. The caftan is pulled over the head. The influence comes from Morocco and other countries of North Africa and may be embellished with embroidery.

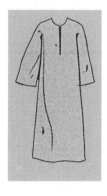

Galanos 1966

As you can see by our short study, there are many major fashion silhouettes with which you must become familiar. These silhouettes are used by today's designers—sometimes on their own, sometimes in combination with other silhouettes. The fashion artist must not only be knowledgeable about contemporary silhouettes, but also of the silhouettes used in the past because this is the well from which future designs will be drawn.

Halston 1976

One of the simplest garment details to draw is the neckline. Its simplicity, however, should not be underestimated as it is directly under the head and therefore takes on an added importance because it helps to frame the face.

Unlike the collar, the neckline is a unit unto itself and generally has no additional parts. Often it is finished off with a facing or binding. A facing is a piece of fabric shaped to follow the contour of the outside edge of a garment—in this case, the neckline. The right side of the facing is sewn to the right side of the garment, and then is trimmed and turned to the inside. This leaves the neck edge with a clean finished edge. To further enhance the shape of the neckline, sometimes it is topstitched—with one or more rows of stitching—or with any various forms of decorative trim.

Another way of finishing a neckline is with a bias binding. The binding is a bias strip sewn onto the right side of the garment and then is folded back on the seam allowance and sewn again to the wrong side. It forms a binding on the outside edge of the neckline. Bias bindings can be in the same or contrasting fabric or color and in various widths.

Often the neckline becomes part of a front or back opening, or it may have a placket as part of the design as in a shirt, jacket, or blouse.

Facing

Bias binding

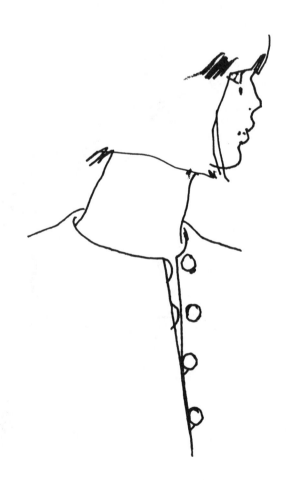

Drawing Necklines

When drawing any neckline, you must be aware that the shape is going around the neck completely and that it relates to the shoulders and chest area as well. As you can see from the turned and profile views of the neck, it is also higher in the back than the front.

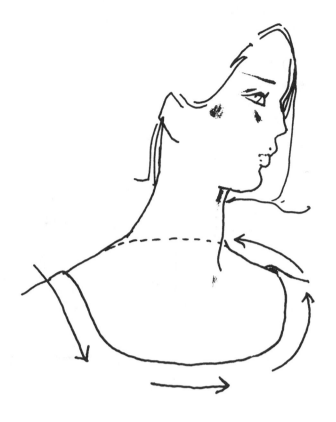

Turned

Profile

Some, such as the jewel (or round) neckline, fit the neck very closely. Others, as in a scoop neckline, descend onto the chest area. And still others, such as a funnel neckline, extend up onto the neck. When drawing any neckline, however, be sure to send both the loop that the neckline makes around the neck and the weight of the fabric.

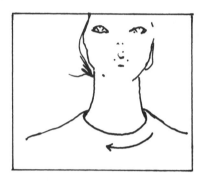

Jewel neckline

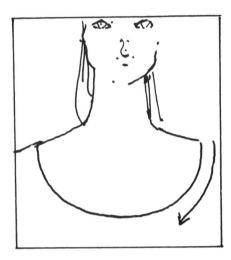

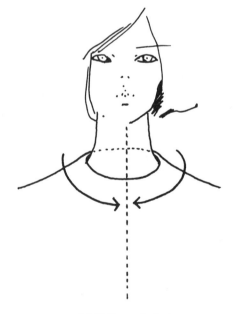

Scoop neckline

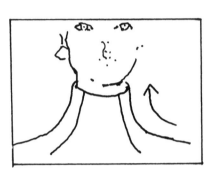

Funnel neckline

Drawing Necklines

The first step in drawing a neckline is to establish the center front line. As I have said before, if center front is even the tiniest bit off, the entire shape will be incorrect.

In a turned view, less of the necklines shows on the side that is farther away from you and more of the neckline is shown on the side that is close to you. There are no exceptions to this rule—except in an asymmetrical neckline. Also notice how the center front line turns with the figure.

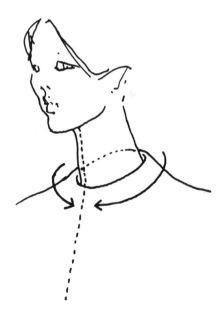

Establishing center front

The loop around the neck indicates fabric.

To draw a neckline:

1 First, draw a dotted line, to show the cylindrical shape of the neck.

2 Draw the neckline shape from the shoulder edge to the center and from the center to the other shoulder edge.

3 + 4 If you draw the neckline from one side of the neck to the other in one step, the perspective can be inaccurate. By stopping at the center and then continuing, you can be assured of greater accuracy. This is especially evident in a "V" neckline, but this error can sneak up in even a simple, round neck.

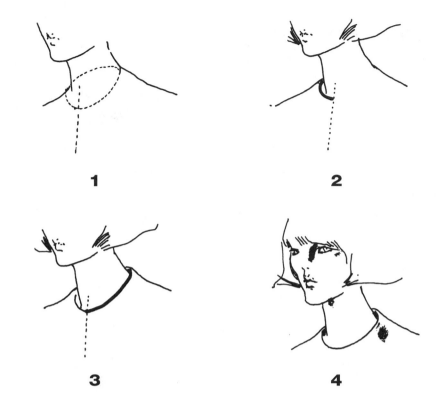

1

2

3

4

Keep in mind that a neckline is a very defined shape, so keep the line smooth—this is not the place for any kind of interesting line. Now add the stitching, binding, or any other trim or detail.

Remember, neckline principles apply to the back of the neck as well as the front.

Neckline Styles

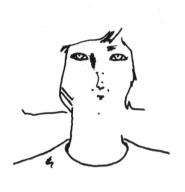

Round or jewel neckline

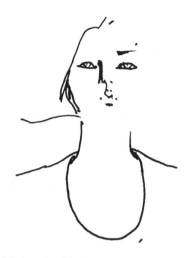

"U"-shaped neckline

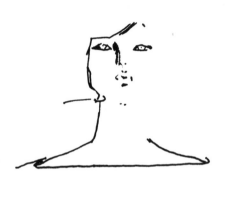

Boat neck

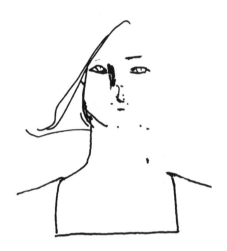

Square neck

"V" neck

Sweetheart neckline

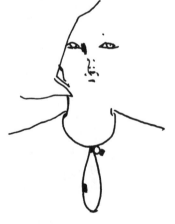

Keyhole neckline

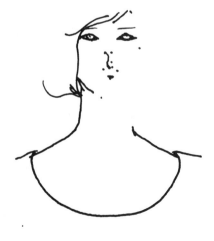

Scoop neckline

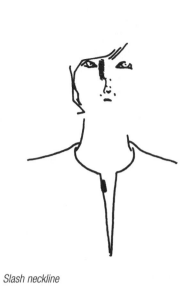

Slash neckline

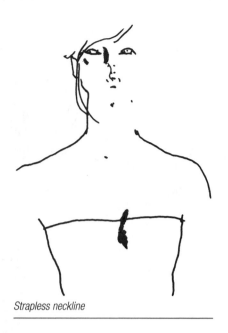

Strapless neckline

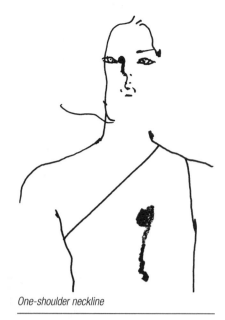

One-shoulder neckline

Camisole neckline

Funnel neckline

Gathered neckline

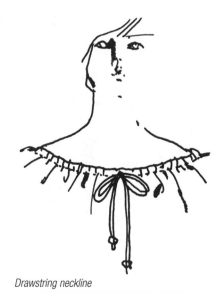

Drawstring neckline

Asymmetrical neckline

Off-the-shoulder neckline

John Galliano/Dior 1997

The collar is the design detail that encircles the neck. What makes the drawing of a collar even more important is that it sets off the face, therefore becoming one of the design elements that we focus on first.

Collars come in all sizes, from a tiny peter pan to a giant bertha that passes the shoulders. They can be low and flat or high and luxurious. They can serve a practical function—such as keeping us warm—or can be an extravagant and luxurious focal point of a garment.

It is important to understand the principles that all collars—regardless of their size or style—have in common. Almost all collars are composed of an upper collar, an interfacing, and an under collar. The upper collar is the portion that we see from the outside or top. The interfacing is a layer of fabric that is used for stiffening, to give the collar body. The under collar, which is often cut on the bias, is the portion that is joined to the bodice. When the upper collar turns over the under collar and rests on the shoulders, the area that folds over and is close to the neck is called the roll line. Because the collar is "rolling" over on itself, at this point, we now actually have six layers of fabric.

Because the collar falls toward the shoulder, it stands up and then turns down. The stand of a collar is the height between the neckline edge and the rolling point of the collar, which determines its drop or roll line.

Collars are attached to the neckline and can go in an up direction, as in a mandarin collar, or can extend in a down direction, as in a shirt collar. Most collars fall in a down direction.

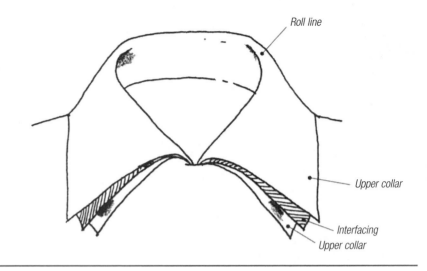

Roll line

Upper collar

Interfacing

Upper collar

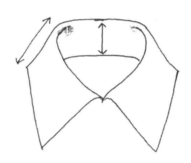

The "roll" of the collar

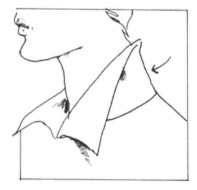

When the collar turns over, six layers of fabric are formed.

The strand of the collar

Collars can go up.

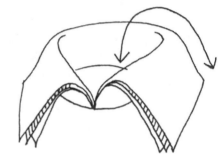

Collars can go down.

Depending on the thicknesses of the fabric, the roll will take on different rounded shapes. Some different types of roll lines and some examples of the fabrics used to produce that particular type of roundness in the roll line are:

- With thin, fine fabrics, the roll takes a very small, round shape. Examples of fabrics that would produce such a roll line are thin cottons including voile and handkerchief linens and fine silks such as crepe de chine, charmeuse, tissue taffeta, organdy, or organza.

- In dress or mediumweight fabrics, the round shape becomes a bit bigger. Examples of such fabrics that would produce such a roll line are mediumweight cottons including muslin and chambray; thin woolens such as flannel and wool crepe; mediumweight linens; and heavier silks including satin and peau de soie.

- In heavier weight fabrics, the roundness becomes a little bit bigger and higher. Examples of fabrics that would produce such a roll line are suiting or coating woolens, flannels, tweeds, mediumweight meltons, camel hair, corduroy, and heavyweight gabardines.

Fine fabrics

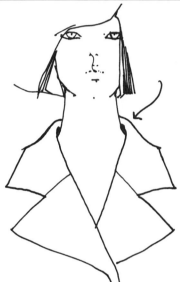

Mediumweight fabrics

Heavier weight fabrics

- In heavyweight coating fabrics, the roll line takes on an even larger and rounder shape. Examples of fabrics that would produce such a roll line are short-sheared fake furs, pile fabrics, heavyweight meltons, mohair, and highly textured or novelty woolens. Also, when you draw a pile or fake fur fabric, the round shape not only gets higher and bigger, but takes on a greater depth.

- Real fur has the same principles as fabric and fake fur. Such flat furs as broadtail and beaver follow the heavyweight coating roundness, but such furs as lynx and fox become so high and round that they seem to be nearly reaching the ears.

Pile fabric

Short-hair fur

Long-hair fur

The next point to consider is the relationship of the collar to the neckline. Some principles of this relationship to consider are:

- The more the shape of the collar conforms to the neckline and has a concave shape, the closer it will hug the neck. A good example is a peter pan collar. The same principle holds true for a collar that goes up on the neck, as in a mandarin collar. The turtleneck is an exception, because it is generally cut on the bias and the stretch quality of the bias cut makes it conform to the neck. Most of the time, a turtleneck is a knit and the knit's ability to stretch allows it to hug the neck closely.

Peter pan collar conforms to neck.

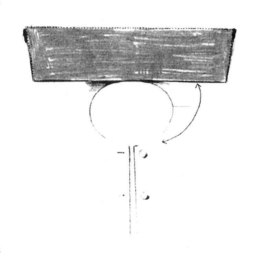

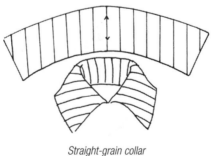

- As the neck edge of the collar straightens out, and has a convex shape, the more it will begin to stand away from the neck. When the collar becomes a straight line, it stands away from the neck even more.

Rolled collar stands away from neck.

Striped Collars

Any collar can be cut on the straight, cross, or bias grain or can be mitered on the bias at the center back. However, these different grain lines are most evident on striped collars. The bias-cut collar has the most stretch to it and is often chosen by designers because of its beautiful roll line.

When drawing striped collars, notice how the angle of the stripes changes as it encircles the neck.

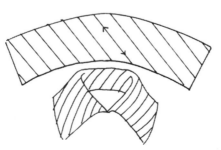

Straight-grain collar

Cross-grain collar

Bias-cut collar

Mitered collar

Drawing Collars

When drawing the collar, the first thing to consider is that the collar goes around the neck, not on the neck. Collars can extend from the neckline up or they can go from the neckline onto the shoulders. Be sure that your drawing follows the perspective of the shoulder and chest area.

Additionally, most collars meet at the center front line. You must pay strict attention to it, because if the center front line is just the slightest bit off, the entire drawing of the collar will be wrong. Block it lightly with a dotted line that goes from under the chin onto the chest area.

To assure more accuracy, draw one-half of the collar to center front and then the other half, rather than from edge to edge. This will give your drawing a feeling of roundness rather than flatness.

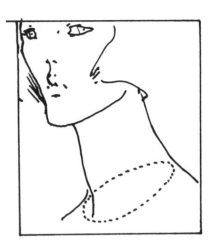

The collar circles the neck.

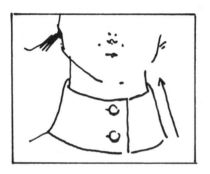

Collars can go in an up direction.

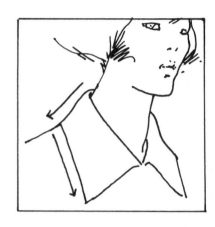

Collars can go in a down direction.

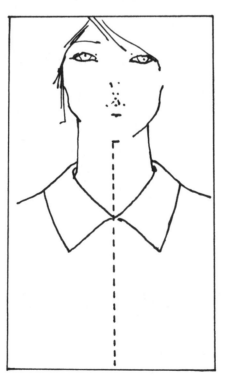

Most collars meet at the center front line.

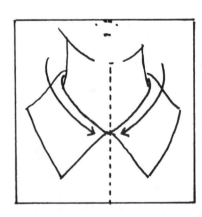

Draw one-half of the collar at a time.

172

Remember that in a ¾ or turned view, the part of the body that is farther away from you is the part that gets the smaller section of the collar.

In a profile view, basically you will be drawing only one-half of the collar. Be sure, however, that your drawing senses the movement of the collar over the shoulders and on toward the back.

Keep the collar and closing lines smooth and clean. Any wiggly kinds of lines will make it look wrinkled. However, you can put a dark accent under the area of the collar that rests on the chest area and at the area where it touches the neck.

In an asymmetrical collar, the principles are exactly the same except that the two sides of the collar are not equal.

For practice, study fashion magazines and pattern books to see and understand the concepts of all the different types of collars. When you see a collar that has a different or unique design detail, analyze it logically for the structure.

Also, before you throw away old fashion magazines, take a marker and trace over every collar. You will see that your eye will begin to understand how they all look from different views. This is a very good exercise to do with other such fashion details as sleeves, necklines, and so forth.

Please note that in the next few chapters, we will study the tailored notched collar and draped collars.

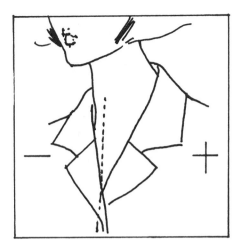

Turned collar view

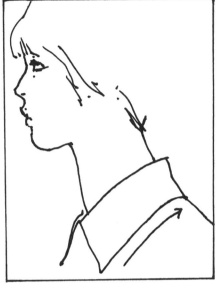

Profile-view collar

Dark accents set off the collar

Asymmetrical collar

Collar Styles

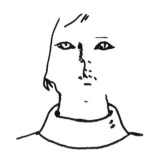

Turtleneck

Mock-turtleneck

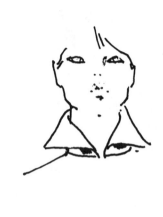

Shirt collar on a band

Shawl collar

Wing collar

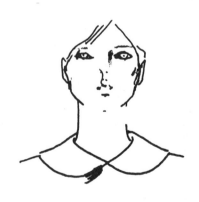

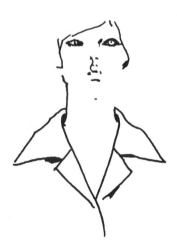

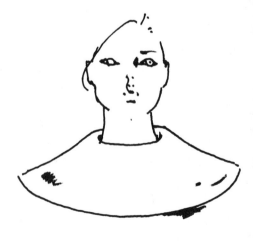

Peter pan collar

Convertible collar

Bertha collar

Pilgrim collar

Puritan collar

Sailor collar

Mandarin collar

Notched collar

Rolled collar

Asymmetrical collar

Cape collar

Collars

175

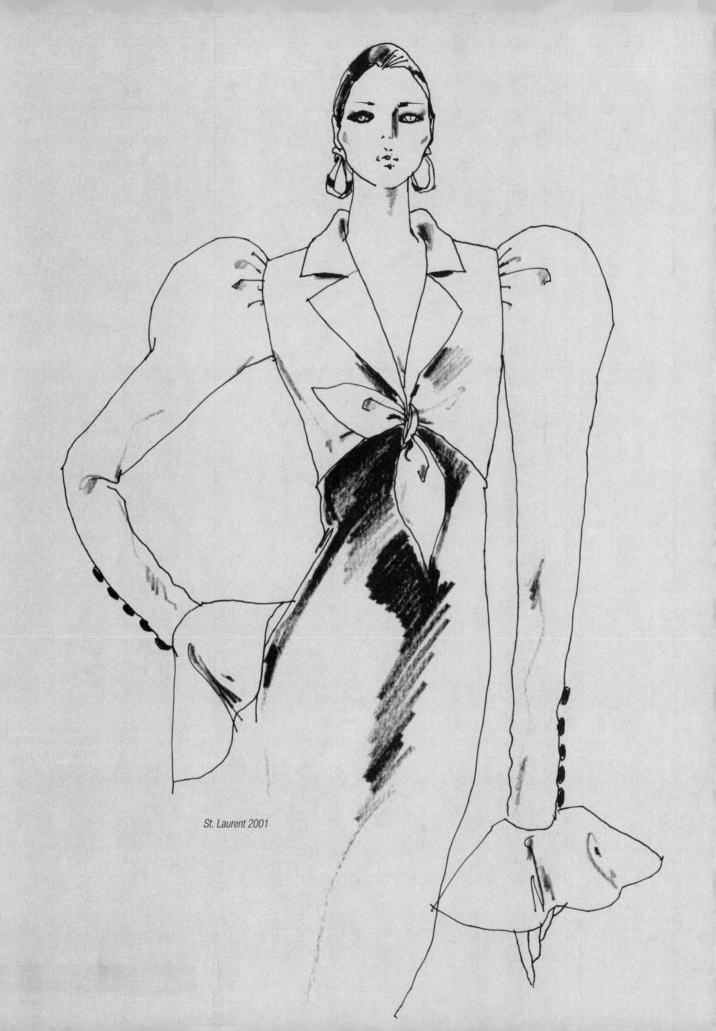

St. Laurent 2001

Sleeves are those parts of a garment that cover and involve the arms. They can be as perfectly simple as a set-in sleeve of a Chanel jacket or as elaborate as the sleeves on an Ungaro ballgown.

When drawing a sleeve, the most important principle to understand is the relationship of the sleeve to the arm. Certain kinds of sleeves, for example, those in a tailored jacket, hang perfectly straight when the arm is relaxed, but folds form when the arm is bent or in movement. Others, as in a dropped shoulder shirt sleeve, are straight when the arm is extended, but folds form when the arm is relaxed.

Each period of fashion has its own look and fit for the sleeve and armhole. For example, the 1960s gave us small shoulders and very high armholes, while the 1980s had very padded shoulders and fullness in the sleeve caps. However, by studying the underlying concepts that apply to any sleeve style, the current fashion will never throw you off. Understanding tailored sleeves, relaxed sleeves, and sleeves that extend from the bodice will not only help you to draw them more accurately, but will actually assist you in choosing poses that best represent them.

Lagerfeld/Chanel 1995

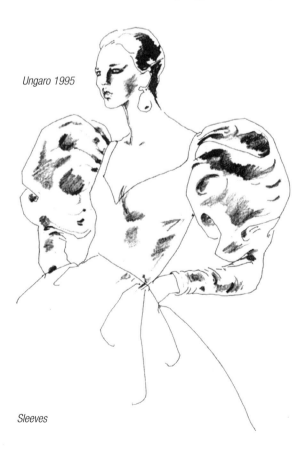

Ungaro 1995

Tailored or Set-in Sleeves

1 A tailored sleeve hangs perfectly straight from the armhole and joins the armhole with a seam. When the arm is hanging straight in a relaxed position next to the body, generally the sleeve is free of excess fold.

By studying the sleeve pattern of a one-piece, set-in sleeve and its relationship to the arm, you can see that the cap is cut high enough to accommodate the shoulder muscle.

2 The armhole of the bodice follows the natural shape between the underarm and shoulder. Rows of gathering stitches are pulled to slightly ease in the fabric, and the puckering is "shrunk" out so that the sleeve will fit smoothly into the armhole. This, as well as the ease at the elbow, allows the arm to move and permits the sleeve to hang straight.

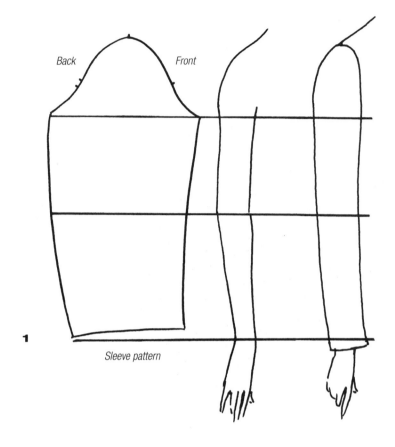

1

Back   Front

Sleeve pattern

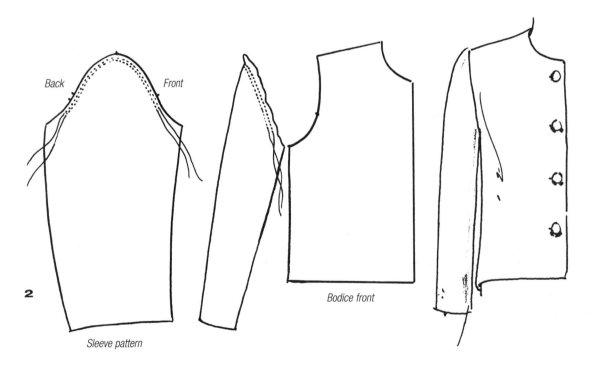

2

Back   Front

Sleeve pattern   *Bodice front*

3 Sometimes, especially in jackets and coats, the sleeve is cut in two pieces. Rather than the seam being under the arm, there is a seam near the back, which curves with the elbow, and a seam on the inside, which curves with the natural bend of the arm. Such two-pieces consist of an upper sleeve and an under sleeve. You can see how the pattern pieces perfectly duplicate the angle in which the arm hangs.

Often, there is an extension at the hem, which is called a vent. In many custom-made suits, these extensions actually unbutton. Most of the time, however, these buttons are just sewn on for the "look."

4 Padded shoulders do not change any of the principles of sleeves. They merely change the silhouette. The shoulder seams of the bodice are extended and the sleeve cap is modified. The pad fills this space to create a broad-shouldered look.

Study examples of set-in sleeves in various positions to learn how different fabrics and different designs change the look of the sleeve. This will help you not only to draw them, but to understand how they work and enhance a garment.

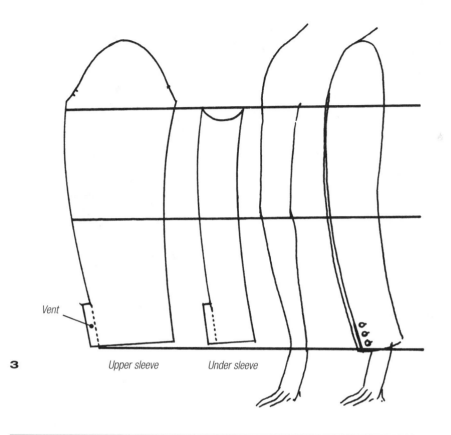

3   *Upper sleeve*   *Under sleeve*

Vent

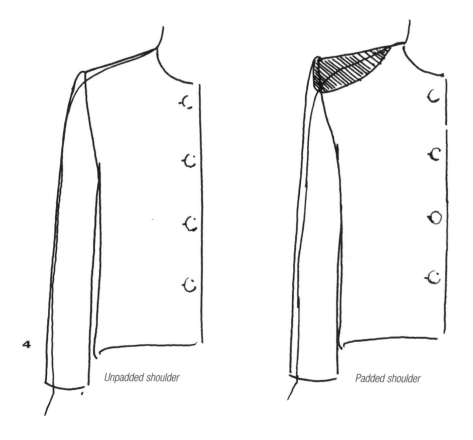

4   *Unpadded shoulder*   *Padded shoulder*

Drawing Set-in Sleeves

1 Begin by drawing in the sleeve cap and the fall to the bend of the elbow. Keep the sleeve cap smooth over the shoulder.

2 Allow for a gentle break at the elbow and draw the inside of the lower half. Notice how the fabric falls on the arm.

3 There will also be a slight break at the shoulder muscle in the back, but the line will be smooth to the elbow and the wrist.

4 In contrast to the upper arm, notice how the fabric falls away from the lower half of the arm. Make sure that the hem encircles the wrist.

5 The finished sleeve should look smooth and unwrinkled.

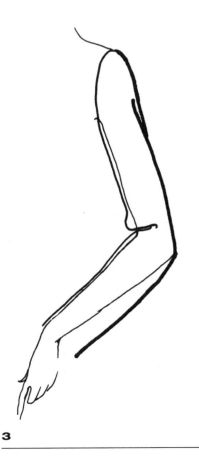

1

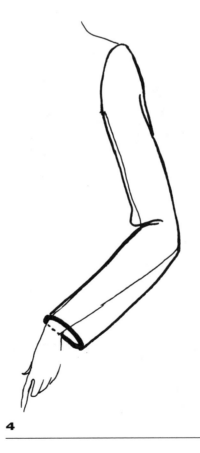

2

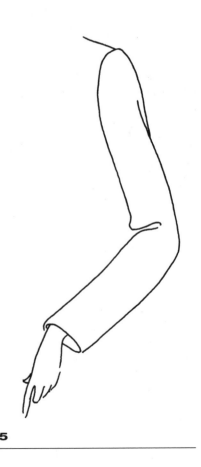

3

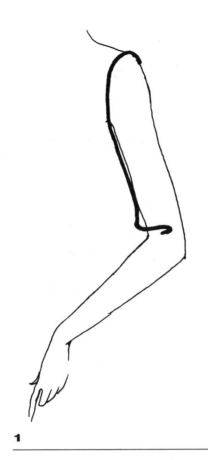

4

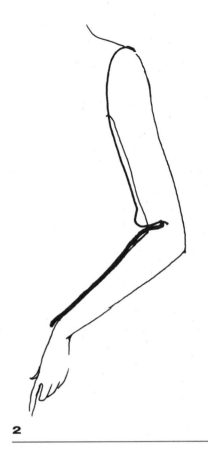

5

Observe how a tailored sleeve
hangs smoothly when the arm is
in its natural position. Folds form
when the arm begins to move.

Relaxed Sleeves (Dropped Shoulder Sleeve)

There are times when folds are a part of the sleeve design and must be drawn as a part of your art. This type of sleeve generally has a lower sleeve cap and a deeper armhole. The armhole also has an angle to it, and because it is not resting on the shoulder, it seems to be dropping off. This is a dropped shoulder sleeve or a relaxed sleeve.

The most familiar of these sleeves can be found on certain kinds of shirts. When you study the way that these shirts hang on the body, you will notice that the armhole is lower, looser, and appears more comfortable and relaxed. Sometimes the design can become oversized and exaggerated and there is an excess of fabric under the arms.

When you compare the pattern to the arm, you can see that there is a shallow or slightly less curved sleeve cap. Because it is set in a bit below the natural shoulder and does not mold it, the excess fabric will form folds. These folds must be a part of the drawing, because they are a part of the design.

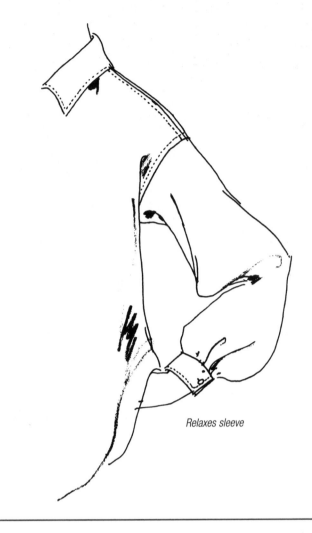

Relaxes sleeve

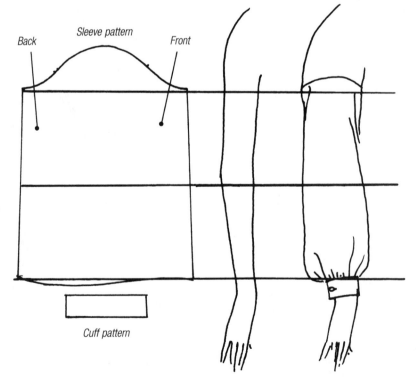

Back   Sleeve pattern   Front

Cuff pattern

Take note of the amount of
space between the arm and the
sleeve. Also, there is a slight hook
that forms at the underarm where
the excess fabric begins.

The arm does not fill the sleeve,
and the armhole does not mold the
shoulder. Because it is unsupport-
ed, this excess of fabric will relax
and folds will form when the arm
hangs in its natural position. Watch
how the folds begin to disappear
when they reach the underarm of
the body.

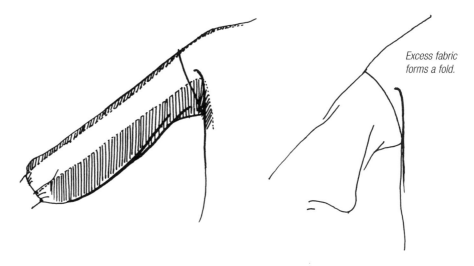

*Excess fabric
forms a fold.*

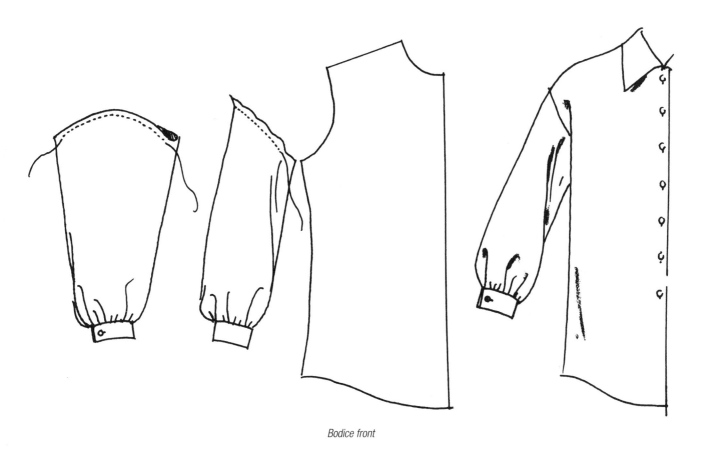

Bodice front

Drawing Relaxed Sleeves

1 Start at the armhole and follow the fold that appears from the armhole to the elbow. Also, keep a gentle fold at the elbow.

2 The fabric falls onto the inside of the lower arm into the cuff or hem. Make sure that the cuff or hem circles the wrist.

3 Continue the back with a smooth line. Notice how the excess fabric falls away from the elbow.

4 Finish with gathers or a hemline.

5 The finished relaxed sleeve should have a graceful flow.

1

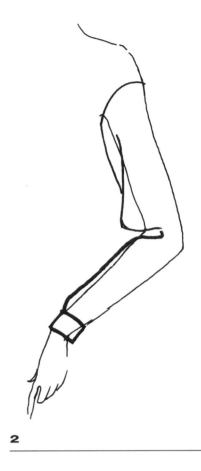

2

3

4

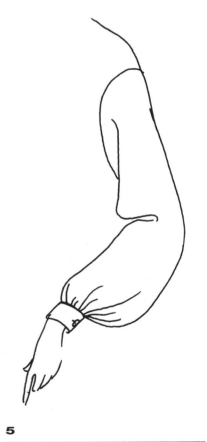

5

Remember, it is not necessary for relaxed sleeves to have a cuff. They can have a loose or a tapered hem. Notice the way the folds work when the arm is in different positions.

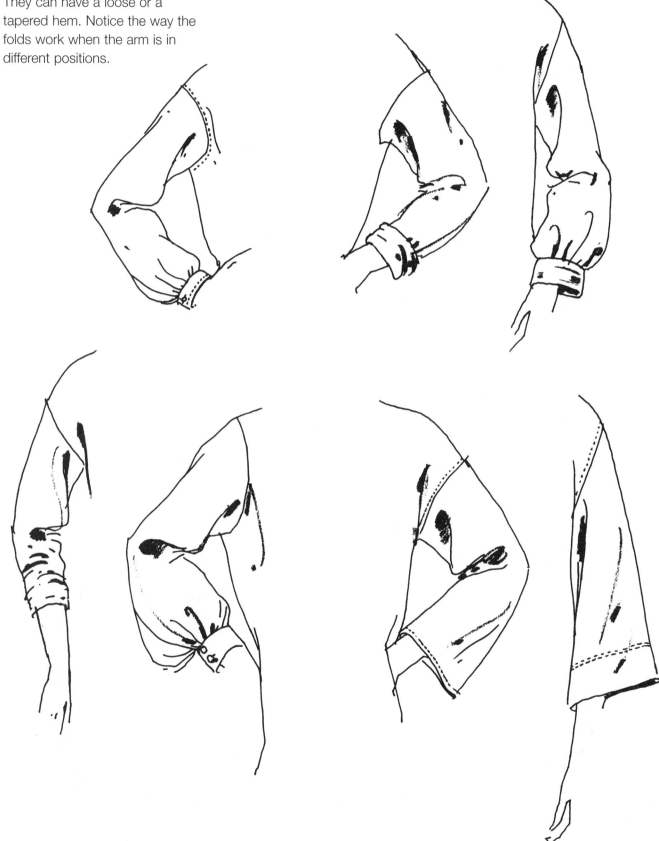

Sleeve Hems

In a tailored sleeve, the sleeve hem curves slightly upward from the front, and then angles down toward the back from the side. Additionally, in relaxed sleeves—whether the hem is plain or gathered—there is also a curve upward from the front, which angles down from the side.

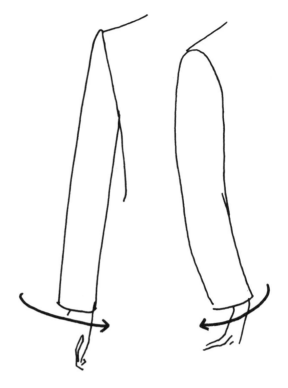

Tailored sleeve hems

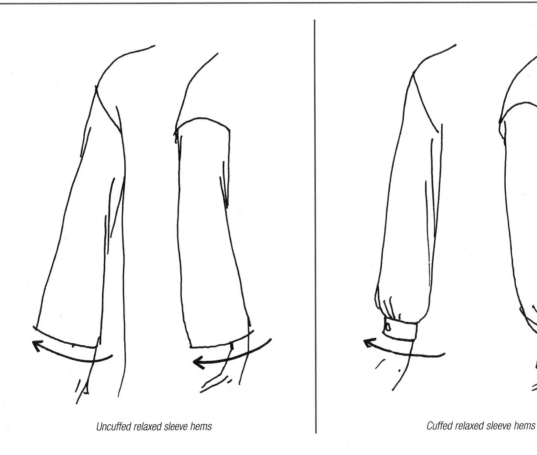

Uncuffed relaxed sleeve hems

Cuffed relaxed sleeve hems

Cuffs and Fullness

Sleeves can also be gathered or pleated into a cuff, which is a rectangular piece of fabric that holds the excess fabric of the sleeve. In a full sleeve, excess fabric is added to the bottom of the sleeve pattern. A full sleeve can be designed in a simple shirt with two pleats, or in a huge, extravagant sleeve on a bridal gown.

Let's examine the pattern piece and its relationship to the arm. Notice how the bottom of the sleeve is larger and blends into the cap. The larger it becomes, the more volume or fullness the sleeve will have. Observe how the back of the pattern piece dips. This is to accommodate the bend of the arm. It will also give the sleeve a graceful flow. It can be gathered or pleated into a cuff that is either narrow or deep, of any width, and can have any number of buttons.

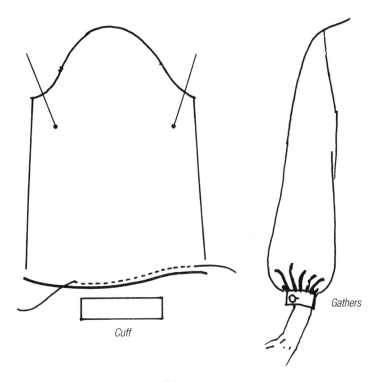

Cuff

Gathers

Full sleeve

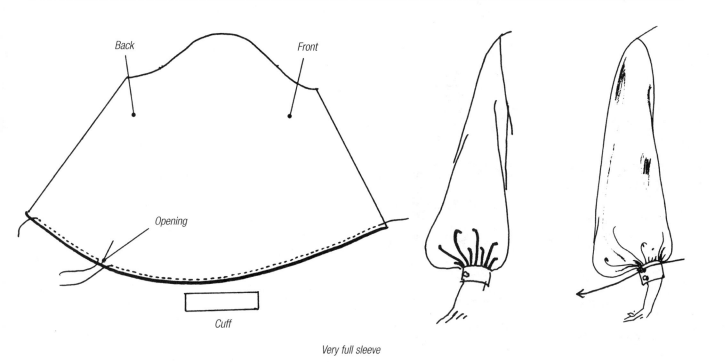

Back

Front

Opening

Cuff

Very full sleeve

Caps and Fullness

The top or cap of the sleeve can be gathered as well. This will give the most volume and drama. A good example of this type of sleeve is a balloon sleeve. Such soft fabrics as lightweight silk, chiffon, or georgette will fall onto the upper arm and fall away from the elbow. Stiffer fabrics, as in a taffeta or organdy, will create a space on each side of the arm.

A full sleeve cap might also taper to a tight wrist, as in a leg-o'-mutton sleeve, and it might be finished at the hem with buttons or a zipper. Remember, different fabrics and cuts will create many different looks in a full, gathered sleeve.

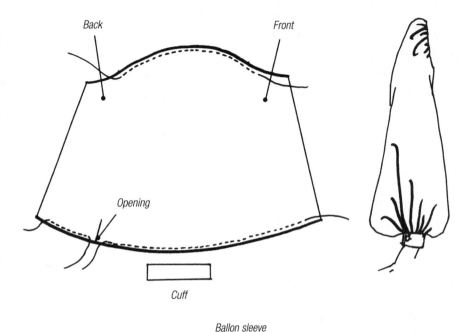

Ballon sleeve

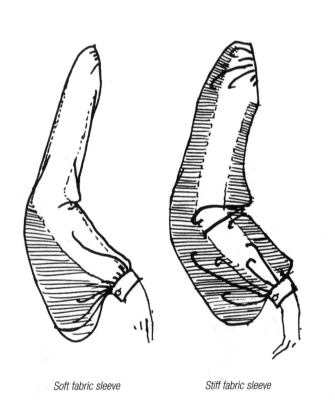

Soft fabric sleeve　　*Stiff fabric sleeve*

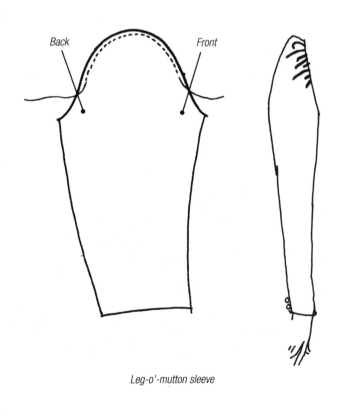

Leg-o'-mutton sleeve

Different fabrics and cuts create many different looks.

Raglan Sleeves

A raglan sleeve has a diagonal seam that extends from under the arm to the neck area. It has many variations, from fitted to loose, from hemmed or gathered into a cuff. A raglan sleeve can be cut in one piece with a dart at the shoulder or with an outside seam to help shape the shoulder. Observe the way different cuts and fabrics affect the look of raglan sleeves.

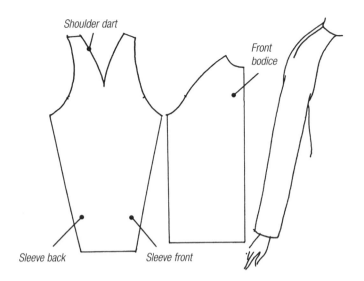

Shoulder dart

Front bodice

Sleeve back

Sleeve front

One-piece raglan sleeve

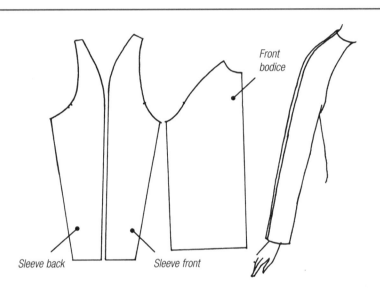

Front bodice

Sleeve back

Sleeve front

Two-piece raglan sleeve

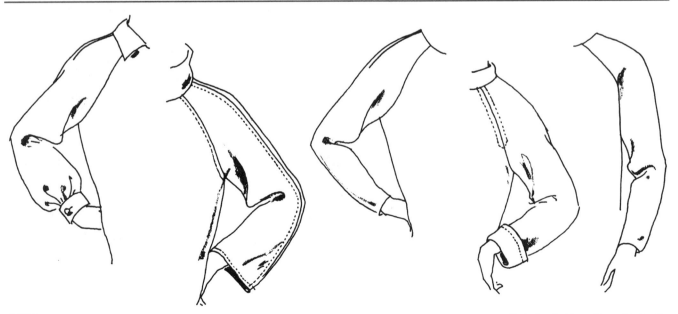

How Sleeves Work on the Arm

Let's study how the sleeve is drawn on the arm. When seamed together, the sleeve becomes a cylinder. It is covering the arm, which is also cylindrical in shape. A cylindrical perspective is formed, which gives the feeling of roundness and depth to the drawing. Notice how the sleeve surrounds the arm, and how any hem from above the elbow takes an upward curve. However, in a bent arm, it is also possible for the hem of the sleeve to curve upward. From this view, it is possible to slightly see into the sleeve or cuff.

On the upper half of the arm, the sleeve fabric rests on the outside and falls away from the inside of the arm. On the lower half of the arm, the sleeve rests on the inside and falls away from the elbow. Additionally, when the arm is raised in a full sleeve, an "S"-type fold forms.

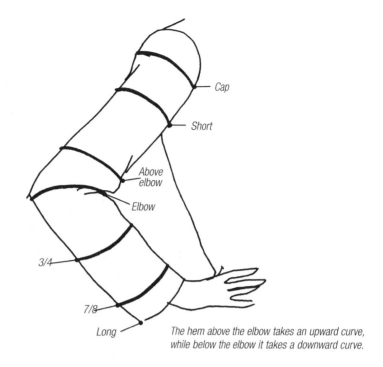

Cap

Short

Above elbow

Elbow

3/4

7/8

Long

The hem above the elbow takes an upward curve, while below the elbow it takes a downward curve.

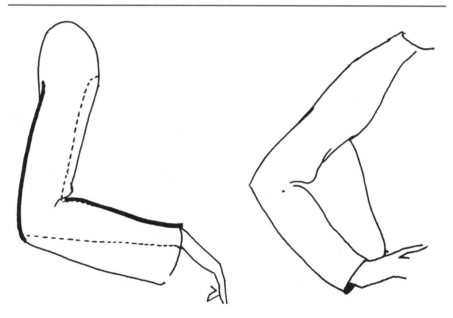

Relationship of fabric to arm

Sometimes the sleeve hem curves upward

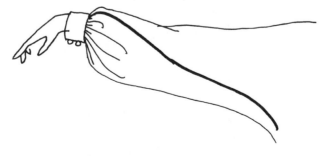

Raised arm showing "S" fold

Armholes

An armhole is that part of the bodice from which the arm can extend. It is also where a sleeve can be attached. Even though armholes have curves, in a front view, it is best to keep them nearly straight with just the slightest of curves. They almost form a parenthesis.

In a turned or ¾ view, both the armholes curve in the direction that the upper body is facing, lying parallel to each other. Notice how the armhole circles from the back. Remember, in a turned figure that breast goes in front of the armhole.

Front view sleeves for slight parenthesis.

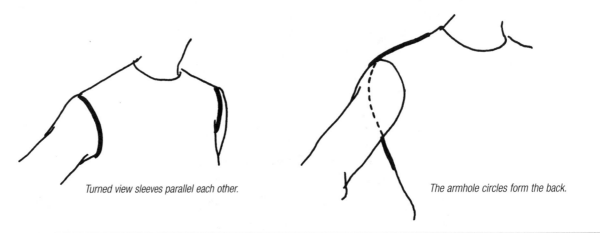

Turned view sleeves parallel each other.

The armhole circles form the back.

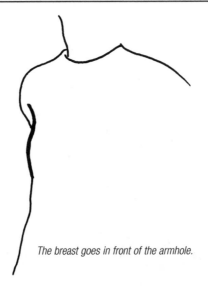

The breast goes in front of the armhole.

In a raglan sleeve armhole, the seam can be drawn straight or slightly curved. It depends on the fit and the style. Also, on a turned figure, you must try to sense the side of the body.

Remember, never "bite" into the fabric when the arm is bent. Make the fold line smooth and flowing. Also, gathers come out of a seam. Don't make these gathers jagged or harsh, with "teeth" marks. Simple, flowing lines will say it much better. In general, keep the folds round and gentle. Also, observe the way that different fabrics affect the way the sleeve falls.

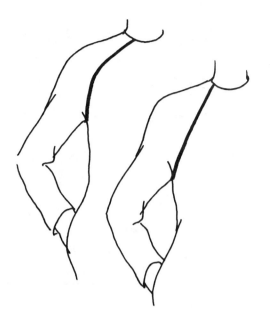

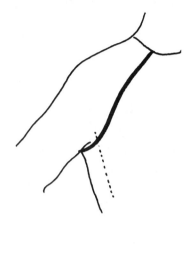

Raglan seams can be curved or straight.

Be aware of the side plane of the body.

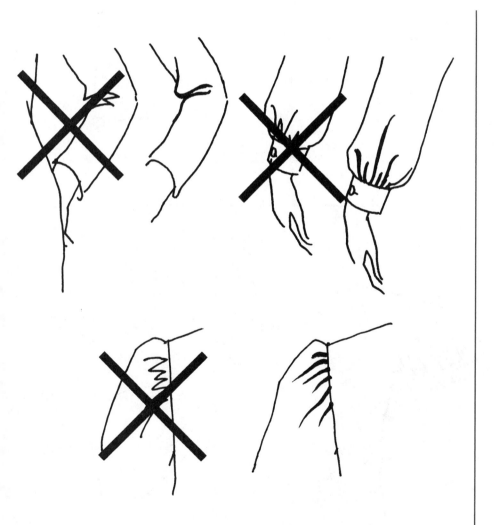

Avoid "bites" and "teeth."

Keep the sleeve folds smooth and flowing.

Sleeves Cut in One Piece with the Bodice

Sometimes, you will want to draw a very dramatic sleeve with a great deal of volume under the arm, but which has no armhole seam. Examples of such sleeves are the dolman and the kimono. This type of sleeve is cut in one piece with the bodice. Because of the great amount of fabric involved in producing this type of sleeve, they are not as common as set-in, relaxed, or raglan sleeves. Also, the pattern pieces are quite large, and it is not easy to fit other pattern pieces with them.

However, just as in the relaxed sleeve, this type of sleeve falls perfectly straight when the arm is extended. Notice the huge amount of space between the sleeve and the arm. When the arm is dropped or is bent, very dramatic folds form. Again, you will see the folds seem to disappear as they reach the underarm. These folds should never extend past the armhole.

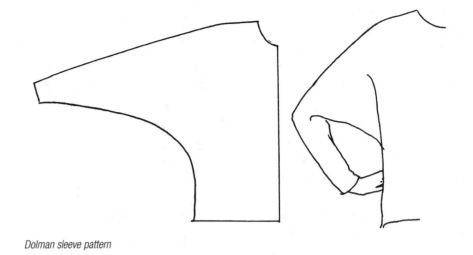

Dolman sleeve pattern

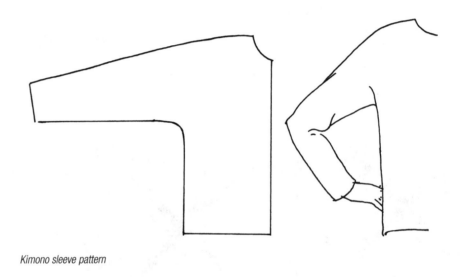

Kimono sleeve pattern

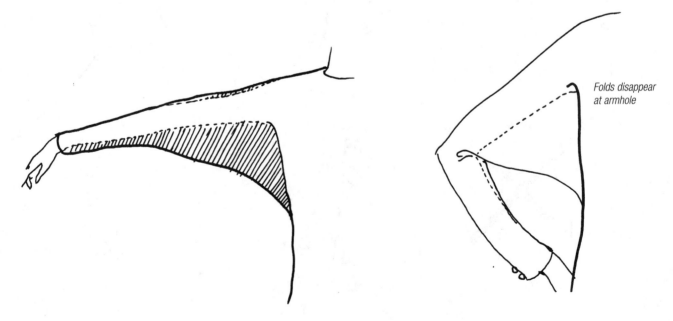

Folds disappear at armhole

Gussets

Occasionally, you might want a sleeve cut in one piece with the bodice, but which is higher under the arm. Without some sort of accommodation, this kind of sleeve would have to be made in a stretch fabric because in any other type of fabric, the seams would rip open when the arm moves. By adding a gusset, which is a diamond or triangular bias-cut piece of fabric, this problem is avoided. A gusset placed under the arm or extending down into the bodice enables the sleeve to have movement, with a smoother fit under the arms, without excess fabric.

Study the great variety of folds this type of sleeve has in various poses.

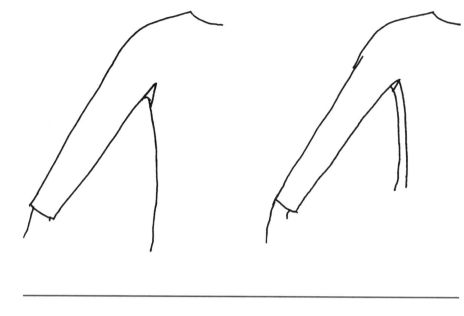

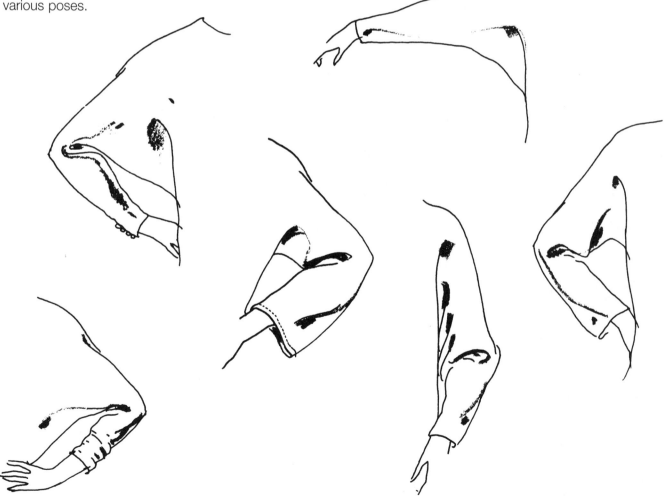

Now that you understand the basic concepts of sleeves and how to draw them, there is no limit to the variations that you can draw. You can take the top of one style and the bottom of another—creating a set-in dolman, gathered raglan, dropped shoulder kimono, short puffed, three-quarter set-in—the possibilities are endless!

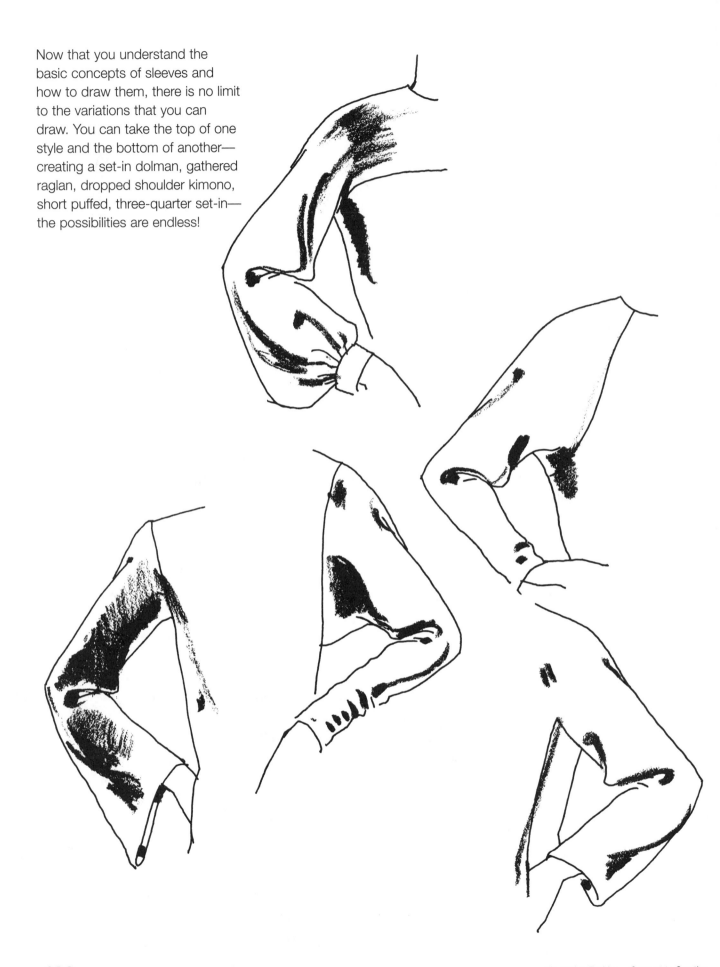

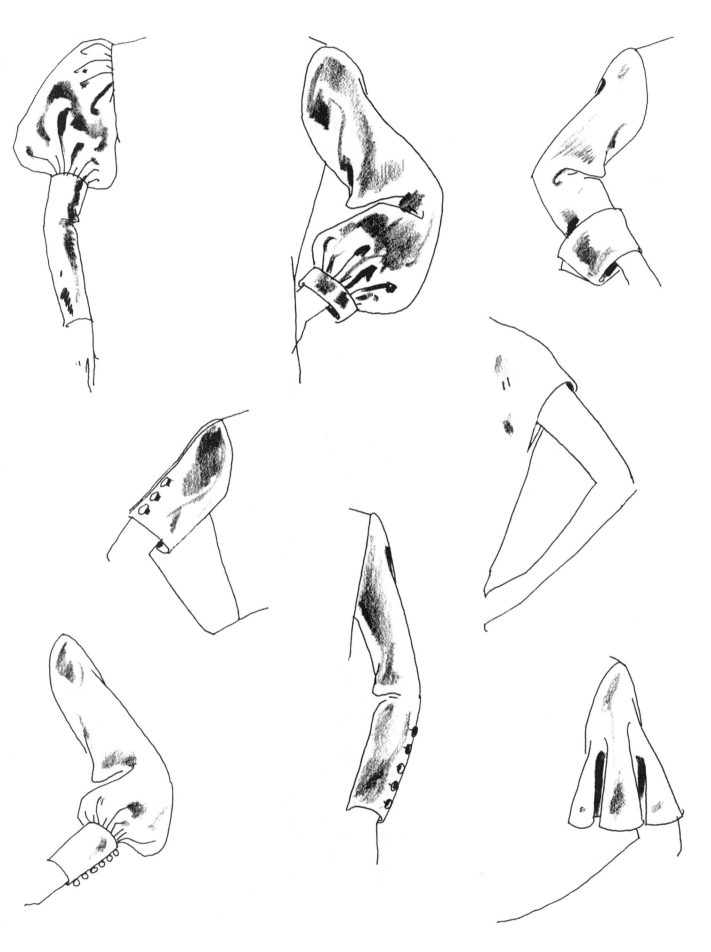

Sleeve Styles

Set-in sleeve

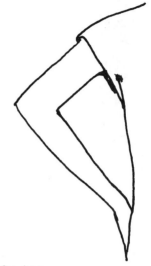

Cap sleeve

Dolman sleeve

Balloon sleeve

Puffed sleeve

Bell or angel sleeve

Bishop sleeve

Kimono sleeve

Juliet sleeve

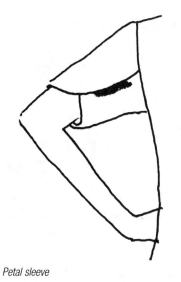

Petal sleeve

Shirt sleeve

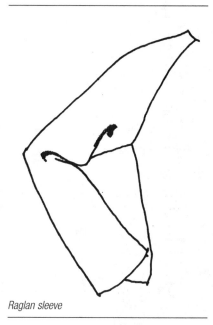

Raglan sleeve

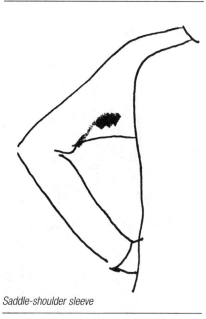

Saddle-shoulder sleeve

Lantern sleeve

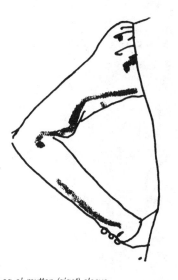

Leg-o'-mutton (gigot) sleeve

Circular sleeve

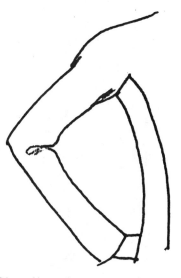

Princess kimono sleeve

Sleeves

St. Laurent 2001

19
Blouses, Shirts, and Tops

A blouse is a particular type of clothing for the upper body, and even though it is similar in many ways, it is usually softer than a shirt. Both may be buttoned up or pulled on over the head. Generically, a top can be either of these, but for the purposes of this book, we have classified them as a more casual, upper-body garment. However, these can range from the tight fit of a ribbed halter top to a long, one-button vest.

The fit of a blouse, shirt, or top changes with fashions of the moment. In the 1960s, bodyshirts were as fitted as a second skin; in the 1980s, shirts were so oversized that they appeared several sizes too large. In the 1990s, cropped tops that showed the navel were a number one fashion item. This trend reached its height in the early 2000s and appeared on everything from sportswear to evening clothes.

Drawing Shirts

When drawing shirts, some important details to observe are:

- Yoke, which is that portion of a garment that extends across the shoulder, front, or back. The bodice attached to it can be plain, pleated, or gathered.

- Flat-felled seams, which are seams that are finished with the stitching showing on the outside.

- Collar band, which is that portion near the collar that stands up and circles the neck. It generally buttons, but can be fastened by a stud in a tuxedo-style shirt. Also, it may remain as a band or have a collar attached.

- Shirt band, which is a band that extends down the front of a shirt to the hem. Buttons generally are attached to it.

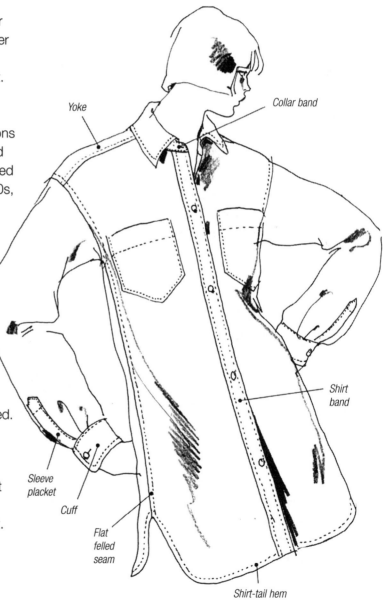

Yoke

Collar band

Shirt band

Sleeve placket

Cuff

Flat felled seam

Shirt-tail hem

- Sleeve packet, which is a slit at the sleeve that is generally finished with a facing. It extends from the cuff toward the elbow. Again, this detail enables the garment to be taken on and off easily.

- Cuff, which is a finish for a sleeve made from a separately sewn-on piece of cloth, which generally is closed by one or more buttons.

- French cuff, which is a cuff that is turned back and fastened with cufflinks. Often used in fancy blouses and tuxedo shirts (and many times in men's wear).

- Shirttail hem, which is a finished hem that is made to look like a man's shirt hem. In women's wear, a hem of this sort can be either tucked in or not.

- Tucks, which are narrow pleats that are stitched in place. These are usually arranged in a series and designated by width, as in an inch, half-inch, quarter-inch, also pin tucks. Pin tucks are only wide enough for a row of stitching.

A tuxedo shirt has a precision to the tucks, while the camp shirt has a great simplicity with the print or cut completely changing its look. The western shirt has its own yoke, pocket, and piping details that rarely change with the prevailing style.

Shirts should look somewhat crisp, with such details as stitching and tucks kept very precise. Shadows on a white shirt are usually done in a light- to medium-gray color.

Tucks

Tuxedo shirt

French cuff

Camp shirt

Western shirt

Blouses and Tops

Unlike shirts, which, regardless of their cut or fabric, follow more specific forms of construction, blouses and tops have more unique details to their design.

Blouses can range from the innocence of a middy blouse to the sultry feeling of a gypsy blouse, from the polish of a stock tie to the romance of a poet-sleeved blouse to the ethnic feel of a cossack blouse. They can be close-fitting or voluminous and extravagant. There is no limit to their variations. Try to keep the feeling of the specific look in your artwork.

Middy blouse

Gypsy blouse

Cascade-front blouse

Poet-sleeve blouse

Stock-tie blouse

204

Wrap blouse

Cossack blouse

Bow-neck blouse

Tops can fit like the second skin of a tank top or a barely existent bandeau. They can be oversized as well, as in a T-shirt or tunic top. If they are very fitted and in a stretch fabric, keep the look close to the body. If the torso is oversized, keep the look of the generous cut. Vests and tunics often are layered over other tops, blouses, or shirts.

Additionally, any shirt, top, or blouse can be worn as a single item or it can be layered over or under other garments as well. Often the pose has to be worked so that all the pieces show. Opening up some of these layers, partially unbuttoning others, or rolling up the sleeves can help when combining many layers.

Tank top

Shell

Bandeau

Crop top

T-shirt

Halter top

Oversized shirt

Cowl-neck tunic

Vest

Cardin 1966

Dior 1948

20

The History of Skirts— Hemlines and Silhouettes

We have come a long way since skirt hems swept the ground and women were not allowed to show an ankle. Until the 1960s, skirt lengths were dictated by a handful of major designers, and women followed their lead. Long, to the knees, or as short as the law would allow, until recently the length of a woman's skirt has always been a major fashion issue.

In the early 1900s, skirts were full length, with just a glimmer of the shoe showing. There were layers of underskirts to help shape the skirts and corsets to keep the waistline as small as possible. Worth, Doucet, and Lucile were responsible for many of the elaborate dress designs of this period.

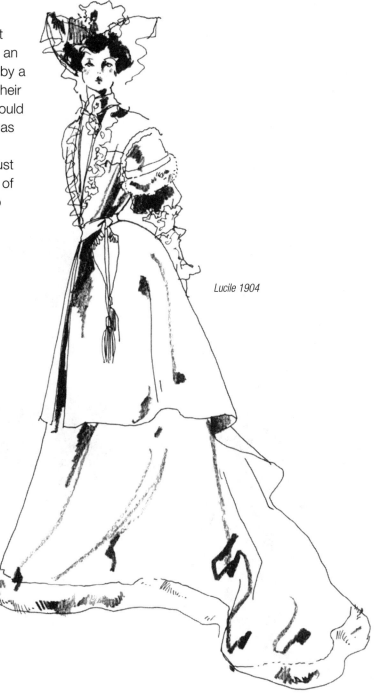

Lucile 1904

Teens

In the early teens, we began to see the skirt silhouette come in closer to the body. Paul Poiret introduced the hobble or peg-top skirt, which was draped upward to the waistline. The hem touched the top of the shoe and the open drape allowed the ankle to show. By the late teens, designers such as Paquin began to raise the hemlines above the ankle.

Paquin 1917

Poiret 1913

1920s

The 1920s possibly gave us the most dramatic skirt length change of the 20th century. By 1926, skirt hems had risen to reach the knee. Never before were such short skirts worn by fashionable women. The 1920s also gave us separate skirt lengths—short for day, long for evening. Chanel, Vionnet, and Patou were early pioneers of the short skirt. With the leg taking on new importance, silk stockings and rouged knees also became quite the fashion. The major silhouette was flat-chested and boxy, with no waistline.

Vionnet 1925

Chanel 1926

1930s

By the 1930s, hemlines once again were lowered. Designers Molyneux and Schiaparelli were showing skirts that reached from below the knee to near the ankle for day. Evening dresses and skirts were almost always full length. The bias cut was very popular and the clothes were cut to be worn close to the body. The silhouette was elegant and flowing.

Schiaparelli 1934

Molyneux 1931

Early 1940s

By 1940, skirt lengths reached to about 15 inches from the floor (approximately the bottom of the knee). During the first half of the 1940s, skirts continued to be this length or slightly shorter. World War II and the restrictions placed on the use of fabric helped bring about this change. Joan Crawford helped popularize the look of Adrian's intricately cut suits with padded shoulders and a simple, straight skirt silhouette.

Adrian early 1940s

Late 1940s

After the war was over, women felt the need to once again feel feminine and fashionable, and the New Look of Christian Dior in 1947 was the solution. Hemlines dropped to just above the ankles, and the skirt's fullness was held out by layers of petticoats. Skirts once again covered nearly the entire leg and silhouettes of cinched waists, padded hips, and long, full skirts were reminiscent of the turn of the century.

Dior 1947

1950s

Hemlines remained basically unchanged through the early 1950s. In 1956, with the introduction of the chemise silhouette, such designers as Balenciaga, Givenchy, and Norell started to inch skirt hems up to just below the knee.

Balenciaga 1956

1960s

For the first half of the 1960s, hemlines stayed at the knee. However, the 60s would change the hemline story forever. From the mid-60s on, there would never be just one dictated skirt length.

In the middle of the 1960s, London's Mary Quant, France's André Courrèges, and America's Rudi Gernreich were the early pioneers of the miniskirt. This is the shortest skirt length in modern fashion. The silhouette was geometric, often cookie-cutter, but above all, modern.

Courrèges 1964

Ungaro 1969

Saint Laurent 1969

Givenchy 1969

1970s

From the shortest micro-minis of the late 1960s, the next logical place for the hem to go was down. And down it went. The midi skirt reached to mid-calf (or slightly longer) and the maxi reached nearly to the ankle. These lengths gave us the mini\midi\maxi debate of the late 60s and early 1970s. Yves Saint Laurent, with his gypsy and ethnic collections, was responsible for the longer lengths and the layered, flowing silhouette that finally would win out toward the end of the 70s.

Saint Laurent 1974

1980s

At the beginning of the 1980s, hemlines were still long. Perry Ellis designed some of the longest ones, but unlike the 1970s ethnic look, the silhouette was spare and sleek. By the middle of the decade, skirts were beginning to shorten and the padded shoulder power suit worn with a short skirt was the silhouette that was quite prevalent. Emanuel Ungaro and Claude Montana helped to popularize both the silhouettes and the hemlines.

Perry Ellis 1983

Ungaro 1984

1990s–2000s

In the 1990s, skirt lengths were—for the most part—no longer a major issue. Women accepted all lengths for different occasions and when in doubt, turned to pants. The only issue with length seemed to be one of "what looks good sells." The use of transparent, lacy, and sheer fabrics (used in many different ways for various looks and lengths) became more important than the skirt length. The silhouettes varied and ranged from retro 1950s and 1960s looks to flowing sheer layers of fabric—and any of the silhouettes could be any length. Geoffrey Beene designed very short skirts in the 1990s, while Karl Lagerfeld experimented with skirts that were layers of lacy, sheer fabric for Chanel.

At the beginning of this century, there were no longer any established skirt lengths. Hemlines at Marc Jacobs and Chanel rose to mini lengths reminiscent of the 1960s, while other designers, such as Yojhi Yamamoto, dropped hemlines to the ankles.

The most significant change, however, was the asymmetrical hem. Suddenly hemlines were dipping up and down, both covering and exposing the legs at the same time. Waistlines often exposed the navel. Fabrics ranged from soft and flowing to all varieties of leather and suede. Unfinished, frayed, or fringed hemlines often replaced conventional hemline finishes.

For decades, skirt lengths were often the most talked about fashion message. Now that they are no longer such an issue, what will replace this controversy? As future designers and fashion artists, the answer rests with you.

Geoffrey Beene 1990

Lagerfeld/Chanel 1995

John Galliano/Dior 2000

Valentino 1983

A skirt is a garment that encircles the lower part of the figure. It generally begins at the waistline, but on occasion can start slightly above or below it. The length, as we have studied previously, can be any-where from a micro-mini to the floor.

A skirt can be a piece of clothing on its own, or it can be attached to a bodice, or it can be the lower part of a one-piece dress. It can be finished with a waistband or facing. Skirts can be gathered, pleated, or flared and can be any silhouette form very slim to extravagantly full.

Let's begin with a chart of different skirt lengths. This is just a reference point for you. As you probably know already, many of these lengths are called by many different names, depending on the decade or the fashion of the time. The names that we have chosen represent the most accurate description of that particular skirt.

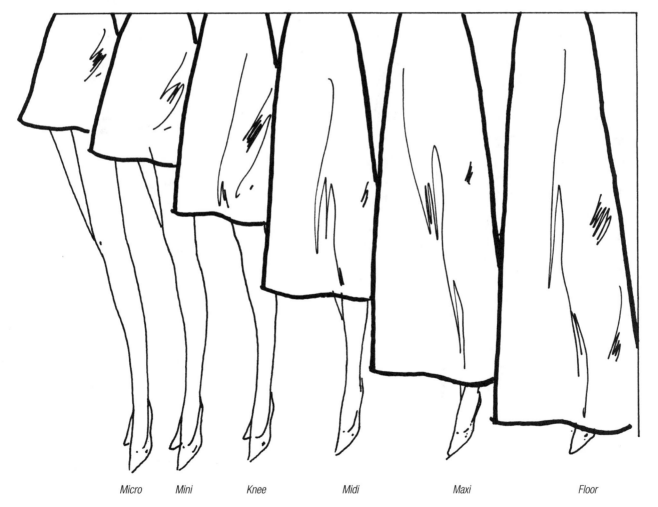

Micro   *Mini*   *Knee*   *Midi*   *Maxi*   *Floor*

Straight Skirts

To draw a straight skirt, first imagine a tube of fabric wrapped around the hip area. Because there is approximately a 10-inch difference, between the hip and the waist, there are several ways to fit the excess fabric into the waist, which include darts, pleats, ease (light gathers), or seams.

As the skirt gets larger at the hemline, the possibilities for fitting the excess fabric to the waistline also include gathers, pleats, or flares. In any skirt, the hemline follows the direction of the high hip. Remember, in all clothing, fabric is an important factor and will affect the way the folds of the hemline will fall.

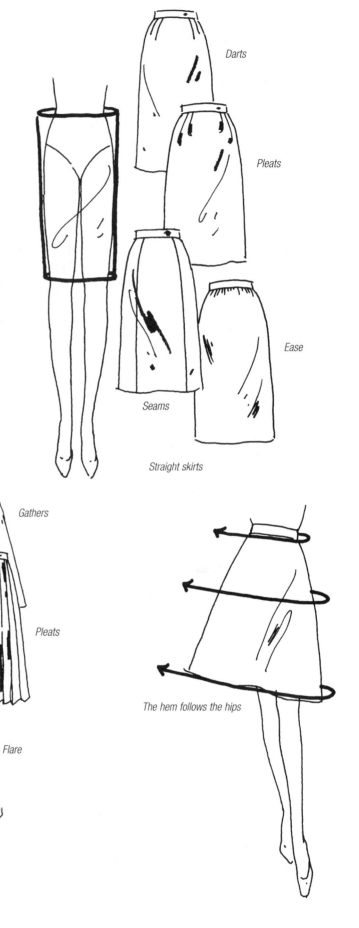

Darts

Pleats

Ease

Seams

Straight skirts

Gathers

Pleats

Flare

The hem follows the hips

Full skirts

Drawing Straight Skirts

Start by blocking in the lower half of the figure. In a straight skirt, the skirt will fall away from the high hip and onto the relaxed hip. There will be slight pulls from the high hip toward the opposite hem. The hemline must never be completely straight or have "points," because the body is cylindrical and the garment that encircles it will round at the edge.

Additionally, the waistband must never be drawn straight, but should be given an upward curve that goes with the cylindrical shape of the body. Keep it even and crisp, and depending on the design, the waistband can be drawn to fall directly on or above or below the natural waistline. It can close with a buttonhole and button or hooks and eyes.

The darts, pleats, or ease should have lines that conform to the roundness of the body. This will give your figure dimension.

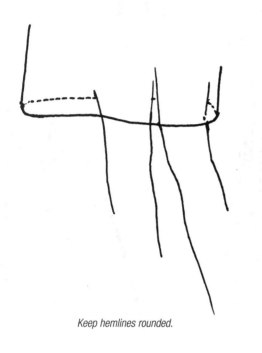

Keep hemlines rounded.

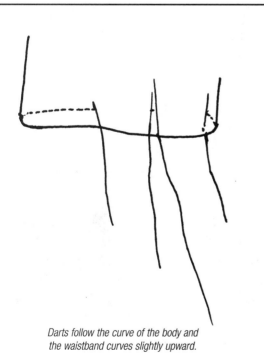

Darts follow the curve of the body and the waistband curves slightly upward.

Gathered Skirts

Gathered skirts are panels of fabric sewn together and shirred or gathered onto a waistband or seam. Double rows of basting stitches are sewn to the fabric and pulled to achieve the desired fullness. Because of this, the relationship between the waistline and the hem becomes a bit more complex in a gathered skirt as opposed to a straight skirt.

Drawing Gathered Skirts

Begin by drawing the lower half of the figure. Start indicating the gathers, keeping the lines rounded to show the form of the figure. (Remember, the helm follows the direction or movement of the high hip.) Draw some of the lines longer than others and some shorter, so that the rhythm is pleasing but not even. Lighten the pressure as the lines get close to the hem. Make sure that the gathers touch the waistband or seam. Also, do not draw these lines so that they look like a graph.

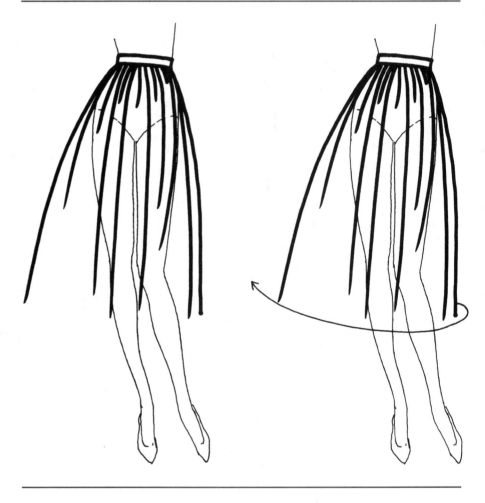

Gathers start at the waistband, not below.

In a gathered skirt, excess yardage is brought into the waistband or seamline, which causes the fabric to make a series of folds at the hem. These folds double back on one another and seem to fall into sections. Depending on the length of the skirt, these sections will take on rectangular or columnar shapes.

To draw the folds at the hem, imagine a double hem. The bottom of the skirt is the first hem. To help you with this concept, draw in a dotted line that follows the sweep of the hem. Next, dot in another line that also follows the sweep, but is slightly above the bottom hem. These "hems" will help you place the folds of the skirt correctly. The folds that fall forward will touch the bottom dotted line. The folds that fall inward will touch the top dotted line. Keep all the lines slightly rounded as they circle the figure. Remember, some of the folds will be wider than others—and none should be exactly the same size.

Additionally, there will be a slight break at the knee when you draw a skirt that goes past the knees.

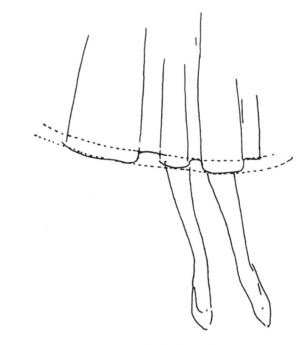

The "double hem"

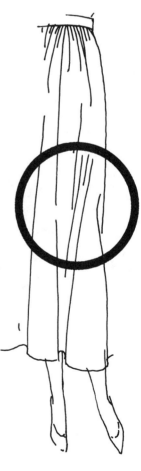

Break at knee

Ruffles, Flounces, and Tiers

A ruffle is actually a small gathered skirt that is attached to a larger one. When used as a hemline detail, they are called flounces. Because we are adding fullness, this will create even more folds at the hem. Also, the rectangular shapes of the gathers might look more square.

Flounces can also form tiers, which follow the same drawing principles as gathers. When drawing a tiered skirt, remember that the tiers of this type of skirt are sewn onto an underskirt—they are not sewn to each other. Generally, the width of each tier stays the same on each tier, but draw each tier as a separate skirt, overlapping them slightly.

Flared and gathered ruffles and flounces

Tiers

Ruffles

Flared Skirts

The hem of a flared skirt has a sweep that is greater than the waistband. By increasing the amount of the flare, the sweep of the hem can range from a gentle flow to a full circle with many ripples. This type of skirt has from two to four panels (or sections), but if the skirt is made of a very soft fabric, there may be more. When spread out, these panels form a circular shape.

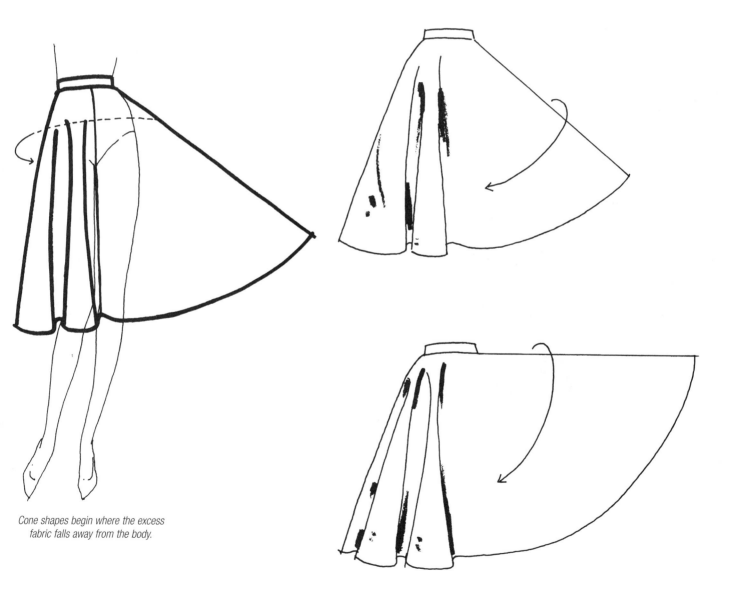

Cone shapes begin where the excess fabric falls away from the body.

In some flared skirts, some of the sections will fall on the bias of the fabric, which will cause a cone shape to form. This cone shape begins at the point at which the fabric falls away from the body.

Another point of interest in some types of flared skirts are gores. A gore is a narrow panel that tapers toward the waistline. Gores produce a cone shape in each section. A skirt that is made with body-fitting gores that flare out near the hemline is called a trumpet skirt. When this type of skirt is longer (near floor-length) it is called a mermaid skirt. Additionally, a straight, gored skirt can have triangular insets. These are called godets.

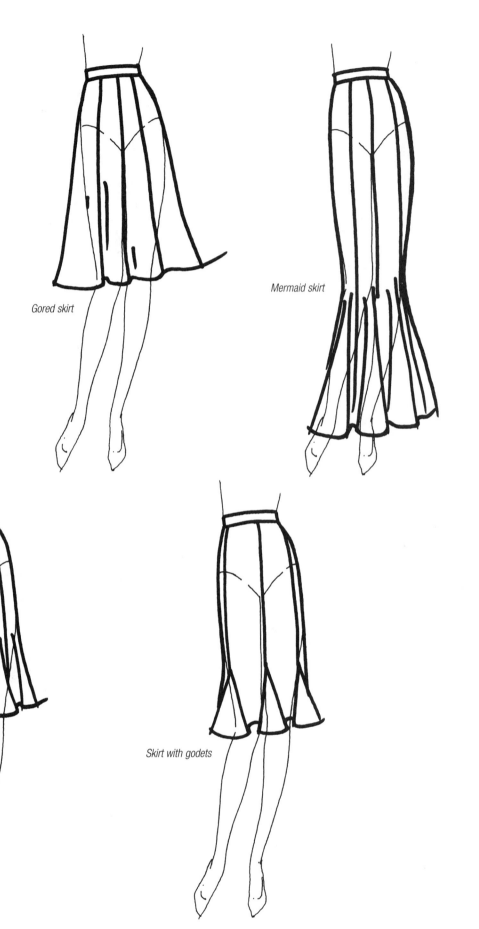

Gored skirt

Mermaid skirt

Trumpet skirt

Skirt with godets

Drawing Flared Skirts

First, draw in the lower half of the figure with a high hip. Depending on the sweep at the hem, bring the skirt out from the high hip. Indicate the cone sections, but stop the lines short of the waistline. This will indicate the excess fall of fabric. These lines (or shadows) should not be rigid.

After determining where the hemline will end, dot in the "second" hemline, which will help you place the folds correctly. (See page 227.) As previously discussed, the folds that fall forward will touch the bottom dotted line and the folds that fall inward will touch the top dotted line.

The amount of cone shapes at the hem will vary according to the sweep of the skirt and the fabric. Such soft fabrics as chiffon or georgette will have small folds at the hem, while a heavier fabric, such as wool crepe or flannel, will fall in bigger folds at the hem. No matter what size they are, keep these folds at the hem rounded, to show that the cut of the skirt is circular.

Cone shapes vary according to fabric weight.

Miters

Notice how the sections of a flared skirt look when the skirt is made of a striped or plaid fabric. The cone shape is formed by the bias. When these sections are seamed together, they form "V" shapes, or miters. Additionally, when a full circle skirt is cut from a striped fabric, the weight of the cone-shaped flares will make the stripes appear rounded. Because it is cut on the bias, the flares will cause many different drapes. Compare how different the same skirt looks when the bias is placed in different directions or gridlines. (For more on plaids and stripes, see Chapter 28, page 315.)

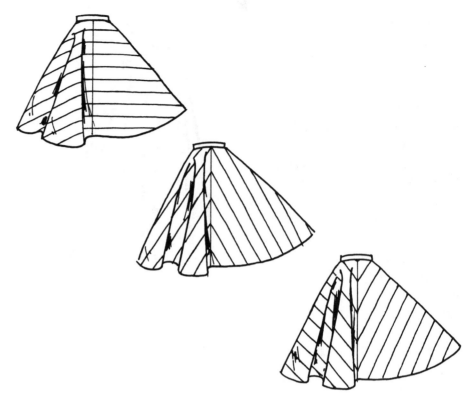

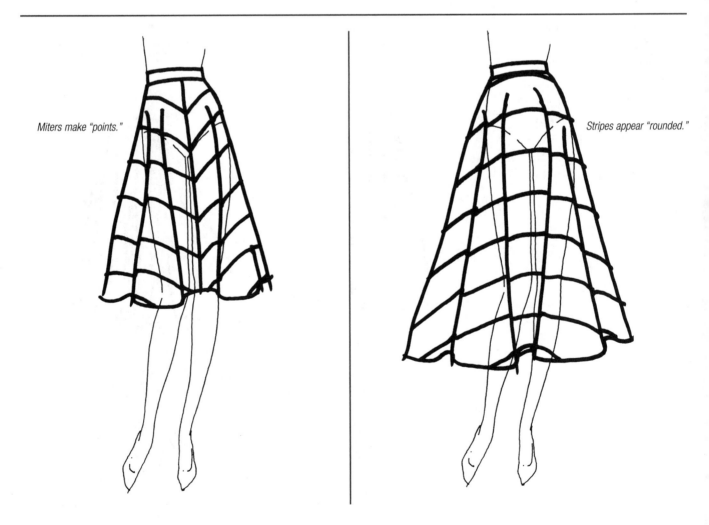

Miters make "points."

Stripes appear "rounded."

Pleated Skirts

Pleats are folds of fabric that are generally pressed flat. However, they can be unpressed and attached to a waistband or seam. Also, they might be stitched down at the top so that the hip area will have a smoother fit. There are many different kinds of pleats, which we will review, but when you draw a pleated skirt, you should follow the same basic principles as for a gathered skirt.

For all your drawings of pleated skirts, sketch in the lower half of the figure with one high hip. Be sure your center front line is accurate. In all pleated skirts, the hem follows the high hip, and you will use the same double hem technique that you learned with gathered and flared skirts.

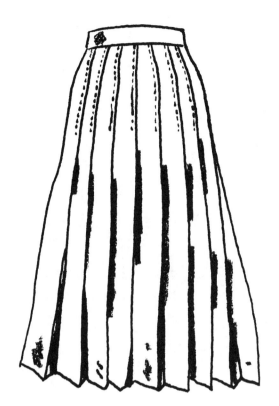

Stitched-down pleats

Pressed pleats

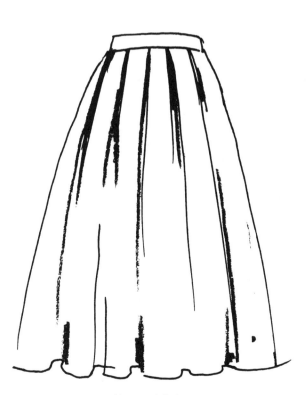

Unpressed pleats

Folded Pleats

The first pleats that we will review are the type in which the fabric is folded to form the pleat. This type of pleat is uniform in size from the waistband to the hem. Some types of folded pleats are:

- Inverted pleats, which fold into each side of the center. The simplest type of pleat is an inverted pleat that runs down the center front of the skirt. Keep the top of the pleat rounded as it passes over the stomach area. Draw the pleats with crisp, smooth lines. Also, there can be topstitching at the top of the pleat.

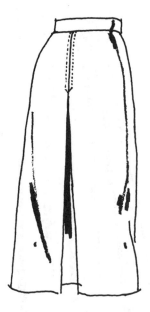

Stitched-down inverted pleat

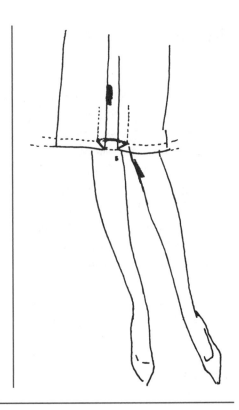

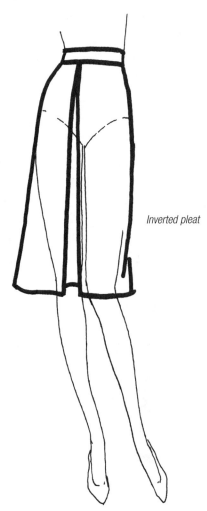

Inverted pleat

- Kick pleats, which are placed near the hem of the skirt. It can be either in the front or the back of the skirt. It is pressed to the side, and sometimes is stitched into place.

- Knife pleats, which are pressed in one direction and are usually ½- to 1-inch apart.

- Side pleats, which can be any width and may or may not be softly pressed.

- Box pleats, which are pleated and folded to face each other. They can be any width and may be crisply ironed or softly pressed, depending on the design.

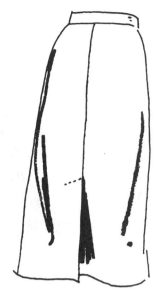

Kick pleat

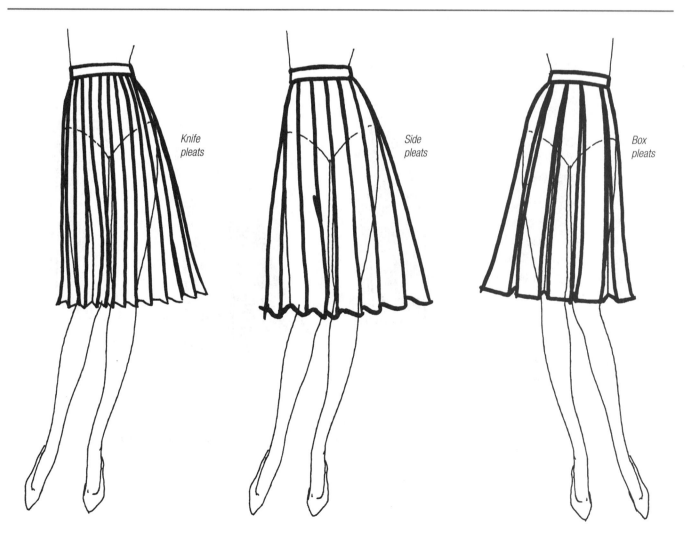

Knife pleats

Side pleats

Box pleats

Flared-type Pleats

The second type of pleat that we will review is not folded, but is based on the flared skirt. Typically, this type of pleat is heat-set and is smaller at the waistband and larger at the hem of the skirt. These pleats are not folded under the waistband (or seam), but fan out from it. They have much more movement to them than folded pleats, with more of a zigzag pattern at the bottom. Two of these pleats are:

• Accordion pleats, which are shaped like the bellows of an accordion.

• Sunburst pleats, which spread out at the hem like the rays of the sun.

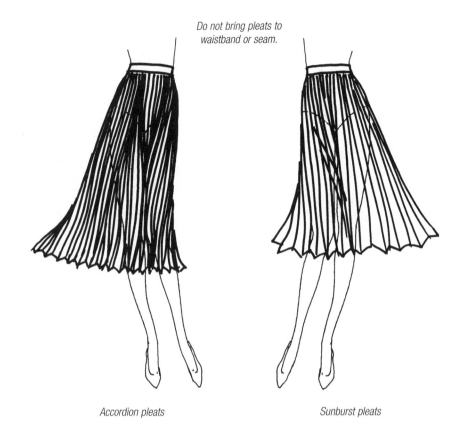

Do not bring pleats to waistband or seam.

Accordion pleats   *Sunburst pleats*

Fabrics can also be very finely pleated. Two examples are:

• Mushroom or crystal pleats, which have very fine pleats (this type is always heat-set.)

• Matchstick or broomstick pleats, which are also very fine (and heat-set), but are made to be irregular. These are versions of the pleats that were developed by Mariano Fortuny at the turn of the century.

When any type of pleat—pressed or unpressed—are formed in groups, it is called cluster pleating.

Mushroom or crystal pleats   *Matchstick or boomstick pleats*   *Cluster pleats*

Remember, skirts can be any combination of straight, gathered, or flared, with or without ruffles, flounces, gores, or pleats. Each skirt will have its own look based on cut and fabric as well. In the beginning, it will seem very complex, but always think of the skirt as its "own" finished design. Let the most important design elements be the basis of your drawing.

Skirt Silhouettes

Wrap skirt

Tapered skirt

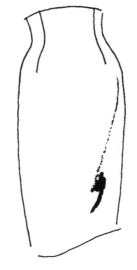

High-waisted skirt

Pegged skirt

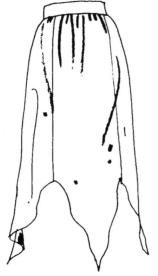

Handkerchief hem skirt

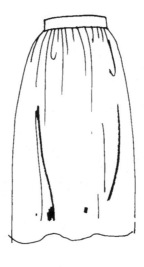

Dirndl skirt

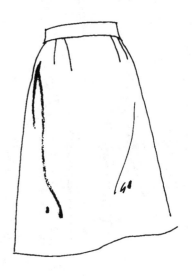

A-line skirt

Slit skirt

Prairie skirt

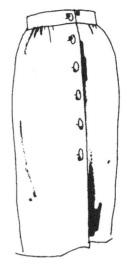

Button-front skirt

Fly-front skirt

Draped skirt

Sarong skirt

Tom Ford/Gucci 2000

22
Pants

A Short History of Women in Pants

The origin of women wearing pants is not known, but as far back as the first century c.e., women from the Middle East and Asia were wearing some form of pants. In a more modern time, Amelia Bloomer, attempting to banish the corset in the mid-1850s, helped to conceive an outfit consisting of a short skirt that was worn over full trousers that were gathered at the ankles. These trousers were called "bloomers" after her. The bloomer costume had a rather short life, but helped to introduce the concept of pant dressing to athletics and sports.

Amelia Bloomer 1850s

The Teens and 1920s

Paul Poiret believed that women's daily lives were becoming more "masculinized," and eventually they would wear trousers. As early as 1911, he introduced harem pants, which were often worn with tunics and turbans to complement their Oriental style.

In the 1920s, French designers Molyneux and Lucien Lelong were designing pajama outfits that could be worn for the beach or for informal luncheons at Deauville. Also, active sports began to require pants. They became fashionable for skiing, and as early as 1921, knickerbockers (knickers) were appearing for golf. By the mid-1920s, breeches or jodhpurs were worn for riding.

Poiret 1911

Lelong 1929

Molyneux 1924

The 1930s

Coco Chanel and other chic women wore pants with turbans and pearls at the Cote d'Azur in the 1930s. Such movie stars as Katharine Hepburn, Marlene Dietrich, and Greta Garbo were wearing man-tailored trousers in public, making this look both glamourous and socially acceptable. Also, in 1931, Schiaparelli designed a one-piece pajama in black wool jersey to be worn at the beach.

Schiaparelli 1931

Chanel 1930s

Dietrich 1930s

Garbo 1930s

The 1940s

During World War II, Sears, Roebuck and Co. offered a "sturdy, comfortable" coverall, which sold for $3.98 in their 1942 catalog. Claire McCardell, one of America's first sportswear designers, often included some pant looks in her collections. In 1949, she designed a wool jersey top and shorts for bicycling.

The 1950s

In the 1950s, because of such actors as James Dean and Marlon Brando, jeans became the fashion especially among younger women. They were often rolled up and occasionally had contrasting flannel linings. Another pants look was narrow, cropped pants and ballet slippers, which was made popular by Audrey Hepburn in the mid- 1950s. American sportswear designers were showing slim pants outfits for entertaining at home. These were often worn with long skirts wrapped over them.

Sears 1942

Audrey Hepburn 1954

McCardell 1949

The 1960s

In 1960, as a major part of his collection, Norman Norell showed culotte ensembles, which cost as much as $825. Because he believed so strongly in them, he offered the pattern to any manufacturer to copy. In 1963, he also designed capes that were worn over pants for travel.

André Corrèges designed sleek, stovepipe pants in 1964. These were worn with sharply tailored jackets and little white boots. It caused a major sensation and was copied at every price level.

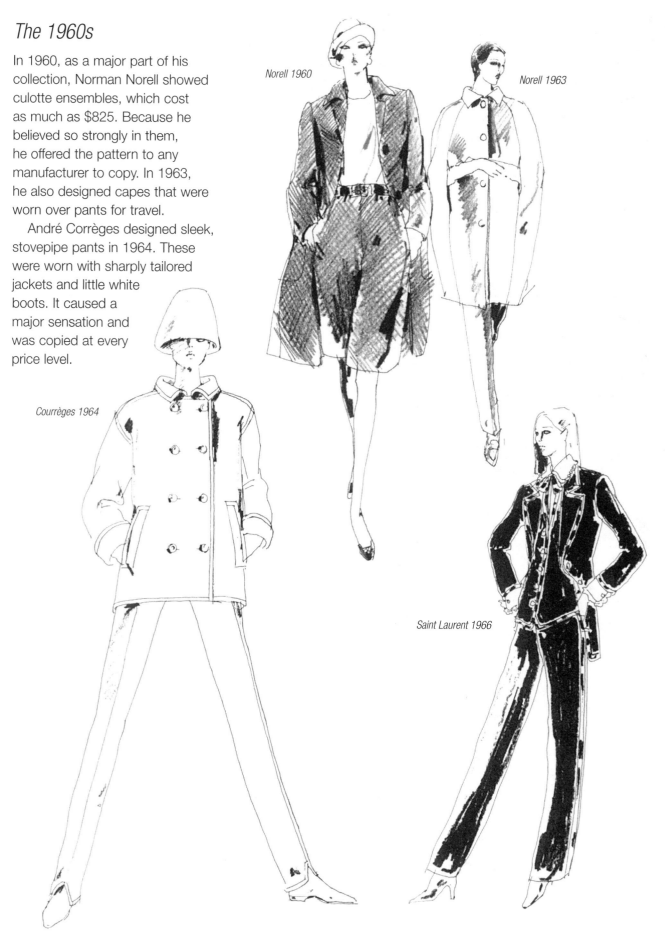

Norell 1960

Norell 1963

Courrèges 1964

Saint Laurent 1966

The 1970s

In the late 1960s and early 1970s, Yves Saint Laurent was the designer who was greatly responsible for putting the final stamp of approval on pant dressing. His beautiful "smoking" or tuxedo suits for evening and his impeccable man-tailored suits for day still have the same chic appeal today as they did then.

The 1980s and on

Giorgio Armani and his relaxed, tailored pants and suits in neutral colors and soft fabrics set the tone for pant dressing in both the 1980s and the early 1990s. No longer a special item, all designers began showing pants as a major part of their collections. From the beautifully tailored pants outfits of Krizia in Italy, to the creative cuts of such French designers as Kenzo, Claude Montana, and Sonia Rykiel, to the clean, tailored looks of Bill Blass, Oscar de la Renta, and Donna Karan—pants were no longer a designer option, but became a necessity.

In the 2000s, pants became sleek and narrow. Usually in the two most popular fabrics, leather or denim, they were boot length and the waistband slid down upon the hip, exposing the navel. These were often worn with a high-heeled strappy shoe or high-heeled boot. The designer jean resurfaced, sometimes frayed or embellished, and prices ranged from Levi's to over-the-top Chanel and Gucci.

Cropped pants and their variations became another alternative. Details such as cargo pockets and drawstrings, featured at the waist, ankle, or down the side of the leg, prevailed.

Today, designers all over the world are designing pants as a necessary part of their collections. Once it was shocking to see pants in a collection, today it would be shocking if they were left out. Designers have come a long way from what we call the classic pant and have begun to experiment with new fabrications and new ideas. It is no longer strange to see pants that are made of georgette, spandex, or suede—or to see a bride walking down the aisle in a pants outfit made of the most elaborate lace!

Saint Laurent 1975

Armani 1983

Armani 1990

Low rise jeans 2000s

Drawing Pants

First, let's take a look at the various pant lengths and styles. Again, as with the skirt lengths, this chart is just a reference point for you. As you probably already know, many of these lengths and styles are called by many different names, depending on the fashion or the decade. Once again, we have chosen what we believe to be the most accurate descriptive names.

Next, let's examine the various parts of pants and the pattern pieces. Pants circle the body at the waist, hip, and leg areas. Unlike a skirt, which encircles the body at the waist, hip, and hem areas, pants encircle each leg as well. Cylindrical perspective takes place in four areas, which are the waist, the hips, each leg, and the hem of each leg.

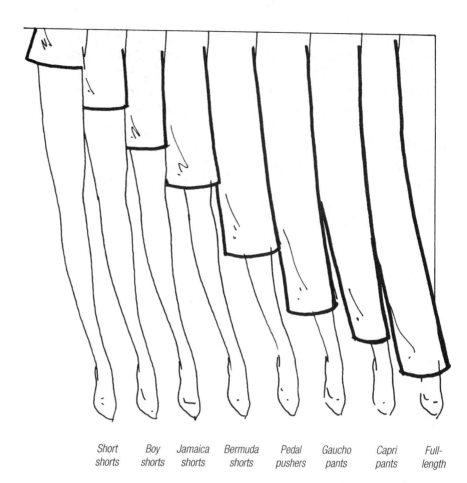

Short shorts Boy shorts Jamaica shorts Bermuda shorts Pedal pushers Gaucho pants Capri pants Full-length

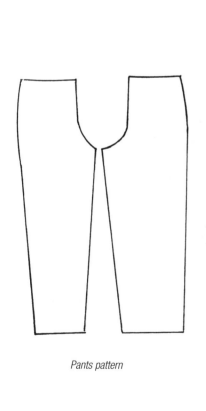

Pants pattern

Cylindrical perspective

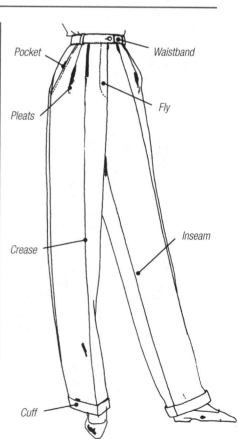

Pocket — Waistband — Pleats — Fly — Crease — Inseam — Cuff

Unlike the skirt, which moves as a single unit, pants move as three separate units. These units are the waist and hip area, the supporting leg, and the nonsupporting leg.

The crotch seam is the center front of the entire garment, but each leg also has its own center front, which moves with that leg. In pants with a crease, the crease becomes the center front. Also, the crease will follow the position of the leg.

1 Let's begin drawing by blocking in the lower half of the figure. Establish the supporting leg and the nonsupporting leg. Indicate the center front of each leg. On the supporting leg, notice that there is a slight indentation just above the knee area on the inside of the thigh. On most pants, the hem will touch the inside of the supporting leg or foot.

2 On wide pants, there will be a slight pull from the high hip to the inside hem. Because of excess fabric at the hem, there will also be a slight ripple at the hem. However, the outside line should be as unbroken as possible. Think of it this way—the inside line can show the approximate position of the leg and the outside line can show the pants width. On the supporting leg, the pants shape or hem follows the direction of the supporting leg and falls away from it on the outside.

3 We have a bit more freedom with the nonsupporting leg. This leg is completely moveable and it should have a graceful and non-static feeling to it. In pants with a classic fit, there is a breakline at the knee that has a soft line, while the other side generally follows the leg shape.

4 In pants with full legs, the inside line becomes straighter and no longer follows the shape of the leg. Instead, there is a slight pull from the inside knee to the outside hem, which somewhat indicates the leg position and excess fabric.

On the nonsupporting leg, the pants fall away from the outside and from the leg on the inside.

Pants move as three units.

Center front of crotch and legs

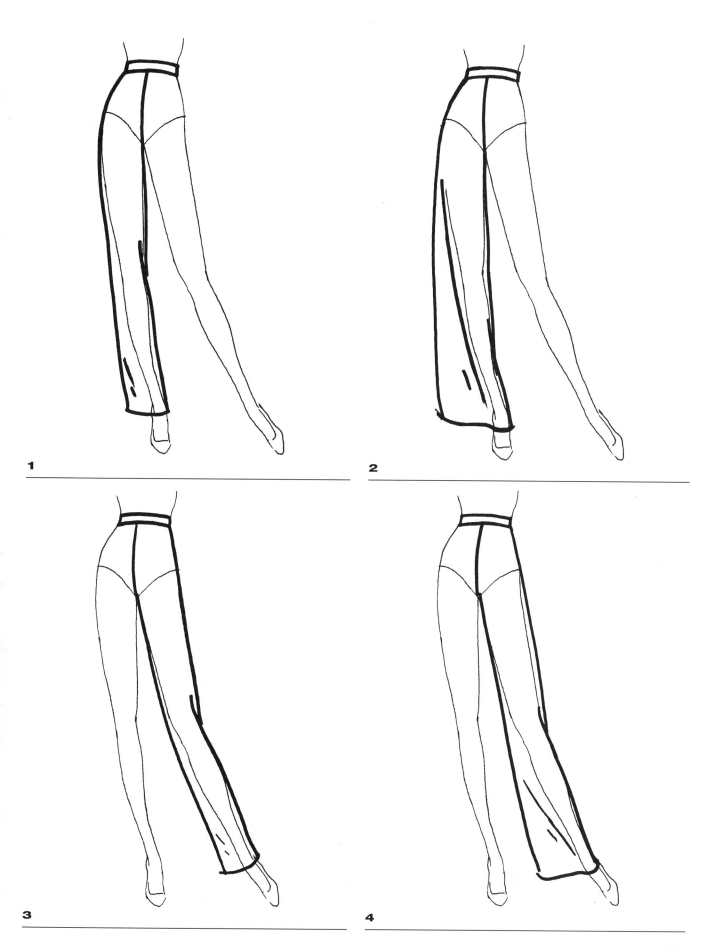

1

2

3

4

Polishing the Details

1 The hem of the pants must always seem to go around the leg. Keep the cuff even with the hemline as well. If the pants have creaselines, the hemline of each leg will make a slight "V" shape at that point.

2 In classic trousers, the creaseline will meet one of the pleats. In pants with elastic waists or drawstrings, keep a light touch in the casing or elastic area—and be sure that the gathers come from a starting point. Check to see that the waist and hip direction follow each other.

3 Pay special attention to the waistband. Does it start at the waist and go up, as in most pants? Or does it go from the waist down, as in a contour waistband? Or does it have no waistband, as in a faced waistline? Make sure that the waistband is even and curves slightly upward.

4 Notice how hems take an upward curve when they are above the knee and a downward curve when they are below the knee.

5 Avoid drawing a "Z" or a "V" to represent the crotch area. A light stroke will say it all.

When drawing pants, it is important to keep in mind that the legs can take endless positions in their various poses, and that all rules have exceptions. We have studied the basic principles and movement of pants, but each pair—depending on the style, cut, and fabric—has its own unique qualities. When designing or illustrating, these differences will allow for endless artistic variations.

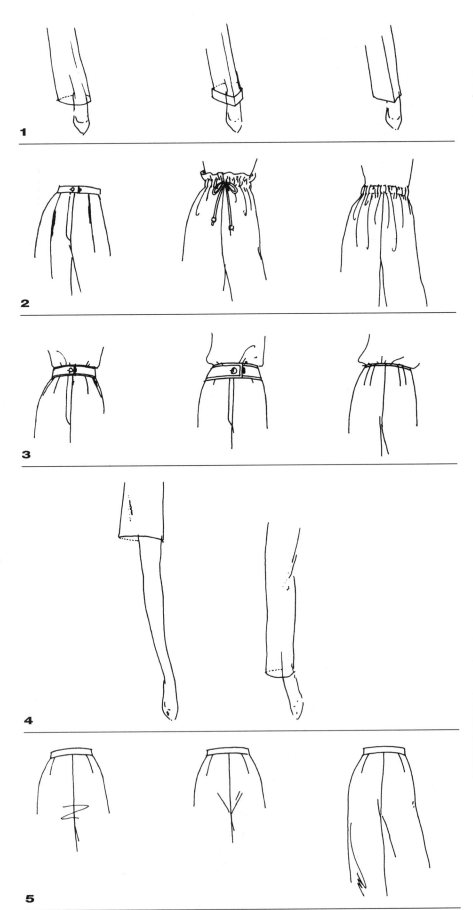

Pant
Details

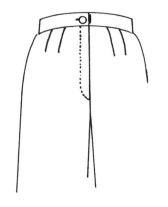

Side pocket

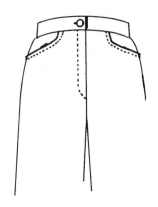

Continental (western) pocket

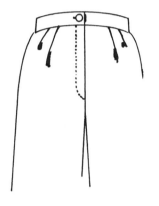

Pleated waistband

Dart-fitted waistband

Gathered waistband

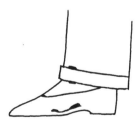

Cuffed hem

Uncuffed hem

Pant Silhouettes

Cargo pocket pants

Tapered pants

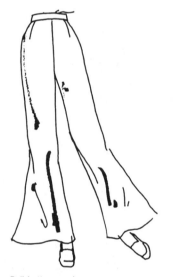

Bell-bottom pants

Straight-leg pants

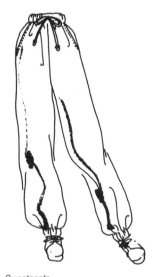

Sweatpants

Sailor pants

Culottes

Gaucho pants

Knickers

Boxer shorts

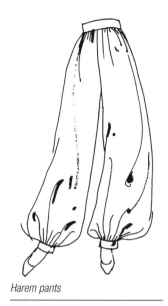

Harem pants

Stirrup pants

Zouave pants

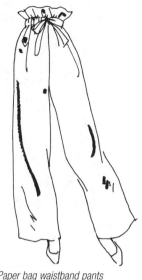

Paper bag waistband pants

Palazzo pants

Pajama pants

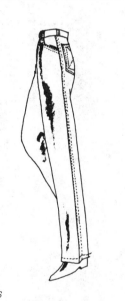

Jeans

Hip-huggers

Draped pants

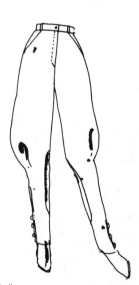

Jodhpurs

Pants

251

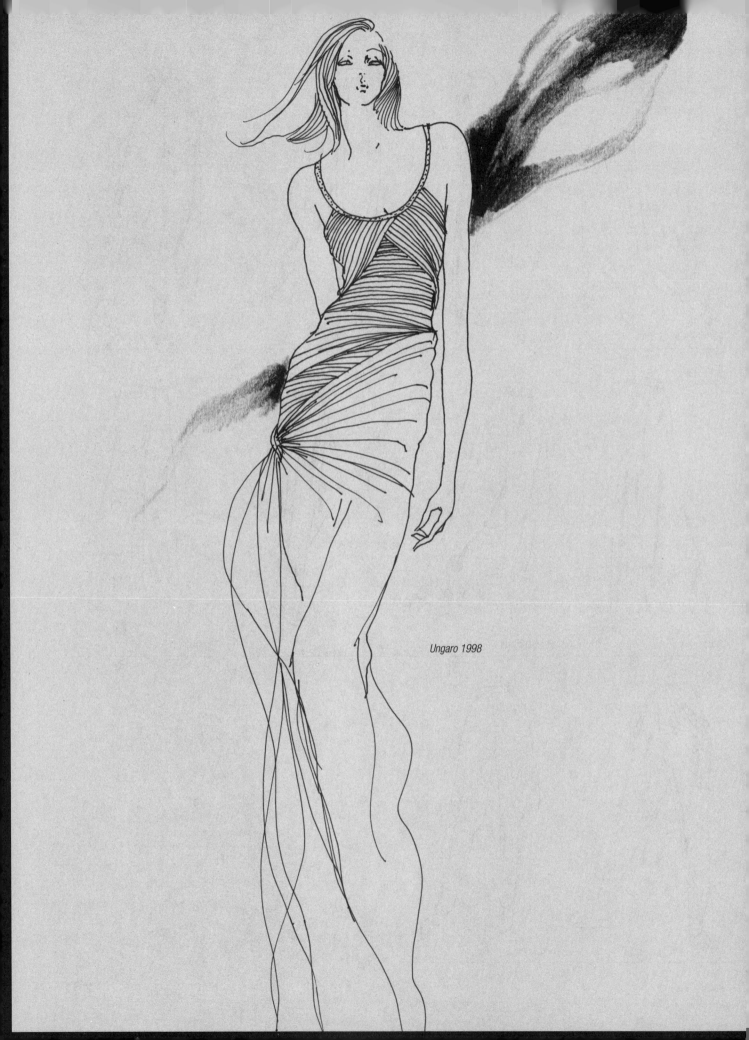

Ungaro 1998

23
Drapery, Bias, and Cowls

Drapery is fabric falling on or away from the body. A draped garment forms folds of fabric, which can hug, wrap, or fall away from the figure. It can be intricately manipulated around a certain part of the body or float completely away from it.

The bias cut was originated by Madeleine Vionnet. She opened her house in France in 1919, but we associate the clinging, elegant evening dresses of the 1920s and 1930s with her. Cowls, drapes, handkerchief hems, and halter necklines were often part of her designs.

Vionnet 1925–26

Alix Grès (Madame Grès), another French couturiere, was famous for her intricately draped and bias-cut gowns. Inspired by the clothing of Ancient Greece, they were often executed in silk jersey. These gowns are timeless in their designs.

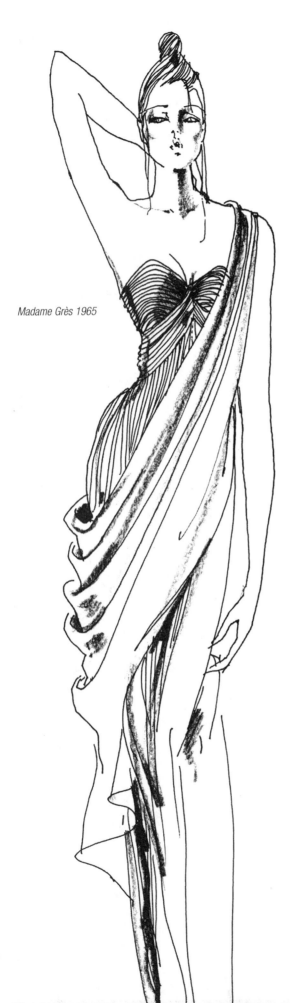

Madame Grès 1965

Madame Grès 1965

Illustrating Fashion—Concept to Creation

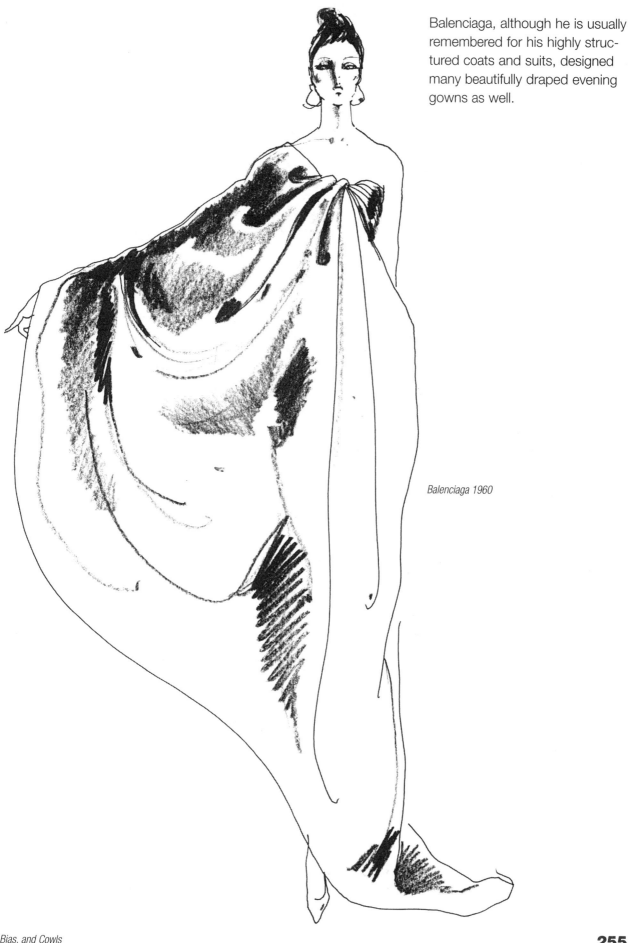

Balenciaga, although he is usually remembered for his highly structured coats and suits, designed many beautifully draped evening gowns as well.

Balenciaga 1960

In the 1960s and 1970s, George Stavropoulos, who was known for his flowing, bias-cut chiffons, and Charles Kleibacker, who was famous for his magnificent, bias-cut evening gowns, continued this tradition in America.

George Stavropoulos 1961

George Stavropoulos 1973

Charles Kleibacker 1964

In the 1980s, Emanuel Ungaro—perhaps more than any other designer—was responsible for the return of the draped and shirred dress.

From the 1990s to the 2000s, drapery still maintained an important place in fashion. The silhouette became elongated and sleek. Bias cuts and circular ruffles in very soft silks were reminiscent of the designs of the 1930s.

Versace cut draped evening gowns so that they revealed as much of the body as possible. John Galliano's soft bias, long slip dresses looked as if they were poured over the body.

Versace 1997

John Galliano/Dior 2003

Ungaro 1985

Understanding Drapery

Draped garments usually involve the direction of fabric called the bias. Fabric is woven with a crosswise and lengthwise direction. The bias is the diagonal direction extending across the grain of the fabric. The bias has a round, very elastic quality. It also has the ability to cling and fall and follow the curves of the body in a very sensual way.

Drapery involves tension points and their relationship to clothing and the body. Let's imagine a square piece of fabric pinned onto the wall. When the fabric falls from one tension point and takes the form of a cone or a triangle, it is called "one-point tension." If you look at a fashion figure wearing a bias-cut gown with a bent knee, the knee becomes the tension point. You can see how the skirt falls from the knee in a cone shape. In a pose with the hand on the hip and a full sleeve, the elbow becomes the tension point and the fabric falls from the elbow in a cone or triangular shape.

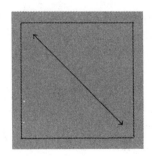

Bias direction

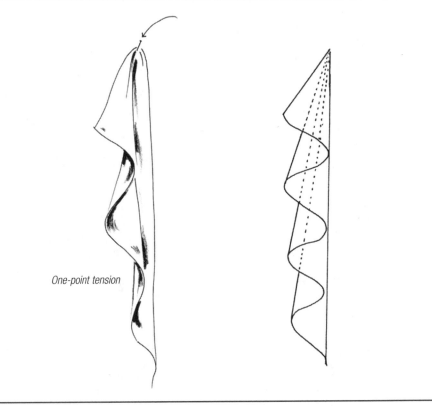

One-point tension

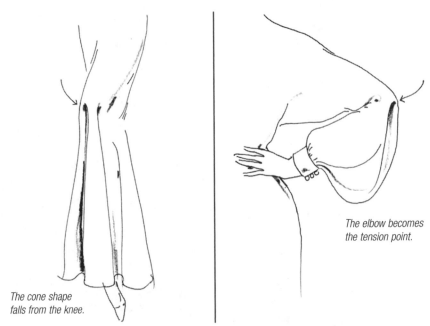

The cone shape falls from the knee.

The elbow becomes the tension point.

A cascade best represents one-point tension. A cascade is a series of open circles that are seamed together. When the inner edge is clipped and forced to lay flat, the outer edge will form cone-shape flares. When opened and held from one point, these flares fall in a circular manner, making rounded, zigzag shapes.

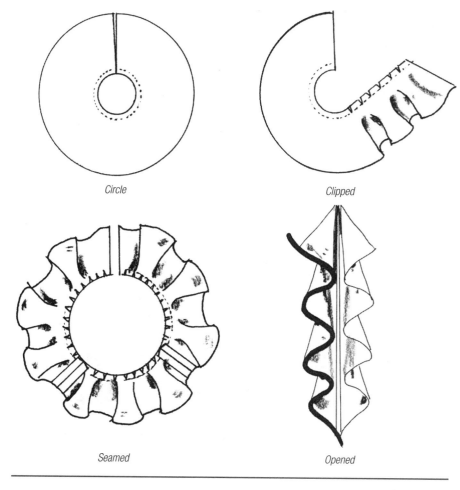

Circle

Clipped

Seamed

Opened

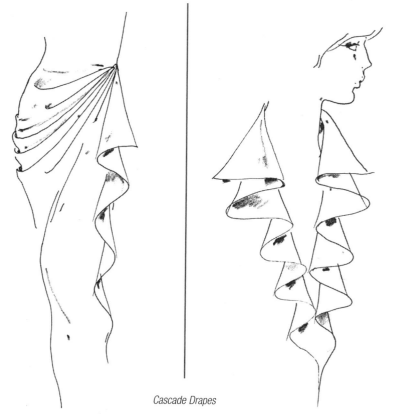

Cascade Drapes

When you pin another piece of fabric to the wall, but this time with two pins—one at each end—you have two-point tension. A cowl is an example of two-point tension. A cowl is either one fold or a series of folds placed on various parts of the garment. It is most typical at the front or back of a neckline, but can be incorporated in skirts, pants, or sleeves as well. They drape best when cut on the bias and when designed in such soft fabrics as crepe de chine, charmeuse, soft jersey, or chiffon.

Cowls fall from the excess fabric or can be pleated or gathered into a seam. The drapes seem to appear looped in back of one another. Also, they can be shallow or quite deep.

Two-point tension cowl

Cowl

Excess fabric forms cowls.

Cowls can fall from the front or back of a garment, on the sleeves or on a skirt, which is called a pannier. A pannier skirt is draped so that the skirt extends from the sides. In cowls, notice how the fabric loops and turns.

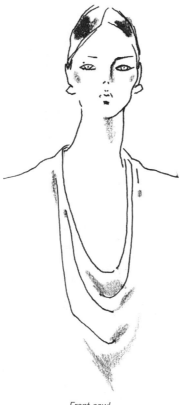

Front cowl

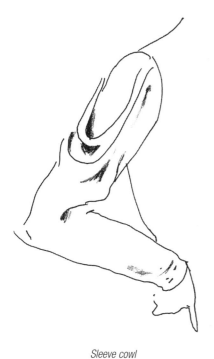

Sleeve cowl

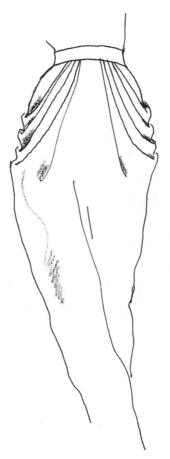

Pannier skirt

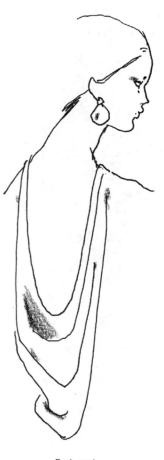

Back cowl

Shirring is another example of two-point tension. The fabric is pulled up or shirred between two seams and is tacked in place over a foundation.

Valentino 1984

Analyzing Draped Fashions

Draped bodices and dresses are other examples of two-point tension. The bias-cut fabric is manipulated over a boned foundation and is held in place with small stitches. The fabric can either be manipulated precisely or casually. Often it has a fluted quality to it.

In both draped and shirred garments, block off the direction the drapery will follow on your underdrawing, making sure that the lines follow the contours of the body. The garments should not have a smooth edge.

Ungaro 1984

When drawing draped garments, there must be a very accurate underdrawing to indicate the direction of the drapery. The feeling of the fabric being manipulated around the body is crucial.

To help you better understand the nature of drapery, let's analyze four draped garments.

This Jacques Heim silk dress from 1951 has a very structured, draped quality. The overall look is crisp and dramatic, with the shape both touching the body at the waistline and then abruptly standing away, making its own definite shape in the peplum. All the drapery meets at the bottom of the belt on the hip. There is a strong diagonal movement across the bodice, with the peplum meeting the bodice and falling into a dramatic, stiff cascade.

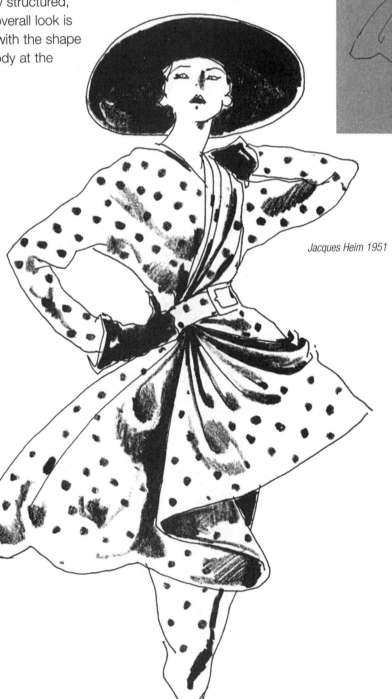

Jacques Heim 1951

The Bill Blass charmeuse dress from 1982 has all the drapery interest in the back. The point where all the fabric seems to meet is at the waistline of the center back. The fabric falls from the shoulders down to the hip and then loops back up into the waistline. There is a concentration of dark shading taking place because of all the lines converging at this point. It is most important to take note of this. From that point the fabric falls to a slight train. Notice how the lines open up as they near the hem. The overall effect has the contrast of a clingy, body-conscious quality at the lower half, as opposed to the dramatic voluminous shapes created in the upper half.

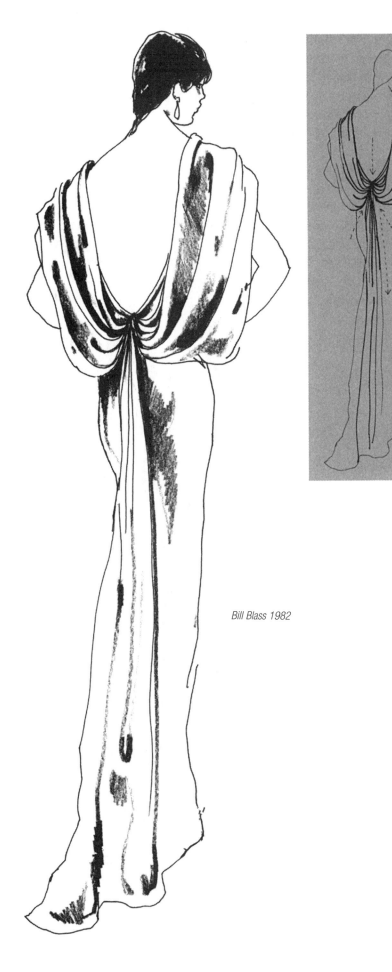

Bill Blass 1982

Jacques Griffe designed this soft, asymmetrical chiffon gown in 1957. All the drapery seems to meet at the side of the empire bodice. The off-the-shoulder neckline should have the feeling of going all around the back until it connects to the opposite side. The skirt has a pannier effect, again draping all around the body. In a draped garment such as this, every line must seem to follow the body contours to their fullest. The points where all the drapery meet are very dense, and then open out when nearer to the hem.

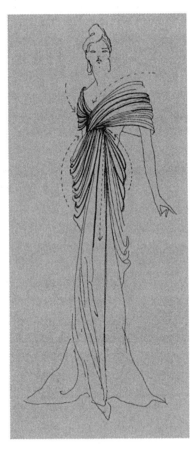

Jacques Griffe 1957

This 1981 Saint Laurent lamé gown is a bit simpler. It spirals the body effortlessly and is caught with velvet bows at the shoulder and above the knee. It is bias cut and body conscious until it flares at the bottom. Because there is not a huge amount of yardage in this particular design, the points where the drapery meet will not be as dense.

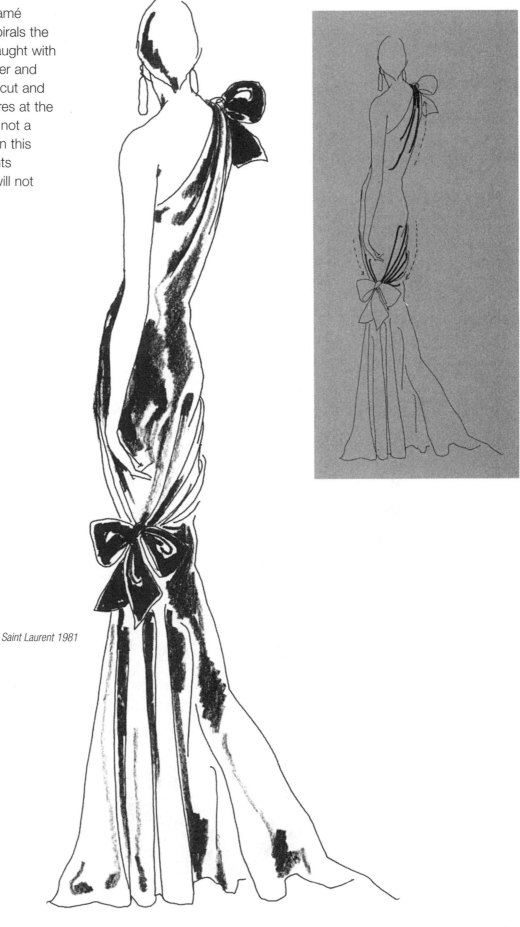

Saint Laurent 1981

Draped garments go back to the ancient Greeks and Romans. When we study a magnificent, draped, bias-cut gown from Vionnet or Grès, it is easy to see why the classic and timeless beauty of this type of garment never diminishes.

Madame Grès 1976

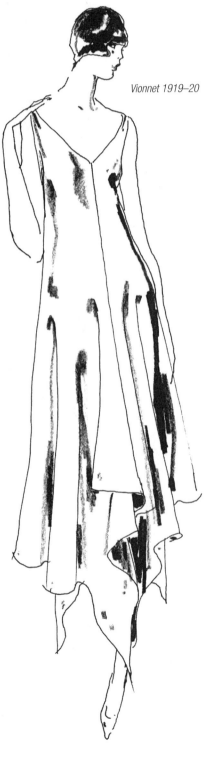

Vionnet 1919–20

Illustrating Fashion—Concept to Creation

A tremendous consideration when drawing draped garments is the care that you must take because of the enormous amount of yardage involved. In spite of the elaborate, complex shapes that are being made by the drapery, the result must look both light and effortless.

Armani 1991

24

Tailored Clothing

Tailored clothing has built-in shape. It is precisely constructed to hold this shape for years. In the finest custom-made jackets or coats, you will notice that:

- The fabric is shaped over a canvas understructure, with the lapels padstitched and taped to roll beautifully.

- The set-in sleeves follow the direction of the arm exactly and hang without any pulling.

- The shoulders are padded, but do not look rigid.

- Pockets are precisely placed to lie flat—they do not gape open.

- Buttonholes are carefully worked, with the finest buttons used for closings.

- The numerous layers of fabric are graded to eliminate at bulk, which retains the sleek, tailored look intended by the designers.

Many hours of handwork and fitting produce a jacket or coat that has an effortless appearance. A magnificent custom-tailored garment has been made in seemingly endless hours of handwork. Many of the methods used to create it have not changed much over the last hundred years. However, modern technology has created many time-saving methods to produce garments of exceptional quality. For example, fusible interfacings replace canvas interfacings, computers speed in the cutting of layouts and of grading different sizes, and modern machine construction methods help to produce excellent, finished products in a considerably shorter time.

Saint Laurent 1995

In this chapter, we will study tailored clothing details and drawing principles that can apply to a coat or coat-dress as well. First, let's look at the parts of a classic, tailored jacket.

The most important thing to consider when drawing a tailored garment are:

- The garment is symmetrical and balanced. Every detail on one side of the center should match the other side. Pockets line up, notches are even, and so forth.

- The line is precise—but not stiff.

- The pose should not be one that distorts the garment.

- The garment should not look wrinkled.

- Folds should be accurately placed and should not look like pulls or a bad fit.

- When you draw one part of the garment, immediately draw the corresponding part. For example, first draw one notch, then the other notch. Draw one pocket, then the other. Don't go down, around, and back up the garment. The flow will be broken and you will make mistakes.

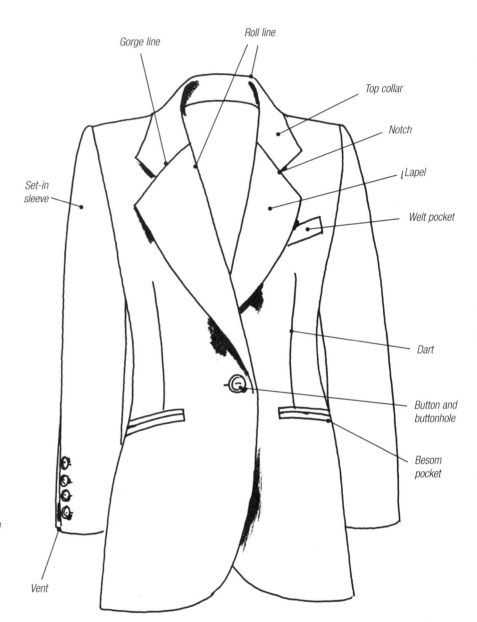

Gorge line

Roll line

Top collar

Notch

Lapel

Set-in sleeve

Welt pocket

Dart

Button and buttonhole

Besom pocket

Vent

Drawing Tailored Garments

1 First, block off the structure on an underdrawing.

2 Indicate the center front line and button placement. If it isn't correct, everything else in your drawing will be wrong.

3 Determine the amount of the opening (or roll line) from the neckline to the first button (which starts at the beginning of the roll line) and mark it. The size of the opening can be from under the collarbone to the waistline or lower. Draw in the "V" opening (roll line). This is the area from which the lapels turn. This "V" must be drawn straight with no wiggles.

4 Sketch in the first button at the end of the roll line and check that it is on the center front line. The buttonhole should go to the left of center front. At the roll line, the jacket lapel is turned onto the chest.

Draw in the closing to the right of the button or center front. Determine the length of the jacket from the button to the hem. Compare it to the distance from the neck edge to the button. Does the hem have a rounded or straight edge? Draw it in.

5 Draw the general shape of the jacket. Is it fitted, semi-fitted, or boxy? The shape is determined by darts and seamlines. Make sure that they follow the body with the correct curves, so that the art will have dimension and will be accurate.

6 Now draw the shoulders. Check if they seem padded, sloped, or natural. The shoulder line should always be crisp and, just as the roll line, should never wiggle.

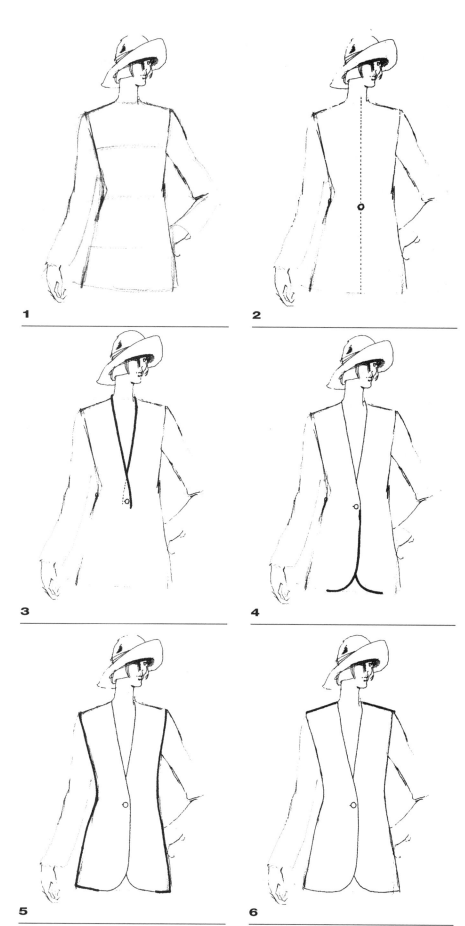

7 Indicate the sleeve length. Check how that length relates to the jacket hem. Add the sleeve vents and buttons. Next, draw the sleeves. Check the details at the sleeve hem.

8 Draw the lapel only. How far does it roll toward the armhole? This is one of the details that will change a jacket or coat the most. Does it start high or low? The gorge line must be straight and you should use a light touch. How far does the lapel notch extend, and where does the top collar meet it?

9 Draw the top collar. It goes around the neck, falls on the shoulder, and onto the upper chest. Indicate the notch opening.

10 Sketch in the pockets, darts, and seams. Make sure they relate to the hem, the center front, and the sleeve hem.

7

8

9

10

Polishing the Details

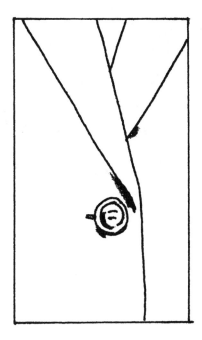

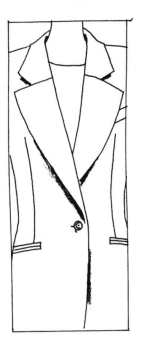

To keep the dimensional quality, let the lapel stop a bit short of the edge. This break will allow the art to look like it is turning. A small shadow takes place here, because the fabric is being lifted off the garment to turn.

There will be a small shadow under the top collar and lapel, because that is where the lapel touches the body. Also, draw in a small shadow to the right side of the opening to show the jacket is hanging away from the bottom button.

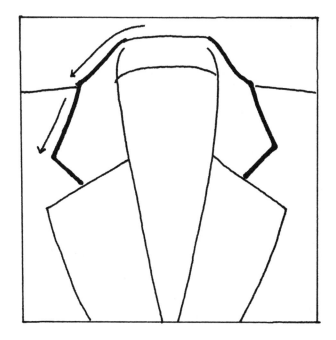

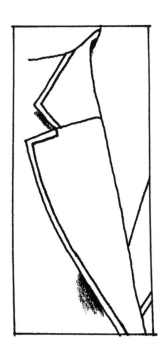

The top collar goes around the neck, falls onto the shoulder, and then onto the upper chest. Indicate the notch openings.

If there is top stitching, make sure that it is delicate and done with a hard line.

Tailoring details

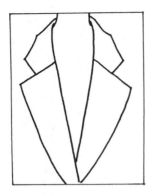

Notch lapel

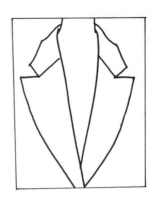

Semi-peaked lapel

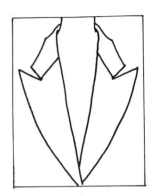

Peaked lapel

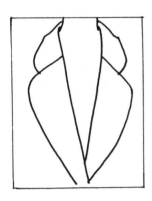

Cloverleaf lapel

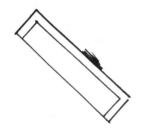

Welt pocket (has opening on one side)

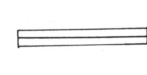

Piped, buttonhole, or besom pocket

Flap pocket

Patch pocket

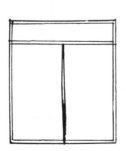

Pleated pocket

Bellows pocket

Keyhole and Bound buttonhole

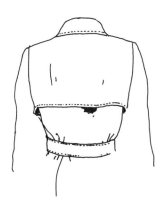

Loose yoke (back view)

Loose yoke (front view)

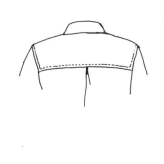

Yoke

Back belt and back vent

Epaulet

Elbow patch

Sleeve strap

Fly front

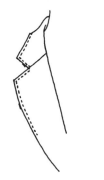

Saddle Stitching

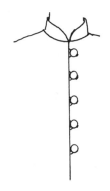

Button and loop closing

Frog

Passementerie

Jacket
and Coat
Silhouettes

Blouson

Bolero

Cardigan

Chanel

Nehru

Spencer

Tuxedo or Smoking

Safari

Norfolk

Riding

Wrap

Pea

Chesterfield

Princess

Trench

Duffle

Polo

Swing

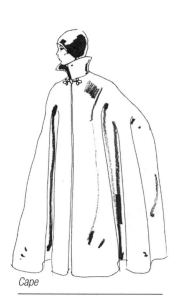

Cape

Tailored Clothing

Norell 1962

25

Analyzing
Tailored Garments

Tailored garments are based on very old and established principles of construction. Technology has changed the way these garments are produced but the pattern pieces remain very much the same. Unlike other garments, a tailored jacket or coat evolves rather than changing drastically. Proportion, detail, fit, and fabric are basically all that makes one decade different from another.

In this chapter, we will analyze four classically tailored jackets from different decades. You will be able to see that even over a 40-year period, the principles of a tailored garment do not change. Although these four jackets are quite different from each other, it will be clear that the same principles apply to all of them, regardless of how fashions change from decade to decade. These same principles should be used when analyzing any tailored jacket, coat, or coatdress. The changes that do occur involve the silhouette, details, fabrics, the degree of construction, and proportion. The jackets that we will analyze are:

- 1950s Irene's ivory and taupe striped wool jacket.

- 1960s Ben Zuckerman's pink wool jacket.

- 1970s Norman Norell's taupe linen jacket with silk velvet top collar.

- 1980s Giorgio Armani's black, white, and red glen plaid wool jacket.

We will analyze them for the silhouette, roll line, notch details, buttons, pocket details, shoulders, sleeves, and other specifics.

1920s

1990s

Irene

Silhouette
- Fitted at waistline
- Hip length
- Front darts

Roll line
- Lapel rolls above the breasts

Notch details
- High notch
- Lapel and top collar practically touch
- Notch opening is very small

Buttons
- Eight-button closing, with the bottom button above the flap; bound buttonholes

Pockets
- Flap pockets

Shoulders
- Small, slightly sloping shoulders

Sleeves
- Straight set-in sleeves, which are shorter than the jacket

Other specifics
- Buttons are placed very close to each other
- Pocket flaps have a mitered stripe detail
- Stripes line up at armhole

Irene 1950s

Jacket from The Ohio State Costume Collection

Ben Zuckerman

Silhouette
- Very slightly fitted
- Above hip length
- Front darts

Roll line
- Lapel rolls high

Notch details
- Top collar is bigger than the lapel—almost shirt-like

Buttons
- Four-button closing, with the last button near the hem; bound buttonholes

Pockets
- Patch pockets at the bustline

Shoulders
- Small, soft shoulders

Sleeves
- Straight set-in sleeves, which are longer than the jacket

Other specifics
- Yoke
- Buttoned pockets
- Welt stitching

Ben Zuckerman 1960s

Jacket from The Ohio State Costume Collection

Norman Norell

Silhouette
- Semi-fitted
- Hip length
- Front darts

Roll line
- Lapel rolls above the waist

Notch details
- Notches of both the top collar and lapel are even

Buttons
- One-button at waistline

Pockets
- No pockets

Shoulders
- Natural shoulders

Sleeves
- Set-in sleeves, which are longer than the jacket

Other specifics
- Black, silk velvet top collar, black button

Norman Norell 1970s

Jacket from The Ohio State Costume Collection

Giorgio Armani

Silhouette
- Fitted
- Hip length

Roll line
- Low at waist

Notch details
- Notch of the top collar and the lapel are even

Buttons
- Two buttons, one at waistline and one below

Pockets
- Two-flap pockets at the second button, one flap pocket above the breast

Shoulders
- Square, padded shoulders

Sleeves
- Set-in sleeves, which are longer than the jacket

Other specifics
- Hand worked buttonhole on lapel; black buttons
- Double row of black topstitching around the lapel, collars, and pocket flaps
- Plaid matches at the armholes and pockets

Giorgio Armani 1980s

Jacket from *The Ohio State Costume Collection*

Saint Laurant
1987 - 1962 - 1978

26
Accessories

Accessories polish off a garment and can give a
fashion figure great drama. Just as designers choose
the accessories for a collection with great care, the
same care should be taken with your artwork.
Studying runway photographs, you will notice that
accessories tend to be dramatic. The small antique
earrings that look beautiful in life would never show up
in a fashion show. The same holds true for artwork.
Think of accessories as part of the garment
design and be aware of their proportion in
relationship to the clothing. Additionally,
when drawing accessories, be
careful to judge the scale of
the pieces on the finished
fashion art.

Ferrè/Dior 1994

Hats

A hat is the accessory worn on top of the head. A hat may fit the head, be pulled down over the eyes, or almost look as if it were just sitting on the top.

Throughout the first half of the century, the hat was almost as important as the outfit with which it was worn. It is very difficult to think of the 1920s, 1930s, or 1940s fashions without imaging a hat. All the glamorous movie stars and smartly dressed women always included a hat as part of their ensemble.

Today, even though hats have taken on a new more casual and fun attitude, most designers use them as the perfect finishing touch to their clothing. Whether it is a huge brimmed hat adding just the chic polish to a suit or an amusing little pouf of tulle worn with a cocktail dress, a hat gives the final statement to the designer's look.

Picture

Cloche

Drawing Hats

There are only two major parts of a hat:

- The crown, which is the section that fits the head.

- The brim, which is the rim of the hat, attached to the crown. This can be small and narrow to large and dramatic. It can be rolled up to frame the face or down to shadow the face with great drama.

It is most important that the hat fit around the head. This can be achieved by indicating a dotted line going around the head. It is advisable to draw the crown first and save the brim for last. If the brim is dramatic, give it all the drama you can conjure. If possible, try to draw the brim in one continuous, graceful line.

In a cloche, or any hat that fits closely or has a close-fitting crown, make it appear as if there is very short or cropped hair under it and really pull it down on the head. Shade the areas close to the face.

Think of a hat as finishing touch, an extravagance. It is one part of the fashion figure that can be treated with an amusing or dramatic quality.

Hat Styles

Fedora

Breton

Tam-o'-shanter

Derby

Cartwheel

Boater

Baseball

Beret

Pillbox

Watch cap

Newsboy

Turban

Jewelry

Jewelry—whether real or costume—is a purely decorative accessory. It is important that they be scaled down on the fashion figure. Think of how big or small the earrings are in relationship to the face, or how long or short the necklace is in the bodice. When drawing jewelry, think of the result that you want to achieve, rather than the individual stones, beads, or details. Also, make sure that the necklace appears to go around the neck. Often the bead or chain closest to the neck will be halved.

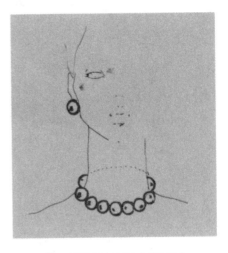

The necklace goes around the neck.

Choker and stud earring

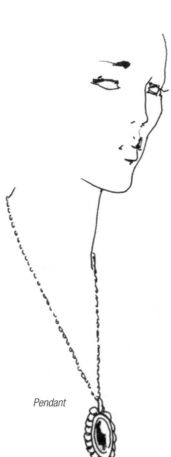

Opera length necklace and chandelier earring

Pendant

Rope necklace and button earring

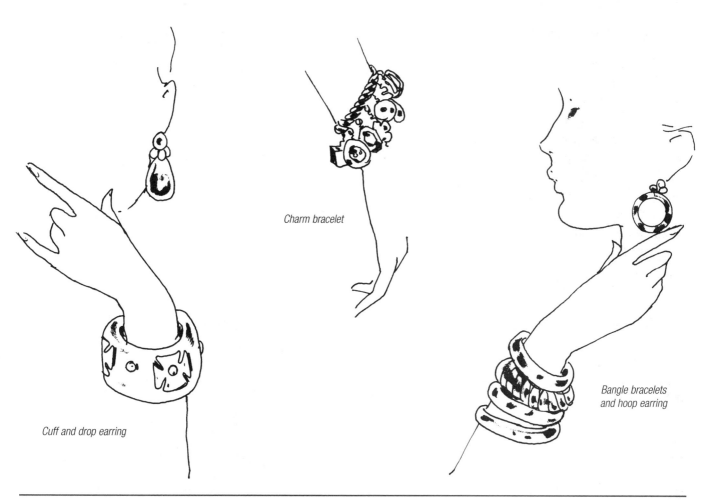

Charm bracelet

Cuff and drop earring

Bangle bracelets
and hoop earring

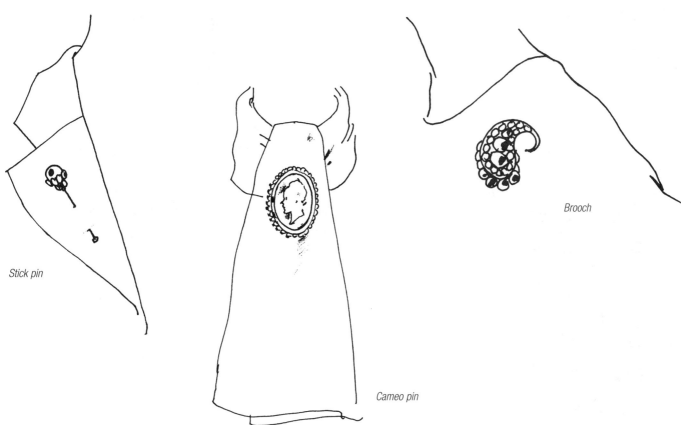

Stick pin

Cameo pin

Brooch

Scarves, Bows, and Stoles

A scarf is the accessory that can encircle the neck, rest on the shoulders, or fly away from the figure. It is a very good means of adding movement to a figure. Scarves can be crisp or soft and fluid. They are finished with rolled hems done by hand or machine, or may be self-fringed. A scarf can be solid-colored, in prints, or hand-painted. They are often edged in border designs.

A long scarf can be tied into a bow, which has five parts, consisting of two loops, a knot, and two streamers. A stole is a long, wide scarf. It can be made of woven fabric, knit, or fur. It allows the figure to have more extravagant arm gestures. Again, treat it very luxuriously and play up the drapery that the fabric will allow. When drawing the streamers of a bow, a long narrow scarf or stole, think of a gust of wind and let it move in a pleasing rhythm. The lines of the fringe can also create interesting movements.

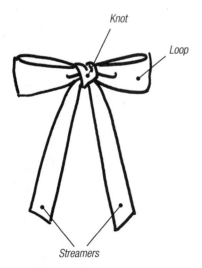

Knot

Loop

Streamers

Tailored bow

Soft bow

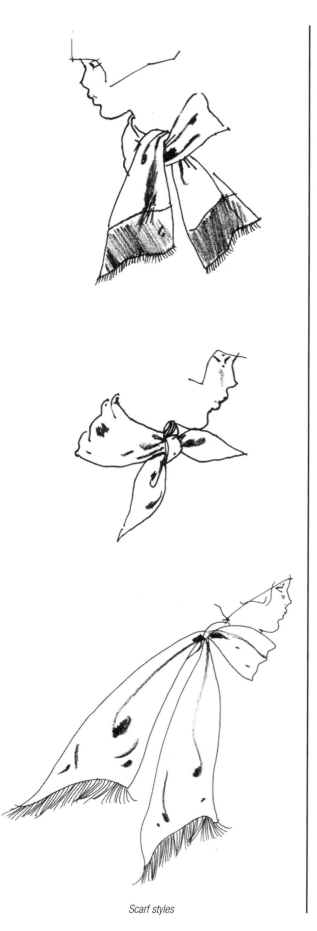

Scarf styles

Stole

Shawls

A shawl is a wrap that is larger than a scarf, and which can be either decorative or utilitarian. It can be made of woven fabric, printed, or knitted. It can also have fringe as a detail. It can envelope the body or be casually draped over the shoulder. When drawing a shawl, remember that it can add a wonderful extra shape to an otherwise simple outfit—play it up to the fullest!

Gloves

Gloves can be worn as a fashion accessory or for warmth in cold weather. They are an additional layer and can be made of anything from a delicate crochet to a sturdy leather. They can be fur or pile-lined, which will give them additional bulk. Make sure that the gloves follow each finger in a crisp shape and lightly indicate the stitching or other details.

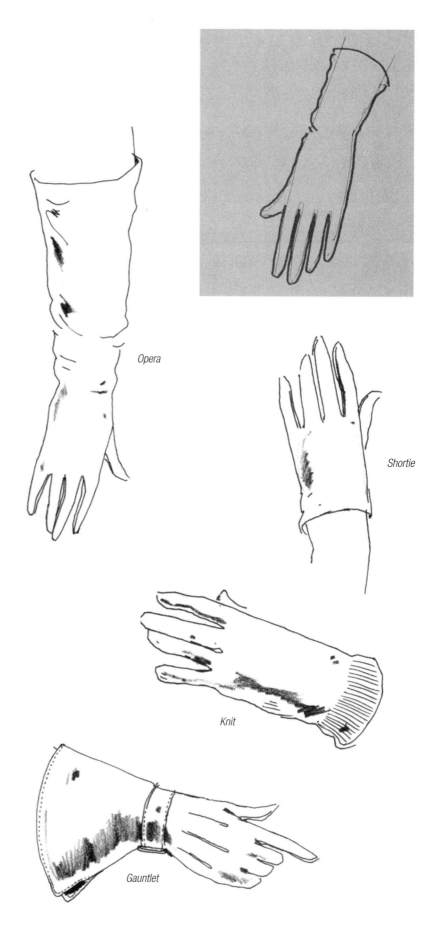

Opera

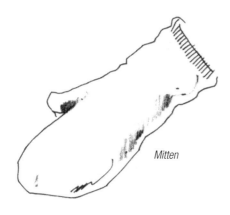

Mitten

Shortie

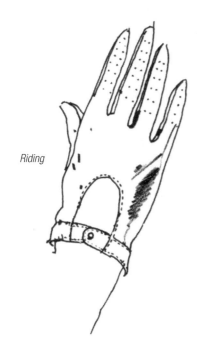

Riding

Knit

Gauntlet

Handbags

Handbags are either carried by hand or hung from the shoulder. They can range from tiny evening bags to near luggage size. Be careful to check the relationship of the bag to the body. Pay close attention to the details and stitching. Keep the shape crisp if the bag is structured. If it is unstructured, draw it with a softer touch.

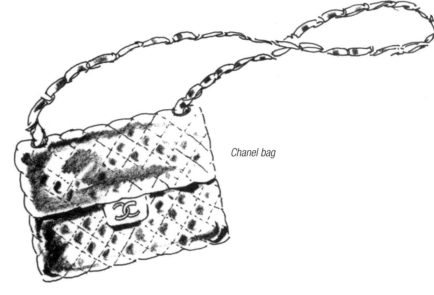

Chanel bag

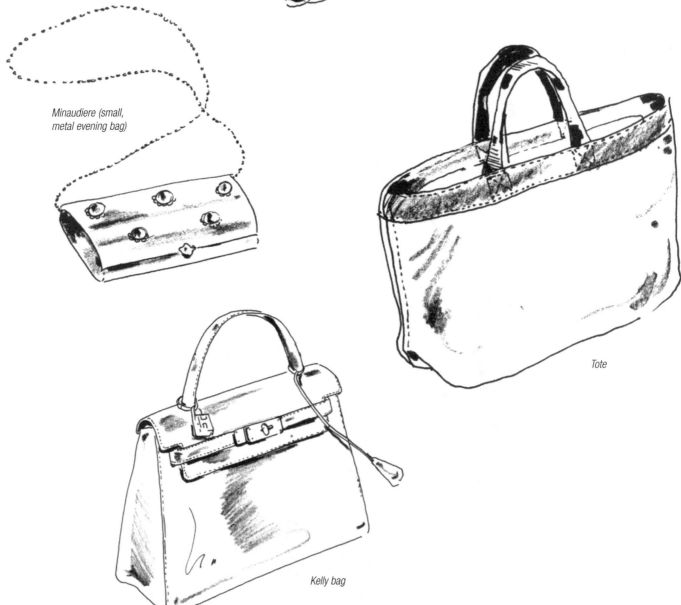

Minaudiere (small, metal evening bag)

Tote

Kelly bag

Shoulder bag

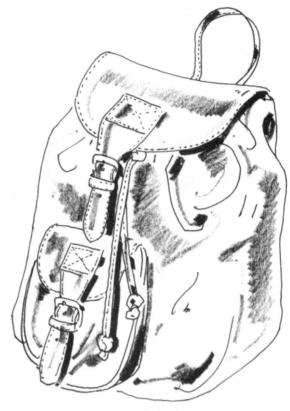

Backpack

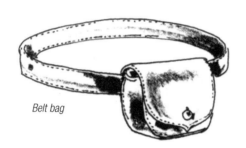

Belt bag

Clutch

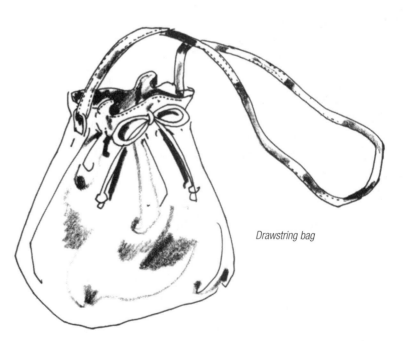

Drawstring bag

Shoes and Boots

Shoe and boot styles change dramatically, from ballet slippers to Louis XV heels, from spikes to platforms, from cowboy boots to combat boots. They can be delicate, sexy, clunky, or purely functional.

Regardless of the style, when drawing shoes the shapes are based on the triangle. The higher the heel, the higher the triangle; the lower the heel, the more shallow the triangle. Also, all shoes have a center front, which turns with the foot. All details and ornaments must accurately relate to the center front.

The flat shoe is based on a very shallow triangle. In the front view, the inside of the shoe will be straighter and the outside rounder. In a turned foot, there will be some foreshortening. The sole of the foot will rest on the bottom of the triangle. The profile foot will fit almost exactly in the triangle.

The higher the heel, the higher the triangle, and the higher the instep. The arch begins to appear. The ball of the foot rests firmly on the ground. For accuracy, it helps if you draw the heel after the rest of the shoe is drawn.

Boots can begin at the ankle and extend as high as the thigh. Remember, there is generally more bulk in a boot, because there is more material. Boots can be made in fabric, leather, suede, vinyl, or reptile skins.

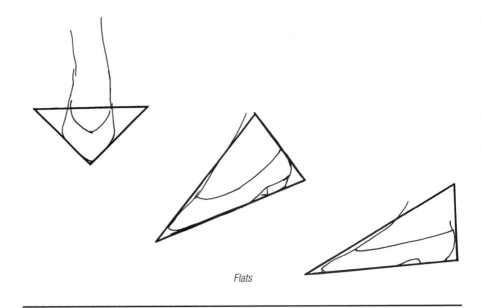

Flats

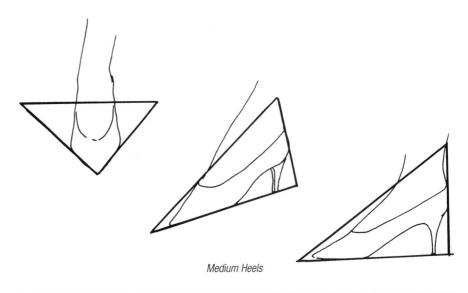

Medium Heels

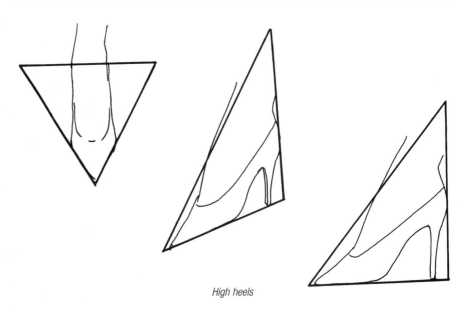

High heels

Shoe Styles

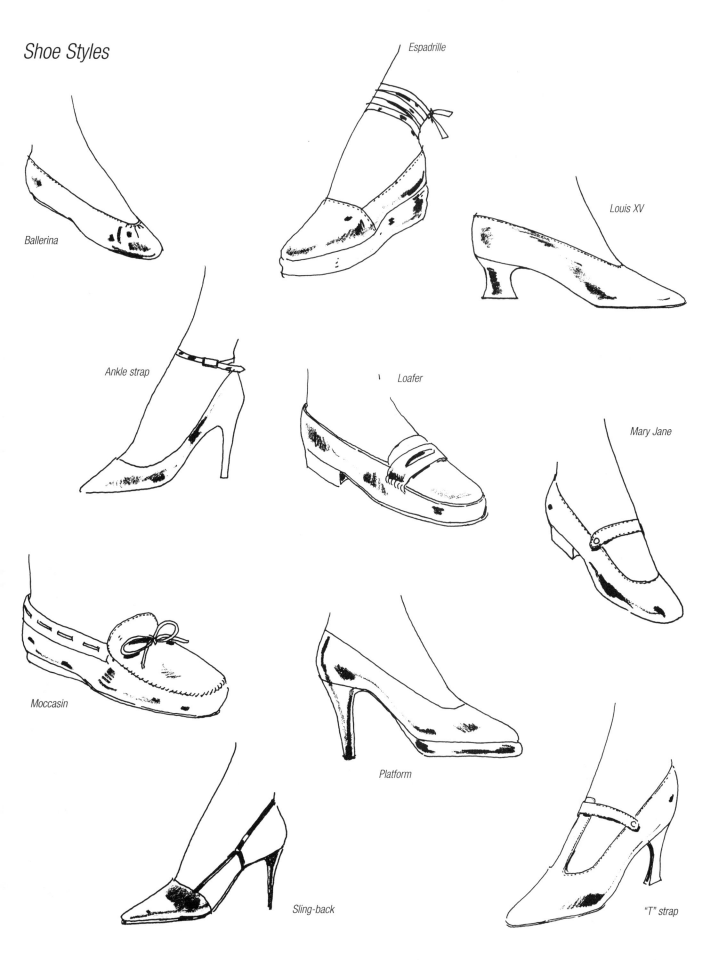

Espadrille

Louis XV

Ballerina

Ankle strap

Loafer

Mary Jane

Moccasin

Platform

Sling-back

"T" strap

Shoe Styles

Ghille

Mule

Clog

Chanel pump

Crushed boot

Spectator

Sneaker

Work boot

Riding boot

Putting it Together

Whether the look has the urbane sophistication of this Bill Blass or the theatrical extravagance of this Christian Lacroix, the most important principle to remember when drawing accessories is that they should be an appropriate part of the total look of the garment. When drawn on the fashion figure, they should blend in well with the other design elements.

Lacroix 1995

Bill Blass 1979

Ungaro 1999

27
Accessorizing the Figure

At this point, let's assume that you have studied and practiced all the drawing techniques that we have examined in this book. You have examined and observed the various parts of the fashion figure, the corresponding garment parts, and you have designed a beautiful garment that you wish to draw. You have worked hard and have developed what you believe is the "perfect" woman for your garment. She has the appropriate attitude and pose. Her face and expression capture the look you want to achieve. You should now begin to think of adding the most perfect accessories. Hats and accessories play an important role in polishing off the fashion figure. Just as the designer will look for the perfect model, hairstylist, and makeup person when showing a collection, the artist must choose them for the drawing.

One of the things to consider when designing or drawing accessories is that what might be beautiful to own, might not be important enough to put on a fashion figure. When a fashion model appears on the runway, she becomes larger than life in a space that is larger than reality. And those perfect little diamond studs that one might wear in real life will completely disappear on the runway.

On the other hand, hats often just add that finishing touch of extravagance and fantasy, giving the model greater presence on the runway. It also gives a fashion look and just the right polish and drama to a piece of artwork. Therefore, when drawing the fashion figure choose an accessory that makes a bold statement— whether it is one clean, modern bracelet or an extravagant gypsy look.

Let's breakdown some of the major accessory looks so that you will be able to incorporate them into your finished art. A fashion figure can be accessorized to fall into one or more of the following categories:

- Classic
- High fashion
- Clean and pure
- Ethnic
- Over the edge
- Retro
- Eccentric
- Combinations

Classic

The classic look is one that always passes the test of time. Classic accessories look good one season after the other and one decade after the other. The fashion figure might wear pearls, bangles, espadrilles, hair bows, lizard belts, pumps, shoulder bags, or gloves. These classic accessories are never really "in" or "out" of fashion. In the 1950s and 1960s, Mainbocher, in his couture collections, and Anne Klein, in her sportswear collections, often used classic accessories. At present, Ralph Lauren's fashions are perfect examples of the classic look.

Ralph Lauren 1980s

High Fashion

A high fashion look often takes a classic look and gives it a twist. Larger or smaller in size, an unexpected use of color, or a controlled, polished form of extravagance. High fashion clothing is always of the finest quality and workmanship. Hats that make a statement, jewelry with a bold but tasteful look, fur or jeweled trims, extravagant shawls and scarves, boots, bags, or other special leather or suede pieces complement the high fashion look. Audrey Hepburn wearing Givenchy will always remain one of the perfect examples of this look. Other high fashion designers include Yves Saint Laurent, Valentino, Oscar de la Renta, and Dior.

Audrey Hepburn in Givenchy 1960s

Clean and Pure

The clean and pure look uses accessories very carefully and discreetly. One perfect piece to pull the look together is often enough. It might be bold, but it is rarely flashy. For half of this century, Mme. Grès made this her signature look. It was a perfect complement to her classically draped gowns. In the 1970s, Halston polished off his simple, classic clothing with jewelry designed by Elsa Peretti. Calvin Klein and Giorgio Armani best represent the clean and pure look today.

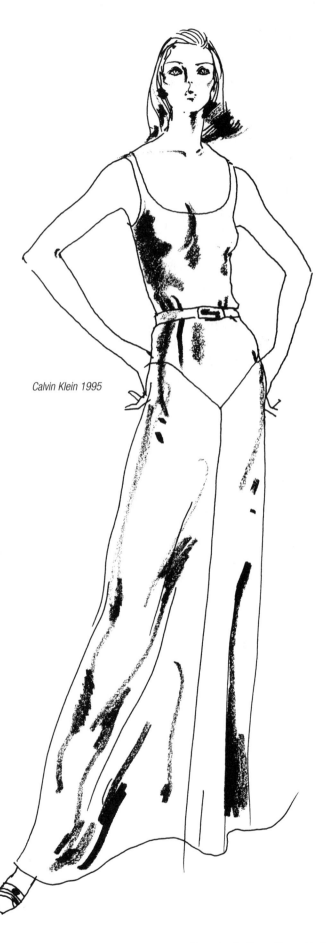

Calvin Klein 1995

Ethnic

The ethnic look uses other cultures and time periods as inspiration. It can be researched with great accuracy, or can be used as a takeoff point for the designer's own creativity. Scarves, turbans, beads, many necklaces and bracelets, embroideries, and elaborately detailed gloves, belts, shoes, or boots help to create this look. Many of these pieces are combined with each other in a very luxurious way. In the late 1970s, Yves Saint Laurent's gypsy looks inspired and influenced many other designers. Saint Laurent often uses different cultures for his colorful, ready-to-wear collections, just as Mary McFadden often turns to other civilizations for her extravagant accessories and her signature pleated evening dresses.

Saint Laurent 1976

Over the Edge

Over the edge takes fashion to its most extreme. Often it is bad taste carried so far that it becomes acceptable. This is fashion that is never based on restraint and sometimes makes a parody of acceptable taste. Karl Lagerfield often exaggerates his Chanel collection in this tongue-in-cheek manner by over-exaggerating or by giving a new twist to classic Chanel pieces—such as quilted bags, black tipped shoes, or chain details. Christian Lacroix is a master of overstatement. He pushes "over the edge" to its limits with his extravagant couture collections.

Lacroix 1994

Retro

Retro turns to the past for its inspiration. A designer picks a certain time period such as the 1930s or the 1960s and then exaggerates the look, or takes elements from it and adapts it to contemporary times. Almost every designer at every level has used retro at one time or another. Yves Saint Laurent has taken the 1940s as a theme for his couture collections and Anna Sui frequently uses retro in outrageous ways for her highly spirited designs.

Saint Laurent 1995

Eccentric

Eccentric is a quirky and very personal approach to accessorizing. It does not appeal to everyone, and often those who follow these designers in a cult-like way are the only ones who appreciate it. The inspiration can come from anything—from hardware stores to religion. Schiaparelli's signature in the 1930s and 1940s were her hats shaped like inkpots, hardware fastenings, or a lobster painted on an evening dress by Dalí. In the last few years, we have had Commes des Garçons, Romeo Gigli, Issey Miyake, and Franco Moschino who used both the familiar and the unexpected in the most original and, many times, humorous ways. Each eccentric puts a personal touch to their designs and accessories, which is often immediately recognizable.

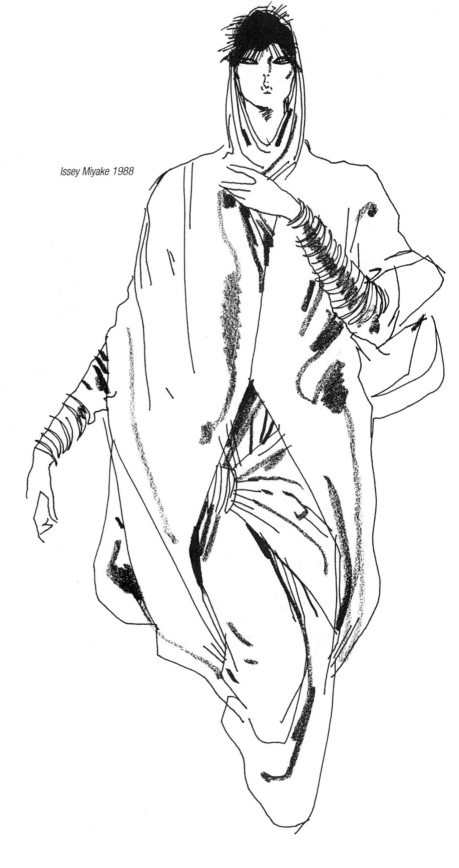

Issey Miyake 1988

Combinations

Often two or more of these looks can be combined—such as high fashion and classic. Also a designer may use high fashion in one collection and ethnic in another.

Combining "Retro" and "High Fashion", Gianni Versace borrows the clean lines of the 1960s, but uses such a high fashion fabric as silver satin to recreate a mini coat typical of that era but with a 1990s twist. The long teased hair, the very heavy eye makeup and high heeled satin boots complete the look.

Planning for a finished piece of artwork is the same as a designer planning a collection. All the thought and care taken before you even pick up a pencil to draw will give you the same results as a well planned, successful runway show.

Versace 1995

Karl Lagerfeld/Chanel 2003

Part 3

Rendering

Bill Blass 1988

28
Stripes and Plaids

Stripes and plaids have been so much a part of our lives that we almost take them for granted. Your first striped garment was probably a part of your layette—a pink and white or blue and white outfit—with a matching striped cap! As a child, we all had our favorite tartan plaid shirt or skirt, which we liked all the more as it faded with all the washings.

Stripes can be as low-key and simple as those on a button down shirt or as striking and colorful as a gypsy skirt in a bright and vibrant cotton. They can be woven into the material as in a subtle shadow stripe or they can be printed as in a bold awning stripe.

Plaids can have the innocence of a parochial school uniform or the sophistication of a rustling silk taffeta ball gown. They can be as old-fashioned as a tiny, woven shepherd's check or as large and modern as an exploded tattersall plaid. However, whether old, small, large, or contemporary, all plaids are based on patterns that are over 1,500 years old!

Some designers, such as Pauline Trigère, have used stripes and plaids consistently in their collections, while other designers rarely use them at all. While they go in and out of fashion, however, plaids and stripes remain classic patterns. And like them or not, understanding the concept of how to draw them is most important. Because they are straight horizontal and vertical lines that extend around the body, they cannot be randomly placed, criss-crossing lines. Instead, they have their own logic and symmetry, which, when mastered, makes them challenging, yet rewarding, to render.

*Givenchy
1995*

Understanding Stripes and Plaids

A stripe is a band of color or texture that may be vertical, horizontal, or diagonal. It can be woven or printed in one or many colors and the stripes may vary in width. Using the center front principle we can begin to understand vertical and horizontal stripes, which when combined form a pattern called a plaid. A plaid is a design of stripes intersecting at right angles.

Both plaids and stripes can be even or uneven. An even plaid or stripe has the lines and spaces in both directions. Even or uneven, they can be printed or woven, in one or many colors or textures.

Even stripe

Uneven stripe

Even plaid

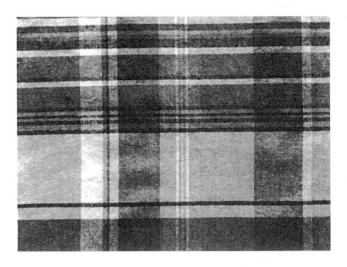

Uneven plaid

Drawing Stripes and Plaids

The most important or dominant color or bar of either a stripe or a plaid falls on the center front of the garment. This bar can also form the edge of a collar, cuff, pocket, or hem, or it can relate to any specific design detail.

Vertical Stripes

(In the next sections, please note that the area being discussed is shown in grey.)

1 Block in a front view figure with the hips and the shoulders in opposite directions. Indicate the center front with a solid line. This becomes the dominant stripe of the garment. All the other stripes work off this one.

The biggest mistake when drawing vertical stripes is to work from one side of the figure to the other. To have correct placement and perspective, work from the center to one side, and then from the center to the other side.

2 Working with only the left side of the garment, divide that side in half at the shoulder (point A) and at the hem (point B). Use only your eyes (do not measure!). Now connect point A to point B.

3 Next, do the same on the right side of the garment. You will notice that because of the crunch of the fabric, the stripe that falls on the side of the high hip has a bend where the waist crunches. It then bows out as it follows the high hip line. Blend them together at the point that they meet.

4 + 5 Divide the sleeves, either by halving them or by lining them up with the garment. The same blending of the line that you did on the side of the high hip is also required at the bend of the arm. At this point, you can accurately divide the body further to render any specific size stripe. The stripes on the finished garment should flow gently with the curves of the body.

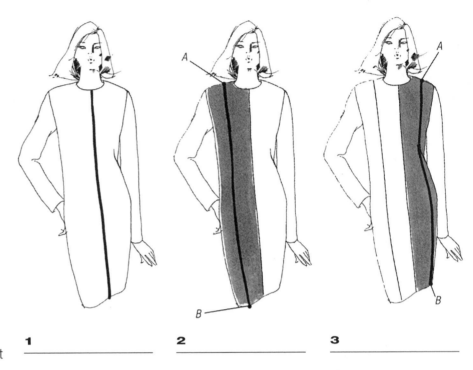

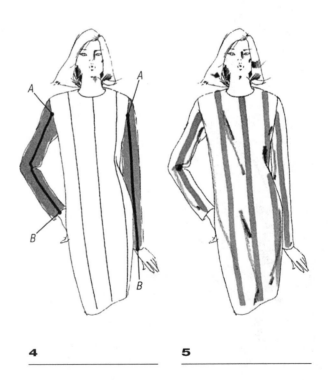

320

Horizontal Stripes

By using the same principles as for vertical stripes, we can divide the figure for horizontal stripes. Begin with a front view sketch of a chemise dress that has opposite hip and shoulder movement.

1 First, divide the distance between the shoulder and hem in half and connect point A to point B. This is the middle of the garment, not the hip. (It might, however, fall on the hip line.)

2 Next, divide the bottom section in half and connect point A to point B with a slightly curved line.

3 Now, divide the top section in the same manner and connect point A to point B. You will notice that the shift in direction from the hem to the shoulders is gradual and smooth.

4 Next, divide and connect the sleeves in the same manner.

5 Continue dividing to render the specific fabric.

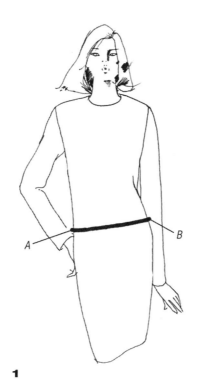

1

2

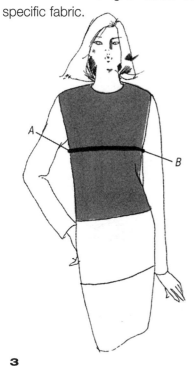

3

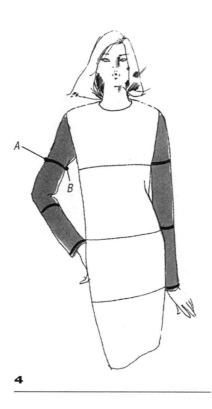

4

5

The Turned Figure in Stripes or Plaid

Block off a turned figure in the same chemise dress that you used for the front view figure.

1 First, indicate center front. Check that the side closer to you is bigger and the side that is farther away from you (the side that shows the breast) is smaller.

2–3 Next, divide the left side and the right side as in the front view.

4 Now, divide the sleeves, either by halving them, or by lining them up with the garment. The side away from you (with the high hip) crunches. Let your line follow it slightly. The side facing you stretches, so your line will be less curved.

5–9 Now work the horizontal divisions in the same manner as the front view. Also, divide the sleeves the same way as the front view.

10 After the initial grid is established, additional stripes may be added to render any particular fabric.

1

2

6

7

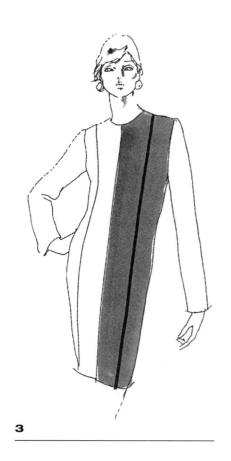

3

4

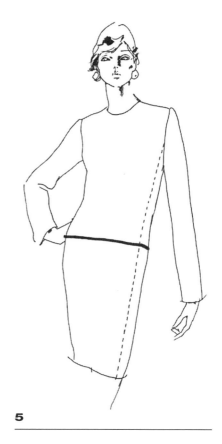

5

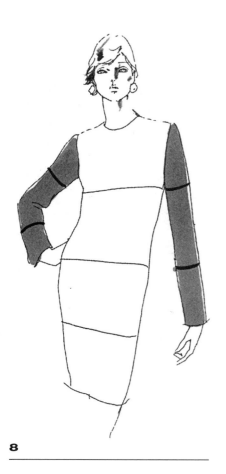

8

9

10

If you extend the horizontal lines, you will see that they meet at a vanishing point. This clearly shows the cylindrical perspective of the figure. The most important principle to remember when drawing stripes or plaids—either for front view, turned, profile figures—is that when you divide each section, you must only work within that section, first from the center to one side, then from the center to the other side.

Drawing stripes and plaids takes a very accurate underdrawing. Regardless of how loose the rendering is, the blocking off must be as precise as possible. Do not attempt to render a stripe or plaid directly on the finished art.

Stripes and plaids are difficult and take planning to draw them accurately and precisely. However, there is a reward that follows all this hard work—when you combine the vertical principles with the horizontal principles you have a grid to block off any plaid or check pattern. This grid can also be used for blocking in all design and construction details, which will ensure greater accuracy and symmetry in your drawing.

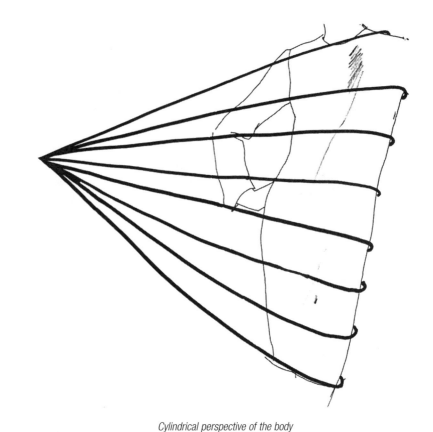

Cylindrical perspective of the body

A grid system also allows for accurate placement of details.

Often stripes or plaids will be cut on the bias. Pay strict attention to the direction on which the individual design detail is cut. When drawing stripes or plaids, some important principles to remember are:

- Plaids and stripes should match at the side seams.

- When plaids or stripes are cut at an angle, as in an A-line skirt, they will meet at points or miters.

- Set-in sleeves match the bodice.

- The positioning and matching of stripes and plaids are unique to each garment.

The most common error when drawing stripes or plaids is beginning at the top and working to the bottom (or bottom to top), or working from one side to the other. This cannot work because of the gradual shift from the direction of the hip to the opposite direction of the shoulder. The correct way to draw stripes or plaids is to begin at the center. From this point you can either work from top to bottom (or vice versa) or from center to one side and then from the center to the other side. Working within a grid system will help you with this problem. Divide the garment in half and continue dividing each half. This enables you to change directions gradually—either vertically or horizontally—and have the stripes or plaids look totally uninterrupted.

Don't distort the stripe or plaid by following every twist and turn of the body. Follow the general movement, paying strict attention to the design details. Soft pencil shadows give garments direction.

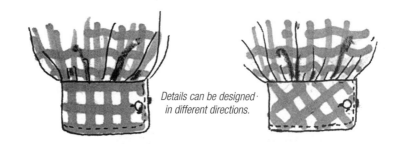

Details can be designed in different directions.

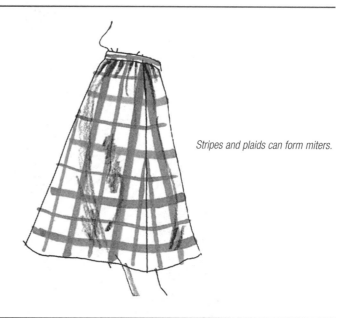

Stripes and plaids can form miters.

Plaids and stripes on set-in sleeves match the bodice.

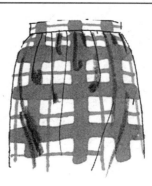

A soft shadow will give a dimensional quality.

Striped and Plaid Garments

The striped fabrics on this Pauline Trigère coat has a diagonal weave. The right side and the left are cut in opposite directions and form a "V" shape. The stripes on the pockets intersect them. When drawing a garment such as this, keep the stripes slightly rounded to follow the flares of the silhouette.

Trigére 1960

This Oscar de la Renta gown has a bold, geometric quality. The scale of the stripe is so large that you can count how many stripes there are. In a rendered drawing, they must be even and they must also seem to go all the way around the garment. Notice how the dark stripe is even all around the hem folds of both the skirt and short cape. It also forms the band of the cape and the bow. Because of the amount of fabric in the skirt, the gathers give the stripe a very close, loopy line, which opens out as the stripes reach the hem.

Oscar de la Renta 1987

Stripes and Plaids

The James Galanos jumpsuit and jacket are made from a very over-sized plaid. Again, the placement is crucial. The bars of the plaid are placed on the hem of the pants, edges of the jacket, lapel, and top collar. They run exactly down the center front of each leg. This strict and perfect attention to detail is why this type of garment is so costly. Make sure that your artwork follows this same precision.

James Galanos 1970

This Pauline Trigère cape and dress ensemble is all of the same plaid. The sweeping cape is straight grain at the closing and turns bias as it reaches the sides and back. The dress is cut completely on the bias. To draw this outfit, you need to carefully grid out the plaid, making sure that the plaid directions are very accurate. Notice the plaid itself was rendered rather casually, but the direction of the plaid is completely precise and accurate.

Stripes and plaids are exact. Whether they are rendered tightly or loosely, the direction, scale, and placement must be perfect. Remember, the more accurate the underdrawing is, the more the finished drawing will look effortless.

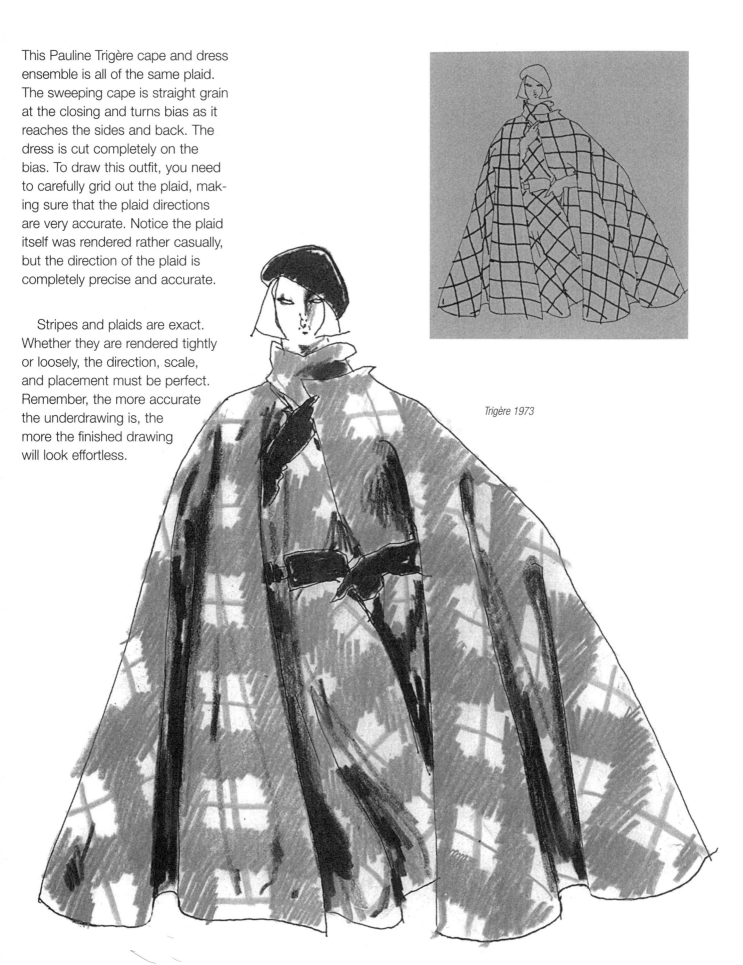

Trigère 1973

Geoffrey Beene 1986/1982

29
Rendering Concepts

Rendering is the artist's way of explaining a fabric. It can help the artist to specifically define a piece of clothing because it shows us how it actually looks. However, rendering does not cover up a bad drawing.

The rendering process begins with the line drawing. Without any shading or color, the line drawing should give us most of the information we need to understand the garment. The lines alone should show us the silhouette and cut, the way the garment falls on the body, the construction details, and the weight and feel of the fabric, or its "hand." After these, all the rest of the information comes from the rendering process.

Rendering will tell us whether the garment is made of taffeta or satin, wool crepe or wool jersey, chiffon or georgette. It will also show us the color, the scale of the print, or the texture of the fabric. It will make the artwork complete.

Many different art supplies or combinations can be used to render the same fabric, just as there are many different ways to render. Rendering can be tight and exact or loose and editorial. It can cover the entire garment or just be indicated. Above all, it is very personal and can have many different approaches.

A fabric category comes in many weights from very light to very heavy. A wool group can range from the lightest, sheerest wool, through challis and crepe, to a heavy wool melton. A family of silks can vary from light silk chiffon or georgette to a silk charmeuse to a weighty silk crepe or heavy silk satin. Because of all the differences within even the general categories, you should never assume that there is just one way to render silk or wool or any other cloth, because the weight of the fabric is the first consideration.

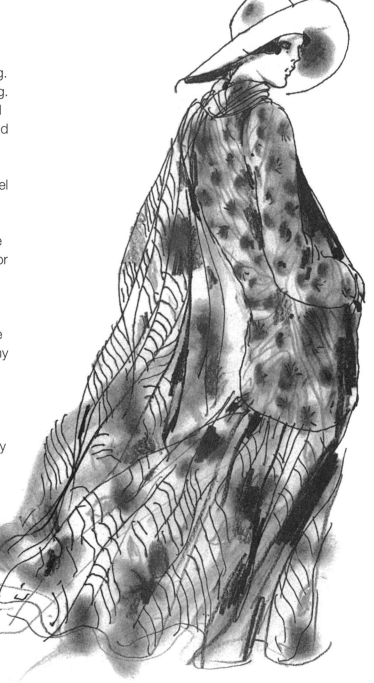

For comparison, if you gathered one yard of silk chiffon and one yard of wool crepe, the results would be completely different. Because it is so thin, the chiffon would gather into less space than the wool crepe. There would be many rounds of fabric at the hem of the chiffon and far less at the hem of the wool crepe. Because of this, it would take many more yards of chiffon than wool crepe if you were to make a similar style garment out of both fabrics.

Another consideration is the "hand" of the fabric, which is that characteristic that is perceived by touching. A fabric can be soft, firm, crisp, fine, heavy, and so forth. For example, a silk crepe has a soft hand, so in a garment it would fall close to the body. Organdy, on the other hand, has a much crisper hand and consequently would stand away from the body.

Silk chiffon

Wool crepe

Silk crepe

Organdy

Fabric Groups

For the purposes of this book, we will group the fabrics into four categories, which include: (1) wool and other textured fabrics; (2) shiny fabrics; (3) sheers; and (4) prints. To help you understand these breakdowns and categories, let's take a look at each one.

Wool and Other Textured Fabrics

In this category there are three weights: lightweight, medium weight, and heavyweight. The lightweight class includes dress weights of sheer wool, wool challis, and bouclé. The mediumweight class includes dress or suit weights of wool crepe, wool jersey, wool flannel, and wool gabardine. Lastly, the heavyweight class includes coating weights of wool melton, fleece, mohair, cashmere, camel's hair, vicuña, and double-faced wool. Textured and patterned wools, which are also a part of this general category, include wool tweed, wool plaids, wool herringbone, and checked wool. Keep in mind that many of these fabrics can cross over to another category simply because of a particular construction. You will have to judge it for yourself.

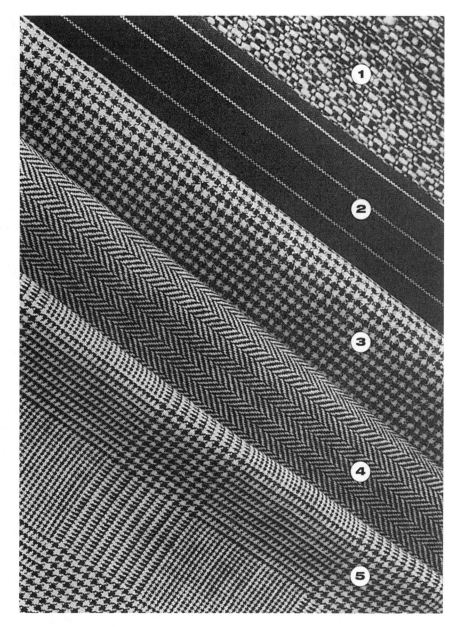

Patterned wools

1 Wool tweed

2 Pinstripe

3 Check

4 Herringbone

5 Glenplaid

Generally, wool fabrics are soft and pliable, sometimes with a rough or fuzzy texture. They are rendered best in a medium that will produce a soft quality, such as a slightly dry brush, a soft pencil, or many combinations, which include using a marker with colored pencils. Because wool fabrics are not shiny (they might have a dull sheen, but this is the exception rather than the rule), there often will be only two values—the base color and a darker shadow color.

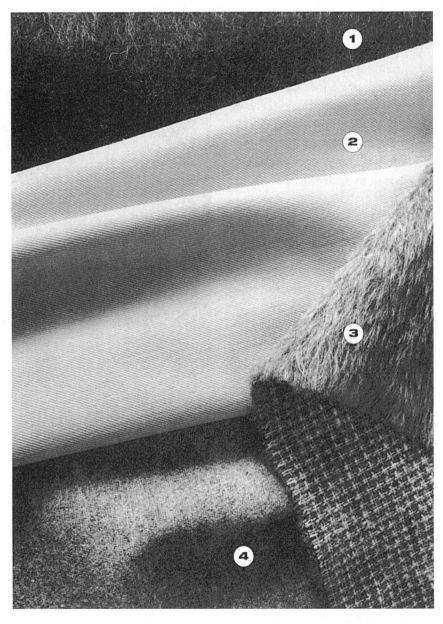

Textured fabrics

1 Melton

2 Gabardine

3 Check

4 Double-faced (reversible)

5 Flannel

Drawing "Wool" Fabrics

The camel hair coat on this page is rendered in marker, using the general color for the main part of the coat and a darker value for the shadows and folds. Remember, the heavier the wool, the more distinct the collar roll, sleeve cap, and hem folds. Don't "over render." Occasionally, leave an edge, and keep the shadows soft.

Watercolor or gouache works well for the overall color with accents in a soft, colored pencil. Some twill weave wools, gabardines, or rougher wools might require diagonal lines to indicate the texture. Tweeds can be rendered with diagonals, crosshatches, and flecks. Often there are two or more shades or colors. Particular textures as in basket weaves, bouclé, slubs, or ribs can be picked up with a sharp pencil or marker. (Linen, raw silk, and corduroy are also rendered this way.)

The layered outfit on this page of many types of textures and weaves can be rendered with a dry brush using india ink and a fine line marker. The double-faced (reversible) wool coat has a herringbone texture on the outside and a windowpane plaid on the inside. The tweed of the jacket is indicated with fine and medium markers, while the diagonal weave of the pants is rendered with a fine marker, as is the corduroy of the vest.

Camel hair coat

Layered look

Mohair, fleece, and heavy wool with "hair" or nap should have a soft edge. This swing coat is rendered with a dark-gray, soft colored pencil and the texture of the wool is indicated with a dry brush and india ink. Do not use a hard outline on any brushed or mohair-type wool fabrics.

When rendering a checked or herringbone garment, you will need to use a grid on the underdrawing.

The large check on this jacket has both verticals and horizontals, with diagonals that go in different directions. Notice that where they cross, a darker tone takes place. The rendering for this jacket was done with a fine marker with colored pencil accents.

Please note: For more specific information on plaids and stripes, see *Chapter 28*, page 315.

Use a grid for accuracy when drawing checks and plaids.

Mohair swing coat

Shiny Fabrics

Shiny fabrics reflect light. They range from the slight sheen of silk crepe to the highly reflective shine of lamé, from the soft shadows of a velvet to the high contrast of an iridescent taffeta.

The hand can be as soft as charmeuse or as crisp as brocade. Surfaces can be as smooth as satin or as slubbed as a doupioni and may be decoratively woven as in a jacquard or brocade. When rendering, keep in mind that crisp, shiny fabrics have crisp, hard edges, while velvets and soft, shiny fabrics have muted, soft edges.

Within this general category, there are three classes, which include the soft shines, the crisp shines, and the decorative shines. The soft shines include charmeuse, crepe de chine, velvet, velveteen, and velour. The crisp shines include satin, taffeta, peau de soie, faille, vinyl, and leather. The decorative surface shines encompass brocade, matelassé, cloqué, moiré, ottoman, jacquard, crocodile, lamé, lizard, alligator, and sequins. Again, keep in mind that any of these fabrics and materials can be in any of these classes due to a particular construction or detail.

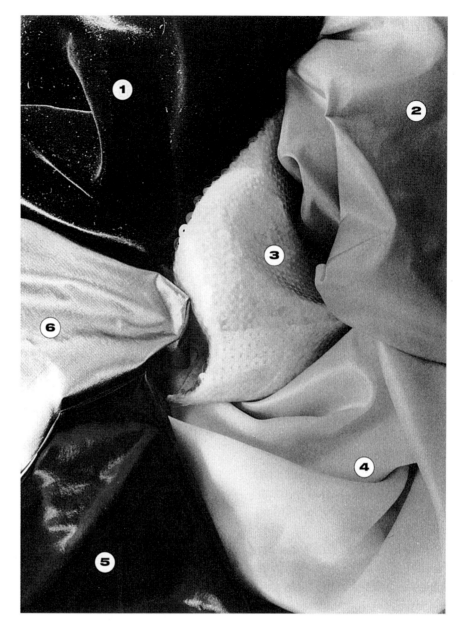

Shiny fabrics

1 Gold-flecked velvet

2 Taffeta

3 Sequined fabric

4 Satin

5 Vinyl

6 Lamé

Drawing Shiny Fabrics

Let's analyze the principles of any fabric with a distinct shine. First, when rendering a shiny fabric, think of a shiny cylinder wrapped around the body. If the light source is coming from the right, you will observe that:

- The lightest value is on the right side.

- The darkest value is farther to the back.

- The middle value is in the front.

When a shiny fabric is on the body, the same principles take place. Let's break the body down into its different planes: breasts, stomach, hips, and knees. Keep in mind that the side plane is the most important. We will use arrows to indicate the cylindrical turns and the gray tones to indicate shadows. Using all this information, you can try your hand at a very form-fitting, shiny fabric dress.

Shiny fabrics have a distinct dark, medium, and light value. The darkest values take place in the folds and shadows. The medium value is the general garment color. The lightest values are on the top folds and highlights. They also take place where the fabric is falling on an extended part of the body, as in an arm, a leg, or a breast. It is almost as if there is a white loop around every dark shadow or fold. Also, remember to leave a light edge around garment details and gathers.

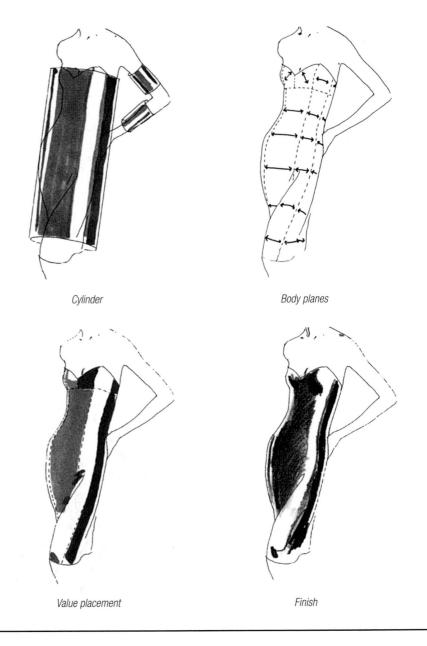

Cylinder

Body planes

Value placement

Finish

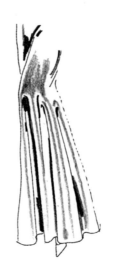

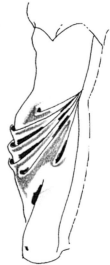

Applying these principles to a long satin dress, first block off the planes of the body. Add the dark tones. Next, add the medium tones keeping the white highlight down the entire figure. Remember, the highlight principles appear on all cylindrical parts of the garment, such as the neck, sleeves, and body.

This backless satin gown was rendered in soft colored pencil, softened by a paper stump or by rubbing tissue over it. Notice the distinct patterns of lights and darks. Satin, charmeuse, and all the soft, shiny fabrics have a certain "round" quality.

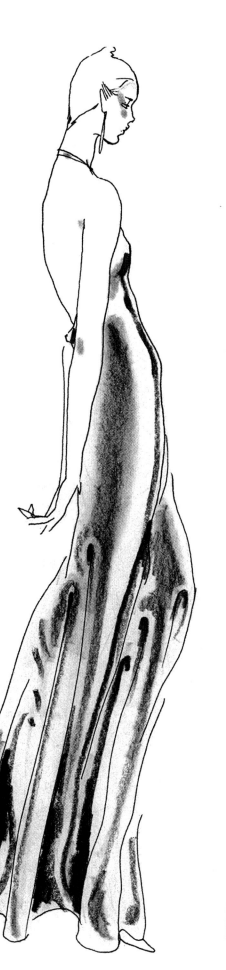

This taffeta dress was rendered
with just a dry brush and india ink.
Again, the highlights are distinct.
Taffetas have a "pointy," crisp
quality. For the base color, you
could use watercolors or markers
along with a dry brush or pencil
for the accents.

Velvets have a very soft edge and there should be a light space along all the edges to keep the "plushy" feelings. This gown and the shadows on the face were rendered in gray eyeshadow with its sponge applicator. Eyeshadow is a wonderful art supply and the sponge applicator gives it a pastel quality. Use an inexpensive brand that is not too oily, fixing it with unscented hair spray. Any color can be used for rendering, but gray is especially useful for shadows. For the face, a set of brown colors works beautifully on top of a skin tone marker.

Sequins, lamé, and beaded garments have very pronounced light and dark patterns. The lamé was rendered simply with a colored pencil. To render sequins, use a medium-pointed marker. On the darks, you can do the same thing with a light-colored acrylic or tempera paint.

Also, charcoal or construction paper works beautifully, because they allow you to work with the whites as well. The charmeuse dress on the following page was executed with colored pencils on construction paper.

Leather and vinyl have hard edges. This vinyl jacket was rendered with three distinct color markers that left definite hard edges and sharp white highlights.

Sequined

Lamé

Vinyl jacket

Sheers

Sheer fabrics are transparent. You can see parts of the body, as well as undergarments, through them. Within the general category of sheer fabric there are two distinct groups, which are the soft sheers and the crisp sheers. The soft sheers include chiffon, georgette, voile, and lace. The crisp sheers encompass organdy, organza, tulle, point d'esprit, and gazar.

In rendering sheer fabrics, there can be many values of a color because of the transparency of the fabrics, which fall over each other. Layers of transparency also eliminate hard outlines. Often a color is used for the edge, or sometimes just a slightly darker value is sufficient. Because the garments have rolled hems, the hemlines should not have a heavy or hard edge, but should retain a very fluid quality.

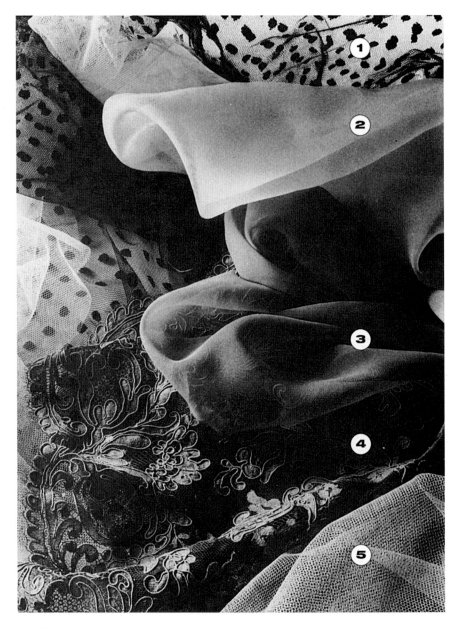

Sheer fabrics

1 Point d'esprit

2 Organza

3 Chiffon

4 Lace

5 Tulle

Drawing Sheer Fabrics

Begin by applying skin tones where it will show through the fabric. This is the method to use when rendering any sheer fabric, especially chiffon or georgette. Use a fine marker to indicate the cuffs, neckline binding, and main folds.

With a wash, colored pencil, or light-colored marker, render the fabric over the skin tone. Try to not leave any hard edges. The outline can be indicated in on an underdrawing or very lightly with a pencil that can be erased.

Apply skin tone.

Indicate detail.

Render fabric over skin tone.

This georgette dress was rendered
with a dry brush. The darkest value
was applied next to the body and
the lightest value was applied
where the fabric hits the air.
Remember, when rendering
sheers, keep a very light touch
and leave no outlines.

Lace

Lace has a net base with a pattern, which is often floral, worked over it. Lace can range from alençon or chantilly to heavy guipure. Lace can be re-embroidered and beaded. Often you will see a dot pattern on the net. This is called point d'esprit.

As with chiffon or georgette, you will render the fabric over the skin tone. The net can be lightly sketched in with cross hatching over the skin tone. On an underdrawing, indicate the motif placement and any scallop or edge design on the hem. First work the skin tones and then render the lace, keeping a rhythm to the line. This lace overlay was rendered with a fine marker over a skin tone marker. The bow was done with a touch of eyeshadow.

The lace top of the dress to the right was rendered with a very fine marker, which again was applied over a skin tone marker. The scallops at the top of the bust were sketched over the dress fabric, which was drawn first.

Instead of a scalloped lace, the design of the dress below uses point d'esprit and a lace motif at the neck. The net and lace motif were done with a very fine marker, while the dots of the point d'esprit were done with a medium-point marker.

Lace

Point d'esprit with lace motif

The tulle section of this ballgown was crosshatched, layer on layer, with a very fine marker. To crosshatch, work each layer in a slightly different direction, working over each previous one to create the shadows. Make sure to pick up the dark accents with a slightly darker line.

This lace and organdy gown on the right is all fine marker with an accent of colored pencil. The organza coat below was also rendered with a fine marker and colored pencil accents. Both use the same tools, but have completely different results and qualities.

Organdy has a sharp quality.

Organza has a round quality.

350

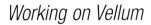
Working on Vellum

Working on vellum is an extravagant and luxurious way to render sheer fabrics. It produces magnificent results. Also, the color can be applied from the back, as well as the front.

Begin with an accurate under-drawing. Draw the garment with a very fine marker, keeping a very flowing line—especially in the draped areas. Indicate the edges and hems in a dotted pencil line, which can later be erased.

On the back, apply the main colors with a marker. The color will be slightly lighter on the front. Don't worry if it streaks slightly. Let the marker dry before turning it over.

Line drawing indicating edges and hems

Apply main colors on the back of drawing.

Now, on the right side of the drawing, render the next layers with marker or colored pencils or both. Keep it very soft and floaty. You can add light or white highlights on the top side because the main color is on the back. Mount it on white paper.

Because this technique is fairly time consuming, it is not used frequently in the fashion industry. However, it is wonderful for a special portfolio piece.

Most outer edges of sheer fabric have no hard lines.

Prints

Prints are designs or patterns reproduced on fabric. Any fabric, from chiffon to satin to wool, can be printed. The motifs can range from a tiny pin dot, to a huge floral in which only several motifs might fill an entire evening gown. They can follow a regular progression, be randomly tossed, have borders, or be engineered to fall on a specific part of the garment. The duplication of the pattern is called a repeat. Also, certain prints have a "one-way" direction or a definite repeat pattern.

Print fabrics

1 Paisley

2 Allover

3 Floral

4 Polka dot

5 Animal

6 Stylized

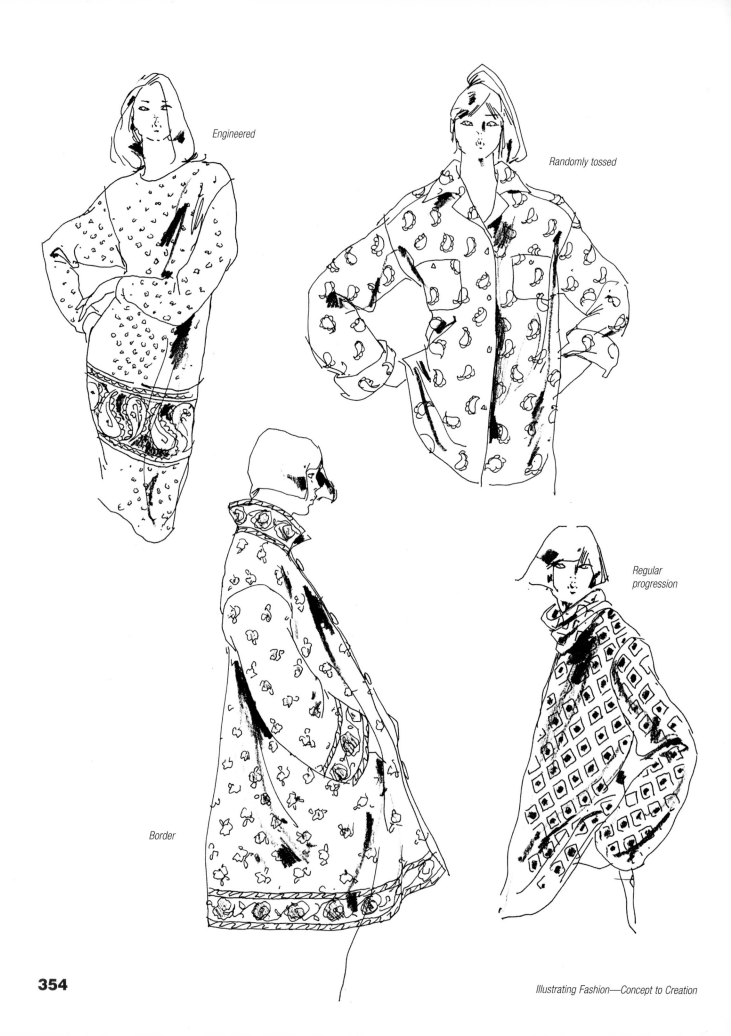

Engineered

Randomly tossed

Border

Regular progression

Drawing Print Fabrics

When rendering a print design, you will want to capture the effect and feeling of the design rather than indicating every detail. Over rendering can make the look too heavy handed. The most important consideration when rendering a print is the scale and the repeat.

To begin, find a print that you would like to render. First, pin the swatch to a dress form or existing garment and walk across the room. If the pattern or print is so small that you cannot determine how many repeats there are, render it for the general feeling.

If the print is medium-sized (average), and you are still aware of the amounts of motifs or repeats that it contains, count them and try to approximate the amount.

If the repeats are very few but visible, determine how many there would be on the specific area such as the bodice, skirt, or sleeve and indicate them on your art.

Small allover pattern

Average size motif

Large scale print

The most important consideration is to be at the correct distance away from the print so that when you render a large motif, it is rendered much smaller, with much less detail. Keep in mind that even if the print is rendered simply, soft shadows will give it a dimensional quality.

Some prints look best when rendered all over, others look best when they are looser. The print and its relationship to the garment will determine this. Determine the fashion message of the print before you begin to render. Is it an impressionistic floral, a bold geometric, or a neat little polka dot? To help you establish the rhythm, direction, and placement of the print, use a grid under your drawing.

Rendered size

Actual size

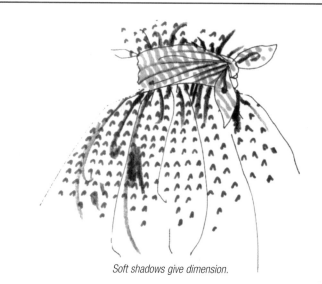

Soft shadows give dimension.

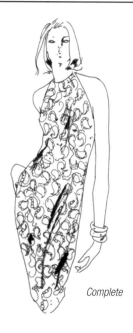

Complete

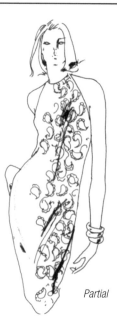

Partial

This classic floral was rendered in two colors of marker all over the garment. The soft accents were done with a colored pencil. As you can see by the grid, there is a strong directional placement to this print.

This large scale geometric print requires extremely accurate placement. The color contrast was not very sharp, so that pattern was not outlined.

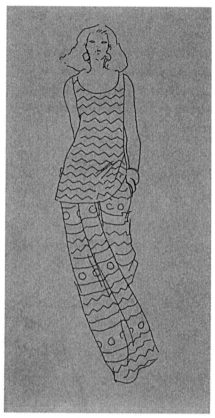

This robe has a border print and a diagonally placed small pattern, which was rendered simply in marker. Notice the paisleys have a one-way direction, with the larger part of the design near the top. The borders must be exactly the same size everywhere.

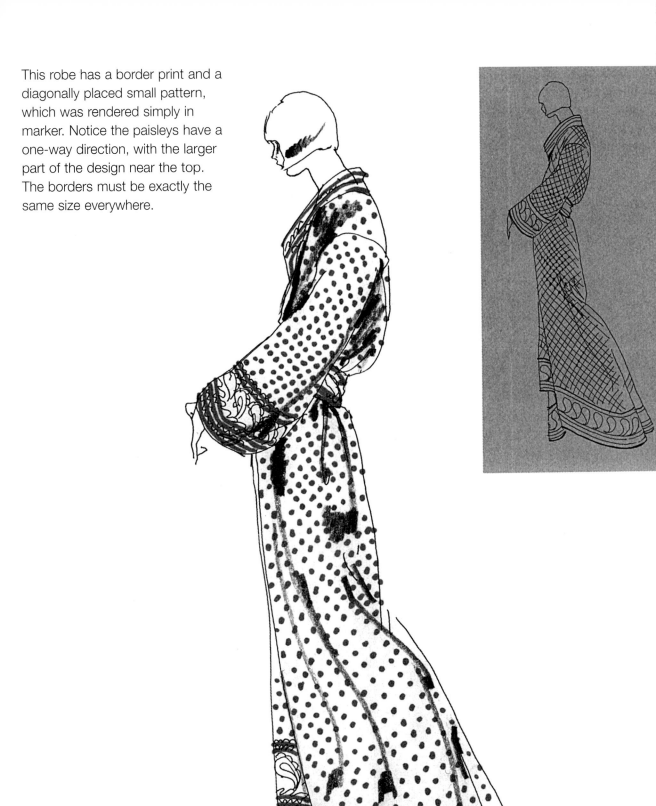

This cowl-back gown has few stylized flowers on a dotted background. There are three colors of marker for the flower and a very fine dot for the background.

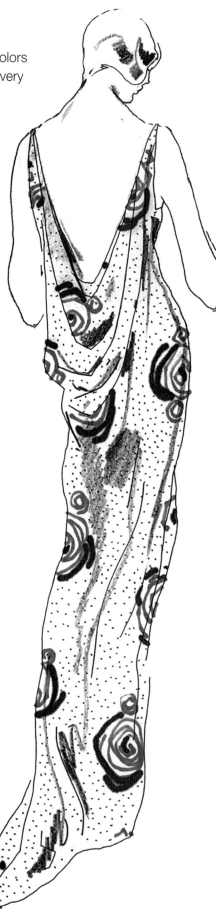

360

Today, prints have many possibilities. A striped fabric can have a floral border, or the print can look like a pieced patchwork. It can mimic a photograph or look like splattered paint. It can be hand-painted down one side of the garment and embellished with beads on the other side. Just make sure that your rendering clearly explains the prints. Also, for greater accuracy, most of the garment should be rendered.

Rendering is a vast subject. There is absolutely no way to include every fabric in one chapter. Fabric possibilities are endless, for example, sequins can be applied to chiffon or wool jersey, and taffeta or flannel can be quilted. Modern technology mixes synthetics with natural fibers so that a particular drape can be achieved. Learning the principles and concepts will help you apply them to a specific fabric.

There are times, however, when several concepts have to be combined to render a particular fabric—cut velvet, for instance, combines the principles of velvet worked on a sheer base fabric. Sequins on jersey combines both the rules of shine and wool. Even if it were possible to cover everything, by the time this book goes to press, new possibilities and combinations will be created. So be open to all new creations and experiment!

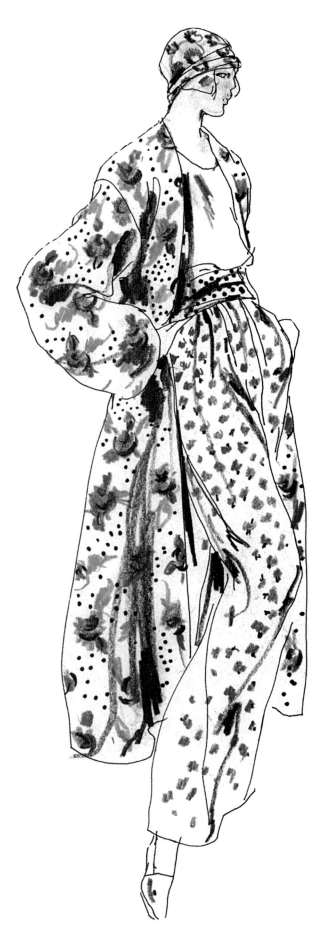

Lacroix 1997

30

Rendering Techniques

Basic Marker Hints

Imagine if all garments were only made in muslin. It would be impossible to tell the color, weight, feel, or texture of them. We would never be able to sense the feeling of a floaty chiffon gown, a textured tweed suit, or a shiny satin dress. We could never imagine glistening beads or sensuous furs. Our eyes would never be able to distinguish between a black and white print or one in blazing colors.

By learning the various rendering techniques, we are able to represent by artistic means the fabrics that we wish to portray in our designs. The viewer will be able to completely understand the character and look of the garment.

There are many techniques for rendering fabrics, and in this chapter I am showing you the techniques that I feel will produce the best results using markers and soft colored pencils. Once you have learned these techniques and have become confident with them, you can adapt them to achieve your own personal results.

Here are some helpful hints for using markers:

- To prevent smudging of the markers, lightly sketch the figure on the marker paper using a 2H pencil. Apply the markers for the specific rendering technique desired. To finish art, work over the 2H pencil with a black or dark grey Prismacolor pencil or with a fine point marker.

- There are some brands of marker paper, such as Bienfang Graphics No. 360, that allow the marker to be used on both the front and back of the paper. This will allow you to do the finished drawing on the front, and apply the marker from the back as well as from the front.

- Lighter color markers are easier to use than darker ones.

- Before using any new marker, draw a 2-inch box. On one side bring the marker to the edge and on the other side stop short of the edge. This will enable you to determine if the marker will bleed over the line or if you should not bring it to the edge.

- For the artwork in this chapter, I used Bienfang Graphics No. 360 marker paper and applied the base color from the back for a softer look. The following applications were applied from the front: Chartpak markers and Prismacolor 30%, 50% and 90% cool grey and black pencils.

Rendering Black and White Fabrics

To render the color black, let us imagine a color range of black fabrics ranging from the lightest black, such as a washed out T-shirt to the darkest black as in a black velvet dress.

To achieve this range, we will work with dark gray markers

1 Fill in the area to be colored black with the darkest color grey that will allow a black line to be seen.

2 With a soft black colored pencil, add the shadows and garment details.

3 For white fabrics, let the paper represent the white color and indicate the shadows with a medium grey soft colored pencil.

(I used Chartpak Cool Grey #7) rather than a black one. Shadows will be drawn with a black soft colored pencil. Because all design sketches are accompanied with fabric swatches, it will be very clear that the actual color is black, not gray.

Rendering Shadows

The properties of different fabrics will result in their unique shadows. There are, however, certain places of a garment that will always result in a shadow. A shadow will always take place in the following areas:

- Any place on the garment that you can put your fingers in or under. This would be under a collar or lapel. It would also take place under flaps and buttons. It would always occur down the opening of a garment, along side the lap over.

- A shadow would always occur when something covers something. For example, in a jacket and skirt, a shadow would always fall on the skirt under the jacket.

- On a turned figure, there would be a shadow along the side plane.

Rendering Tweeds

A very effective way of rendering tweed fabric is do a rubbing over a piece of sandpaper. Different weights of sandpaper can simulate different weights of tweed fabric.

1 Start by applying the background color of the fabric.

2 Lay a piece of sandpaper under the drawing of the garment and gently rub in the colors of the tweed with the side of a soft colored pencil or pencils.

3 Indicate the shadows by going over the original marker once again with the same color. This will result in a darker shade of the color. An alternate way would be to use a gray or black soft colored pencil. Draw in the garment details

Different grades of sandpaper allow for different effects

Rendering Plaids

On your underdrawing, indicate the grainline directions of the plaid (see Chapter 28 on Blocking Stripes and Plaids).

1 Apply the background color with a marker.

2 Indicate the vertical bars with a soft colored pencil.

3 Indicate the horizontal bars with a soft colored pencil. Darken the area where the horizontal and vertical lines cross.

Plaids can also be rendered with markers and colored pencils

4 Draw in the secondary plaid lines.

5 To simulate a medium to heavyweight woolen or a plaid with a diagonal weave, work diagonal line with a soft colored pencil over the dominant bars.

Rendering Furs

Think of fur as a tire or balloon circling around the neck or wrists. **1** Indicate the fur trim in the appropriate areas of the garment and apply the background color of the fur with a marker.

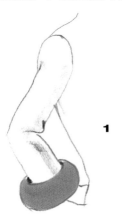  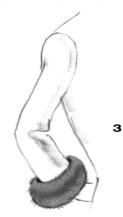

Mink or Sable

2 For **mink or sable**, draw a line across the center with brown eyeshadow and applicator or soft brown colored pencil.

3 Gently draw in the outside edge with a very soft colored pencil line. Indicate the hairs over this line. Indicate the inside hairs with a white soft colored pencil.

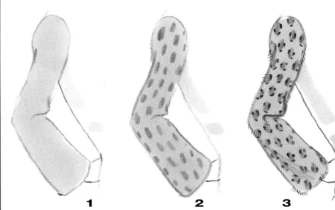

Fox or Long Hair

For **fox** or **long hair** fur, follow to step 2, but work long, graceful lines to indicate the longer hair of the fur.

Leopard

1 For **leopard**, color the background with a tan marker.

2 Randomly work irregular ovals with a soft brown colored pencil.

3 Draw a broken outline around the brown in a soft black colored pencil.

Rendering Satin and Taffeta

1 Indicate the background color but do not bring the color to the edge. There should be a bit of white paper exposed.

2 Using the marker a second time or a soft colored pencil, indicate the areas that will be in shadow such as under the breasts and

down the side plane. If the knee were protruding, a shadow would fall on the lower part of the leg.

3 Give yourself a light source over one shoulder of the figure. Imagine that this light source is going to go down the figure. The areas that protrude, such as the breasts or top of the leg, will catch the light and the non-protruding areas will

just get a glimmer. Using a soft white colored pencil, duplicate this light source. Work the pencil in a soft round motion. You will notice that on this particular pose the light falls strongly on the top of the breasts, eases on the stomach and hip, gets stronger on the leg that is protruding, and then eases down once again.

1   2   3

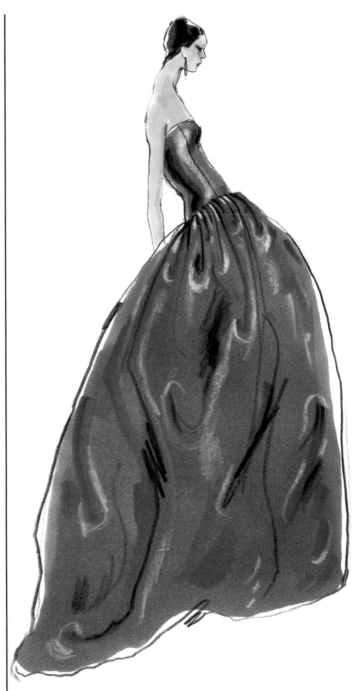

4 For light colors or white fabric, indicate the shadows with a medium grey soft colored pencil.

5 On gathers and drapery, lightly work soft white colored pencil around the folds.

6 For satin, keep the white highlight soft.

7 For taffeta, keep the white highlight a bit crisper and pointier.

Rendering Leather and Vinyl

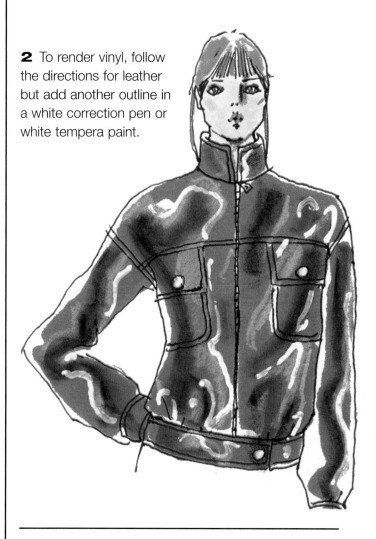

2 To render vinyl, follow the directions for leather but add another outline in a white correction pen or white tempera paint.

Rendering Velvet

When rendering velvet, bring the marker color to the edge. Gently rub a soft white colored pencil around the edges and folds.

1 To render leather, follow the directions for satin, but outline the soft edge with a soft white colored pencil.

Rendering Sequins

1 Block in the background color, leaving a little white space around the garment.

2 Using the marker a second time, shadow in the side plane and under the breasts. If the leg is protruding, shadow under the knee. For even more drama, you can shadow on top of the marker with a dark grey or black soft colored pencil.

3 Using a Sharpee Marker or any round tip black marker, draw in dots going down the light source. Scatter additional dots randomly on the figure.

4 Using a whiteout pen, work white dots over the black ones and over the color as well. The black dots will ultimately become reflections for the sequin and the white ones will become the actual sequin.

On the areas that protrude, such as the top of the breasts or a leg, work the whiteout pen even more.

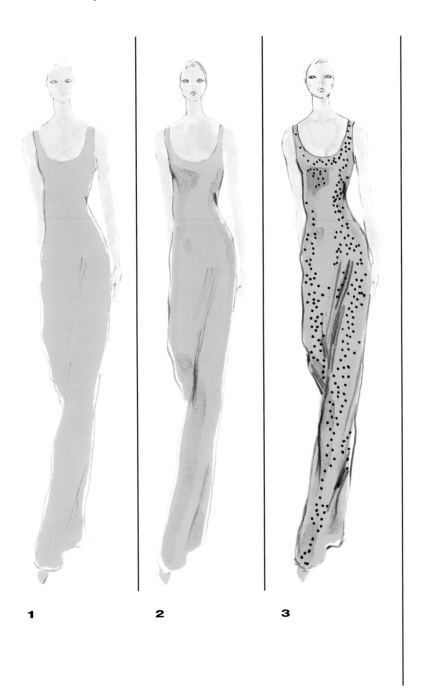

1   2   3

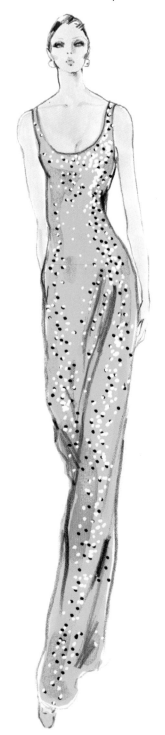

4

Iridescent Beads or Sequins

1 Leave background the white of the paper. Indicate the shadows with a light grey marker.

2 Indicate accent shadows with a soft grey colored pencil. With a darker grey marker, draw in small dots going down the light source.

3 Dot over the grey marker with a whiteout pen.

4 Lightly rub shades of yellow, lavender, blue, orange, and green colored pencils over the whiteout to create iridescence.

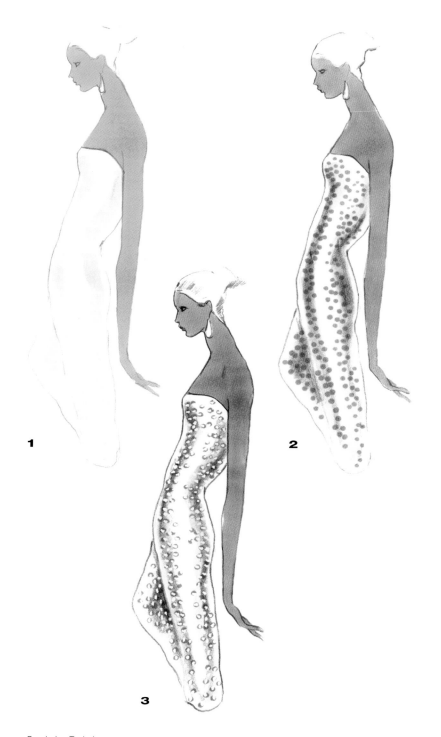

1

2

3

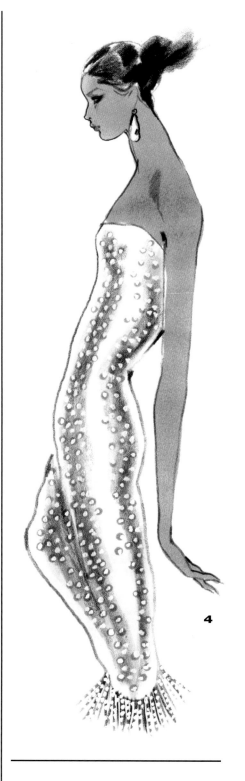

4

Beaded Fringe

1 Draw in light lines with a fine tipped marker.

2 Dot over the line with the whiteout marker.

Rendering Chiffon

1 Color all the skin tones not covered with fabric with a marker. Indicate the chiffon lightly with a soft colored pencil.

2 Indicate the shadows and folds with a darker shade of soft colored pencil.

3 Indicate the skin tone under the chiffon with a soft skin tone colored pencil. Draw in the garment details with a darker value of the colored pencil.

4 With a dark grey soft colored pencil, indicate the darkest shadows and emphasize the important design details. Do not draw any dark or hard lines around the outside edges of the chiffon. Keep them soft.

Rendering Tulle and Lace

1 Color all the skin tones not covered with fabric with a marker. Color all the additional fabrics that are not tulle or lace with a marker. Lightly indicate the shape of the skirt.

2 To render the tulle, rub the side of a soft colored pencil over a piece of tulle. Indicate the skin tone under the lace with a soft skin tone colored pencil.

3 To darken the folds of the tulle, rub a second time using more pressure on the side of the colored pencil. For accents use more of the point of the pencil.

To indicate the net base of the lace, rub very lightly over a piece of tulle on top of the skin color.

4 Indicate the motif of the lace with a very fine tip marker or a very sharply pointed colored pencil. Do not outline the lace or tulle with any dark or heavy line.

5 Neck facings and hems are often finished with the scalloped edge of the lace.

1 Indicate the background colors with a marker.

2 Using a soft colored pencil or marker, draw in the basic shapes of the dominant motif. If there is a stripe, draw in the dominant color.

3 Draw in the secondary shapes with a soft colored pencil.

4 Add in the final details. Use a soft grey colored pencil to indicate the folds and shadows.

5 Follow the same steps for a dark background color.

Sonia Rykiel 1977

31
Knits

The main difference between knits and woven fabrics is that knits stretch and therefore darts and seams can be eliminated. Because knits stretch, they can fit very tightly, and because of their construction, they will not rip apart. Also, they are not finished with conventional hems and facings, but with ribbed, rolled, or crocheted edges.

For a tight-knit garment, think of a ribbed poor-boy sweater, a spandex body dress, or a bodysuit. Usually these garments are smaller than the body and until they are put on we might find it difficult to determine the fit. On the other hand, knits can be extremely oversized and luxurious. The body seems to disappear under the garment, the neck is buried under a deep cowl, and the sleeves extend past the fingers. Sometimes, as in a classic sweater, the fit can be somewhere between the two extremes.

Knits are extremely versatile and can be used in many different ways and combinations. Knits can range from a very flat surface to a very textured appearance. Garments can be knit of simple, solid colors or intricate patterns can be employed that use many contrasting colors and textures. Yarns of every size and texture are available to be used in many different combinations. Knit fabric can be combined with woven fabric for interesting contrasts. Also, knits can be beaded or embellished. Today, knits can be used for anything from caps or gloves to dresses, pants, coats, or sweaters. Because of modern technology, infinite combinations of colors and textures can be produced.

Body-conscious rib knit

The basic breakdown of knitted garments are:

- Hand knit, which are garments that are completely knit by hand.

- Handloomed, which are garments that are handmade on a knitting machine.

- Cut and sew, which describe knitted yardage that is cut and seamed together with a serger.

- Computer knits, which can be designed in many complex patterns because the technology allows for many color and design options.

Twin set

Oversized and luxurious cowl neck

382

Yarns come in thicknesses that range from thin, fingering yarn to heavy, bulky yarn. In terms of gauge (stitches per knitted inch) the knitted swatches below show the basic breakdown of different types of yarn.

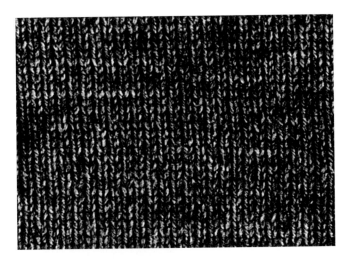

Fingering yarn will knit approximately 7 to 9 stitches per inch.

Sport yarn will knit approximately 5 to 7 inches per stitch.

Worsted yarn will knit approximately 4 to 6 inches per stitch.

Bulky or chunky yarn will knit approximately 3 to 5 stitches per inch.

Knits

Fibers can range from the most luxurious to purely utilitarian. Some luxury fibers are:

- **Cashmere**, which is fiber that is obtained from the downy wool of the cashmere goat from the Kashmir regions of India and Pakistan.

- **Angora rabbit hair**, which is a soft, fuzzy fiber obtained from the underhair of the angora rabbit.

- **Mohair** which is a long, white, lustrous hair fiber obtained from the angora goat.

Other natural fibers used for knits are cotton, wool, linen, and silk. Also used extensively are manufactured fibers, which include rayon and acrylic.

Yarns can have many textures and weights. When drawing garments that are knit from these yarns, be careful to not have a hard line on the outside edge. Try to have your line duplicate the lines the following yarns:

- **Bouclé yarn**, which has a curly looped texture. A marker or pencil works well. Keep a squiggly rhythm to the outside edge.

- **Mohair yarn**, which has a fuzzy texture. A dry brush works well.

- **Angora rabbit hair yarn**, which has a furry and soft texture. A dry brush is very effective. Keep the strokes gentle and fur-like.

- **Chenille yarn**, which has a thick velvety texture. A heavier marker or soft pencil can give you the rich hue that is just right.

- **Metallic yarn**, which has a sparkly, shiny, glitzy quality. Markers, pencils, or brushes all work well. Thrown in some dots to indicate a "sparkle."

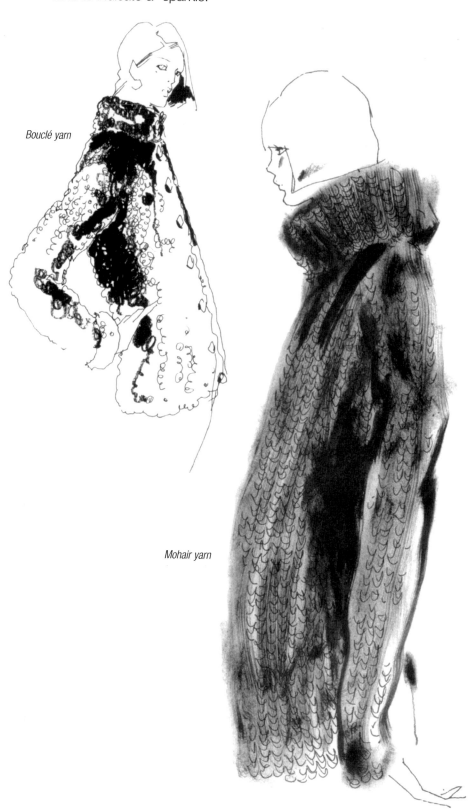

Bouclé yarn

Mohair yarn

384

Angora rabbit hair yarn

Chenille yarn

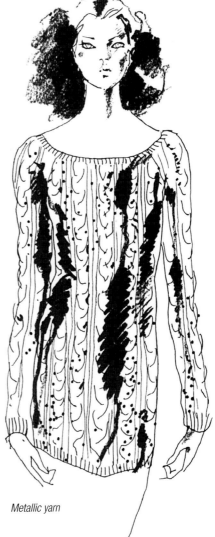

Metallic yarn

There are many more yarns as well. Any of these yarns (or others) can be combined in stitches to produce different types of knit stitches and patterns (that are shown on the following pages). These include:

- **Flat stitches**. Included in this category are:

- **Stockinette**, which is a basic flat stitch used to create a jersey fabric. This is made by knitting one row, then purling the next. Used in many different types of knitwear from cashmere and Shetland sweaters to sweatshirts.

- **Purl**, which is the reverse side of stockinette. It is used for the same type of garments as the stockinette stitch.

- **Garter**, which is a stitch that is done by knitting every row. The example shown here has the garter courses separated by rows of stockinette stitches.

Stockinette

Purl

Garter

- **Textured stitches**. Included in this category are:

- **Cable**, which is a stitch that produces a rope-like pattern in which groups of stitches cross over and under each other.

- **Pointelle** (lace), which is a stitch that forms holes in the fabric by the use of transfer stitches or by dropping stitches.

- **Fisherman**, which are stitch patterns that can feature cables and zigzags.

- **Ribbing**, which are stitches made by a knit one, purl one construction. This forms rows that have a vertical striped effect. This stitch is more elastic than plain knitting and is used when a tight, shaped fit is desired. Many times it is used for finishes, as in waistbands, neckbands, and waistbands.

- **Popcorn**, which is a stitch that looks like a small pompom. It is often done in a contrasting color as a novelty effect.

Cable

Pointelle

Fisherman

Ribbing

Popcorn

- **Knit patterns**. Included in this category are:

- **Fair Isle**, which are patterns that are often done in many contrasting colors. These have knit floats (on the back) that connect the stitches. The patterns can be anything from abstract geometric shapes to animals and flowers. These patterns are usually used in scarves, caps, and sweaters.

- **Intarsia**, which are flat knit patterns that are knitted in solid colors so that the patterns on both sides of the fabric are identical. They are usually done in geometrical patterns and used in sweaters.

- **Argyle**, which is a type of jacquard knit that is made in several colors to form diamond or harlequin designs. It is used extensively in hosiery and sweaters.

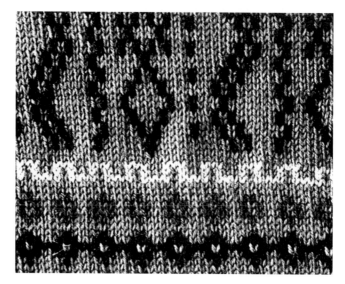

Fair isle

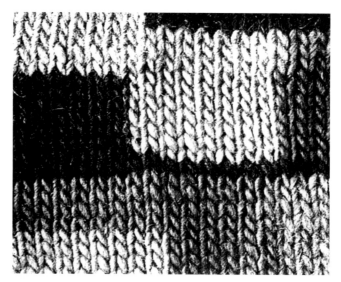

Intarsia

Argyle

Knitted clothing can use any combination of the knit stitches and patterns shown on pages 386–388. When drawing them, it is very important to keep the line soft and rich and to let the line quality duplicate the feel and texture of the knit.

Keep folds round and avoid any pointed edges—keep hemlines and collars round. Try to avoid any hard edge unless it is a very flat knit, such as a T-shirt or fine-gauge yarn such as cashmere.

On a patterned knit, block the stripes or pattern off lightly or on an underdrawing. Patterns tend to have a "step" rather than a round shape.

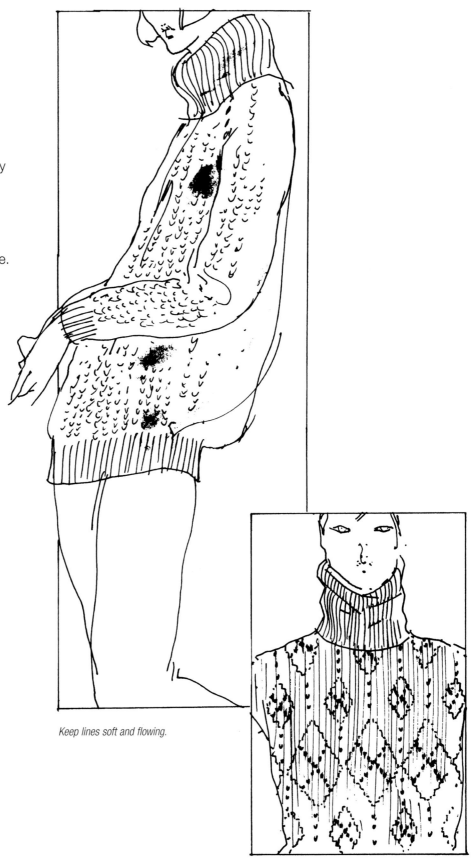

Keep lines soft and flowing.

Patterns have a "step" rather than round shape.

The following details appear on many knitted garments:

- **Ribbing**, which is used to finish off necklines, sleeves, and hems. It is also used on cowl, mock-turtle, and turtlenecks.

- **Full fashioned**, which is a method that shapes the garment detail as it is knitted and is often used at the armhole. Notice the small marks it makes as a result of the stitches being brought together.

- **Rolled edge**, which is a style of finishing where the edge of the knitted garment is allowed to curl naturally.

Ribbing

Full-fashioning

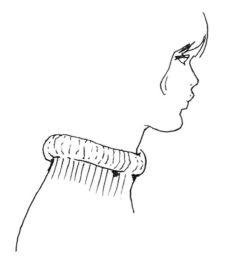

Rolled edge

Styles of Knitted Garments

Cardigan

Turtleneck

Mock-turtleneck

Cowl neck

Poor-boy

Slip-over

Sweater vest

Beaded sweater

Twin sweater set

Christian Dior 1950

Part 4

The Extras

Bill Blass 1994

32
The Walking Figure

Think of a chiffon dress billowing in the wind. The excess of fabric leaves the figure and flows into the air. If we were to sketch this dress on a figure that was standing still, the fabric would fall and the movement of the dress would disappear.

The walking figure (sometimes referred to as The Runway Figure) is an option that allows us to show not only the garment, but also the garment in motion.

We generally use this figure when the garment has an excess of fabric in one or more areas. A straight skirt and fitted sweater do not have this excess, but a fuller skirt and a top with a scarf do.

Notice how we can move the excess fabric of the skirt to one side and allow the scarf to leave the figure and ripple out into the air.

Lacroix 2003

Drawing the Walking Figure

The walking figure starts out the exact way a traditional standing figure does.

1 Begin by sketching the front view action figure with opposing shoulder and hip movement. More movement will be created if you bring the leg past the balance line. You will see that there are no changes at this point, but rather than indicating the non-supporting leg on the ground, we will lift it and move it towards the back. By lifting the non-supporting leg off the ground and moving it back it will become foreshortened.

The Foreshortened Leg

2 Begin by sketching in the outside lower muscle in one continuous slightly rounded line.

3 Draw a guide line from the knee to ankle following the shape of the outside muscle.

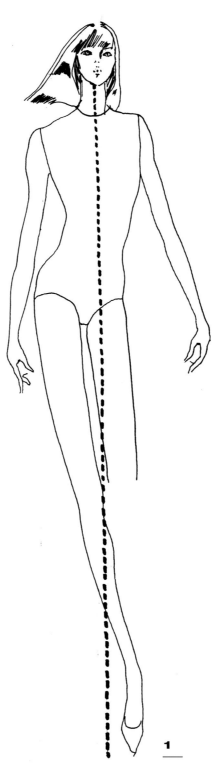

1

Front view action figure with opposing shoulder and hip movement

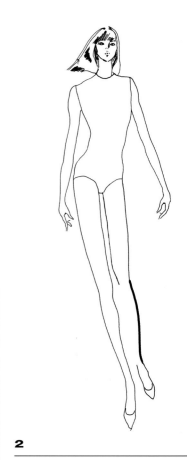

2

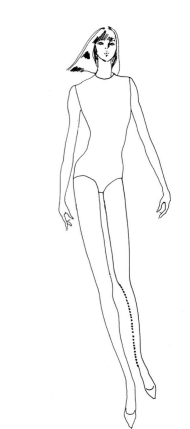

3

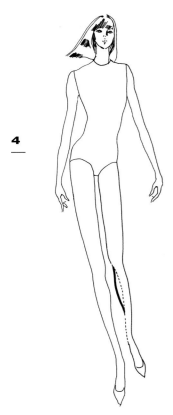

4

4 You will notice a small hollow in the middle of this shape. Place the inside muscle in this hollow. Erase guide line.

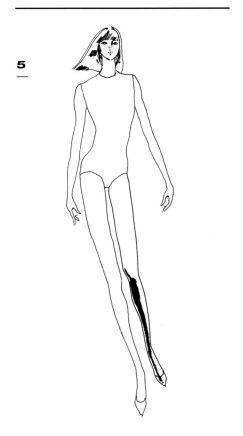

5

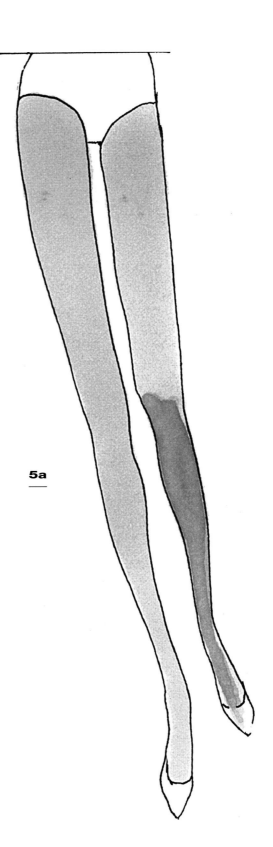

5a

5–5a Shade from the knee down to the foot by going over the marker a second time, shadowing in colored pencil or grey pencil.

The Walking Figure

When drawing skirts, there is
a shadow near the front leg.

When drawing pants, notice how folds form at the knee on the foreshortened leg. The pant hem becomes rounder as well. Many fashion publications that once photographed garments in a studio, now photograph them directly at the fashion show, on the runway. These are the most ideal photo references to use when drawing the walking figure.

A Brief History of Men's Fashions

Women's clothes have been influenced by menswear as far back as the 1930s, when Marlene Dietrich was photographed wearing an adaptation of a man's suit. Additionally, Yves Saint Laurent has been designing tuxedo suits for women for the last 30 years.

Until the 1960s, the male fashion model was merely a hanger for clothing or a backdrop for women. However, the "mod" fashions of the mid-60s put a change to that forever. The male peacock was born and his place in fashion became established. Today, almost every important designer of women's clothing also designs a menswear collection. Male fashion models are becoming almost as famous as their female counterparts, and the runway shows are almost important as the women's. Such names as Giorgio Armani, Calvin Klein, and Ralph Lauren not only design menswear, but also use it to influence their women's collections.

After the War of 1812, pants were becoming widely worn in America instead of silk breeches or stockings. The evolution of the three-piece suit, however, resulted from the waistcoat, frock coat, and breeches that were worn only decades before. And since the beginning of the 20th century, men's suits have consisted of basically the same parts—tailored jacket, pants, and vest. At the turn of the 20th century, men wore sack suits, which were business suits of worsted, flannel, or tweed, with a loose-fitting, single- or double-breasted jacket.

Sack suit 1905

Just as the flapper look influenced women's wear, in the 1920s, men too were looking for a younger, more youthful image. They wore snug-fitting, natural-shoulder suits, which were often topped by ankle-length raccoon coats.

In the 1930s, despite the Great Depression, the male fashion image was the highly sophisticated screen idol, personified by such movie stars as Cary Grant and Fred Astaire. The elegant cut suit of the English-inspired drape suit (extra fullness at the chest and over the shoulders) was a major influence for menswear and is still inspiring designers today. Additionally, zippers were just starting to replace the button fly.

The 1940s and the war brought an austerity to menswear, and the restrictions of fabric gave men a narrower silhouette. Synthetics allowed fabrics to become lighter and easier to care for. The end of the decade brought back the double-breasted suit with broad shoulders and wide lapels.

The 1950s gave us the man in the gray flannel suit. A single-breasted, straight hanging, natural-shoulder cut, which popularized the "Ivy League" look and Brooks Brothers. Toward the end of the decade, the "Continental" suit arrived from Italy with its sleek, shaped, side-vented jacket and uncuffed trousers. The movies also brought us the "rebel." Marlon Brando and James Dean made leather, jeans, and T-shirts the look of youth.

The 1960s forever changed the way men were going to look. In the beginning of the 60s, President Kennedy popularized the two-button, natural-shoulder suit and a trim, clean, youthful appearance.

The second half of the decade brought us the English Mod Look, Carnaby Street, and the Beatles. The look of men's fashions was finally liberated with the advent of the Nehru suit, the turtleneck replacing ties, colorful, patterned shirts, and sometimes even beads!

English Mod suit 1960s

Drape suit 1930s

The 1970s gave us such designer names as Bill Blass, Pierre Cardin, and John Weitz. It also brought the double knit leisure suit, belted vests, and the unconstructed suit, which had no shoulder padding or hand tailoring.

The 1980s brought in the "power suit," which was highly shoulder-padded and had a low roll to the lapel, with a slim-hipped silhouette. Giorgio Armani, Calvin Klein, Hugo Boss, and Ralph Lauren were now creating entire menswear collections. Designer underwear was becoming as popular as designer suits.

Contemporary menswear is about soft dressing. The shoulder pad of the power suit is being replaced by an easier fit and a more relaxed attitude. The look is more about texture and fabrics. Unisex cologne is being marketed for men and women, and both sexes are borrowing items from each other. Such women's wear designers as Donna Karan, Dolce and Gabbana, and Gianni Versace are entering the menswear market. People who wear designer labels for work are wearing J. Crew and the Gap for weekends. Such active sports manufacturers as Nike, Adidas, and Reebok are adding clothing lines to their labels.

Still, when all is said and done, men's fashions change at a slower pace than women's, therefore the male fashion figure remains a bit more consistent. Most figure drawing principles and clothing details remain basically the same as with drawing women's clothing— balance, movement, gesture, center front, collars, sleeves, or pants. The blocking off of the male head, arms, and legs changes more in emphasis than rules.

Relaxed suit 1990s

Power suit 1980s

Drawing the Male Fashion Figure

The male and female fashion figures, with the exception of muscular emphasis, are drawn without many differences. The distinctions are mostly in alignment, emphasis, and attitude. For example, the female is more fluid and the male more angular.

Although the female figure is a bit smaller, I use ten heads to draw both men and women. If you are drawing them side by side, the male figure will be taller.

Because the bone and muscular structures differ between men and women, and because there are so many variables between the sexes themselves, for the purposes of comparison only, let's study the basic differences. When comparing the male fashion figure to the female figure, we can see that a man's:

- Shoulders are wider and squarer, his neck is thicker and a bit shorter, and the arms have more defined muscles.

- Chest is bigger, with a much greater width in the back, and the torso is a bit longer.

- Waist is a bit larger and lower (and not much smaller than his hips), and the hips are narrower.

- Knees are more prominent, the leg muscles are more defined, and the hands and feet are bigger.

- Body is generally broader and straighter, with shoulders that are wider than his hips.

- Supporting legs does not angle in as much (in a resting pose) because the pelvis is smaller.

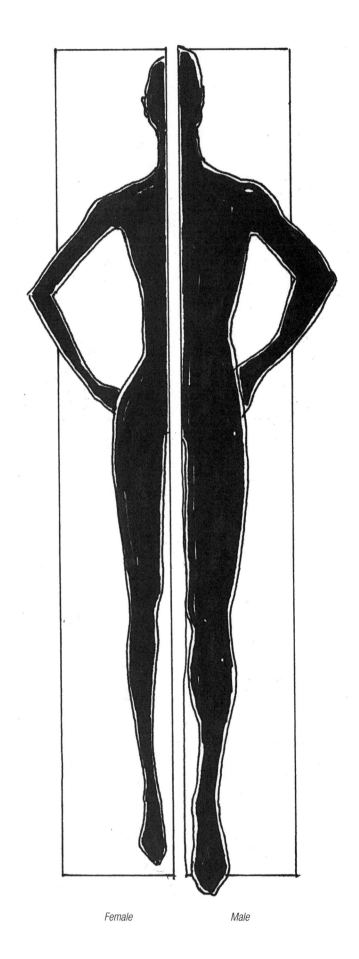

Female   Male

404

The illustrations on this page
show the male fashion figure in
both a front and turned view.

Now let's study the specifics of
the male fashion figure.

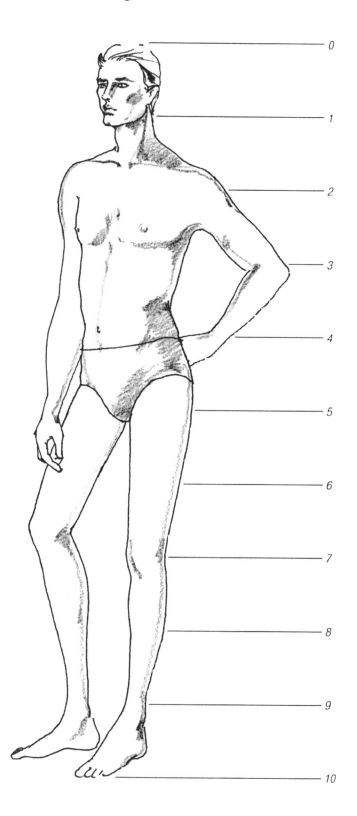

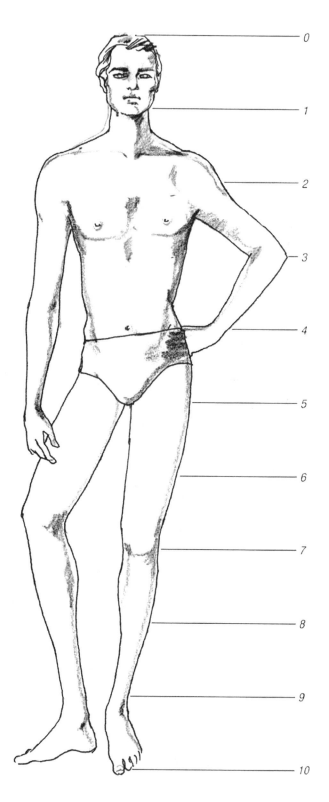

The Neck, Shoulders, Arms, and Hands

Again, let's look at the differences between the male and female fashion figure. On the fashion figure male you will notice that:

- His neck is thicker in relationship to the shoulders and has more bulk.

- His arms and shoulders are thicker and more muscular.

- His wrists are thicker.

- His hand is squarer, with the fingers blunter and less tapered.

The Torso

The torso of the male fashion figure differs in subtle and not-so-subtle ways from the female. When examining the torso of the male figure, take note that:

- His torso tapers slightly to the hips, but has little curve.

- His waist and hips have less difference between them.

- His hips are narrow.

- His stomach muscles are more defined.

The Legs and Feet

The legs and feet of the male fashion figure are quite different than the female's. Upon studying those parts of the anatomy, you will see that:

- His legs and feet have more muscular definition.

- His knees more prominent.

- His calves and ankles are more defined.

- His feet are larger and more angular.

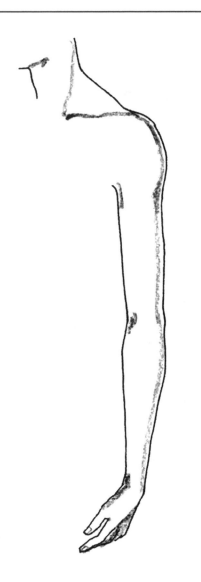
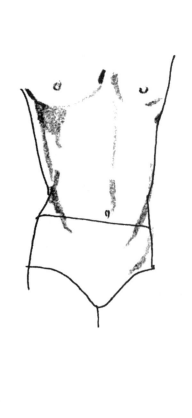

The Head

Because men do not wear makeup, the features will have a more natural quality. However, the blocking off of the head will be the same as for women, except:

- The general head shape will be more angular.

- The eyes are narrower with less upper lid.

- The eyebrows are lower.

- The lips are narrower and the lip line is wider.

- The jawline is squarer and more pronounced.

- There is a heavier, more pronounced chin.

On the turned profile head, please note:

- There is a slight indentation in the forehead.

- The eyebrows extend out further.

- The nose is generally straighter.

- There is less curve between the mouth and nose.

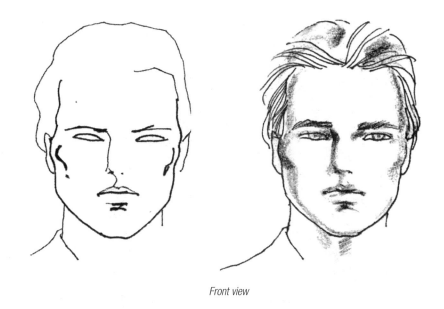

Front view

Turned view

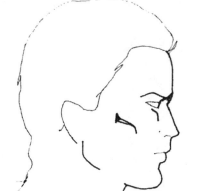
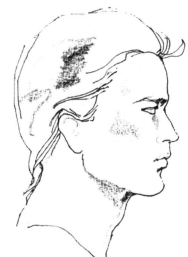

Profile view

Again, because makeup cannot be
used to create an attitude, the
different facial types of men are
more clearly apparent.

Elegant

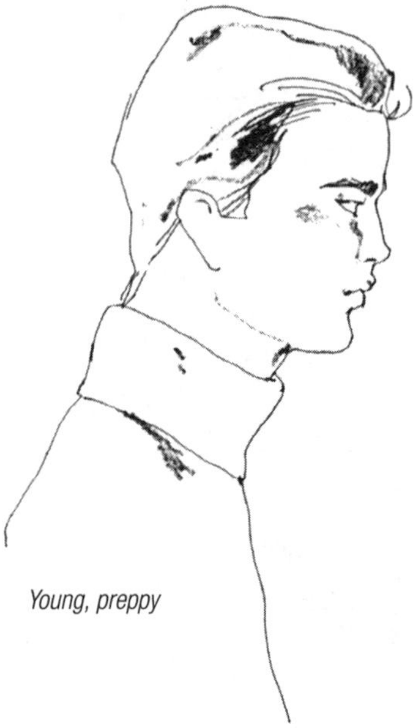

Young, preppy

High fashion

Intellectual

Slightly older

Sportsman

Drawing Men's Suits

The big changes in men's suits are often in the shoulder and lapel. When drawing men's suits, the basic tailoring details and principles are identical as in women's wear, except:

- Men's garments close left over right on the body (which means right over left on a drawing).

- The shoulder line should be kept crisp, with the collar hugging the neck.

- The sleeve cap often is less defined on a natural-shoulder suit.

- The roll line and closing must always be straight and precise.

- The shape is not as exaggerated as on a woman's suit.

You will easily start to discern the differences when you examine the various details, such as the specific folds and drapes in a single- or double-breasted suit, a layered look, and a coat. Also study the differences in attitude in a sportcoat look, a casual and relaxed ensemble, a layered outfit, trendy dressing, activewear, and the classic tuxedo.

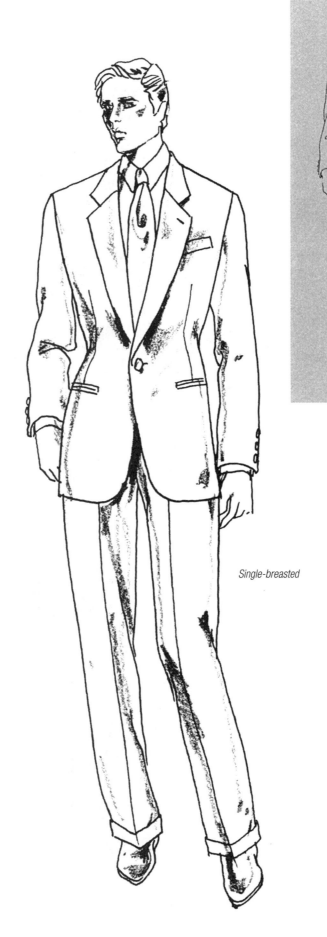

Single-breasted

Double-breasted

Sportcoat and vest

410

In the male fashion figure, the poses tend to be more solidly rooted with less arm exaggeration. The arms and hands remain closer to the body unless they are in some specific activity, such as holding a glass, lifting a collar, unbuttoning a jacket, or resting in the pockets. Activewear, just as with women, should have the appropriate poses, for example, running, exercising, throwing a ball, and so forth.

Although high fashion menswear changes seasonally, much of men's clothing remains classic. Often the width of a lapel, the padding of the shoulder, or the taper of the pants will be all that separates one season from another! However, just as with women's wear, different ideals are in or out of fashion based on similar reasons. The muscular swimmer of one season is soon replaced by the intellectual scholar of the next. But even though menswear has come a long way from the self-consciousness it once had, it is still not as free as women's wear, for the most part.

Please note that because of the very similar methods used, specific details for drawing shirts, pants, knits, and tailored garments can be found under those various chapters in this book.

Casual sportswear

Sportcoat

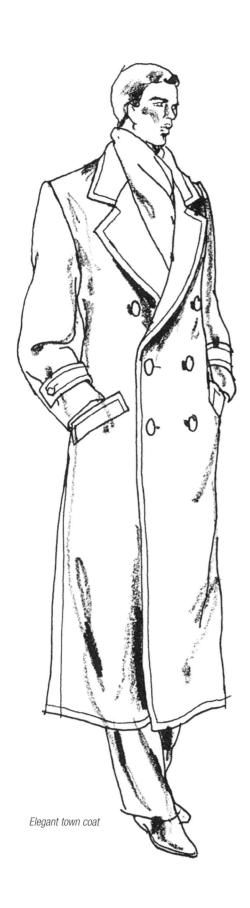

Elegant town coat

Trendy

Active

Layered

Tuxedo

34
Children

It can be lots of fun to draw children. The most important thing to remember when drawing them is that children are not scaled down adults. They are not chic or sophisticated—they have a light, playful quality. Their poses are not elegant or graceful—they are animated and sometimes awkward. Their faces do not convey an attitude—they are innocent, unselfconscious, and expressive. When you draw children, try to retain a lively and spontaneous quality. Some other important factors and hints to remember are:

- The size ranges of children's clothes usually correspond to their approximate age.

- Children's body proportions, facial expressions, and poses change greatly from year to year.

- The younger the child that you draw, the more "round" qualities that should be apparent in your drawing.

- Children's heads get smaller proportionally as the body lengthens. (This is the biggest difference between drawing adults and children.)

- Knitting and pattern books are excellent sources for children's photographs.

Children's ages range from infants (and newborns) to teens. First, let's break them down into different age groups and study them. For the purposes of this book, we will use the age ranges of infants, toddlers, two- to three-year olds, four- to six-year olds, seven- to ten-year olds, young teenagers, and teenagers.

Infants

First, let's look at infants. An infant is a baby from birth to the age when it begins to walk. Its head is one-quarter of the total body size. Everything about an infant is round, from the head and its features to the torso and the arms and legs. The legs turn inward and the knees have exaggerated dimples. Because infants don't walk or even crawl, the only poses available are lying down or propped up.

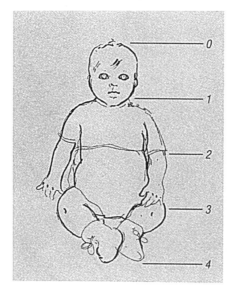

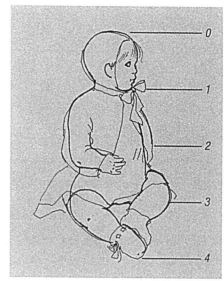

Toddlers

A toddler is approximately one-year old and four heads high. Because they do not walk easily on their own, the poses will be sitting, crawling, or lying down. Everything about their bodies is still round and undefined, and the fact that they are in diapers makes this even more apparent. The arms and legs are chubby and have very little definition to them. Because the spine is curved, the stomach protrudes and makes a round shape. There is little distinction between boys and girls.

The head is still about one-quarter of the body. The shape of the face is round, with the cheeks making it even rounder, and there is no jaw definition. It appears as if the head is resting on the shoulders. Their eyes are large and round and their eyebrows very light. Their lips are soft and mouths never seem to be completely closed. Noses should be kept short and small. The hair is usually just starting to fill in.

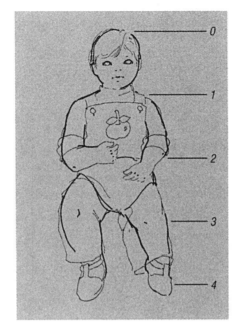

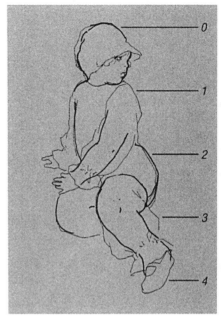

Two- to Three-Year Olds

Because a child usually begins to walk easily by two years, the poses will now be standing and more active, but awkward. The figure is approximately 4 to 4½ heads high, with the biggest change in the length of the legs. The legs have become longer, straighter, and strong enough to support their bodies. The arms and legs are a bit more defined—but still pudgy. Because the spine still curves inward, the stomach still protrudes.

The face is slightly more defined and the child now has a neck that shows. The mouth is a bit larger because teeth are coming in. Hair is more defined, but there is still little distinction between boys and girls.

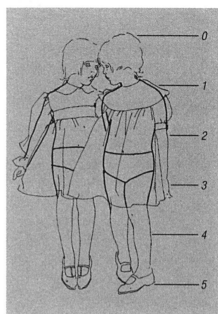

Four- to Six-Year-Olds

Many changes take place during these years. The poses become more animated and active. The figure is approximately five heads high. Legs grow longer. The torso loses some baby fat, but there is still no waistline. The stomach protrudes less. But the biggest change is that girls and boys begin to look very different. Because of this change, the clothing also separates the girls from the boys. The child now has a combination of "fashion" and "innocence."

The face becomes slightly narrower and the eyes less round. The nose becomes more defined, with a roundness to the tip. The mouth is larger because all the teeth have grown in. Eyebrows are darker and the hair becomes more styled.

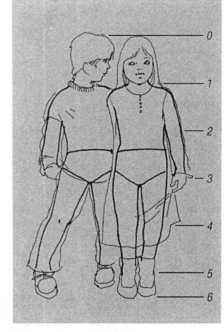

Seven- to Ten-Year Olds

Because the child is now in school, the poses and gestures begin to lose their cuteness. The figure is approximately six heads high. Even though muscle tissue begins to replace baby fat, the waist is still not defined. The arms, legs, and torso become longer and slimmer, and the knees and elbows become more apparent.

Baby fat is disappearing from the face, however the cheeks are still much rounder than an adult's. The nose is still small, but the bridge is becoming more defined. The mouth begins to lose that "pursed" look.

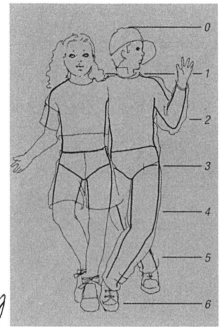

Young Teenagers

The figure is beginning to mature and is now between seven and eight heads high. The figure is more slender, with the torso becoming elongated and a waistline appearing. The arms and legs are longer.

The face begins to develop bone structure and the features become more adult-like. Hair styles are more grownup.

In girls, hips and breasts begin to develop and the waistline begins to appear. In boys, the muscles of the shoulders, arms, and legs are more developed. A boy's hips are narrow and the waistline is lower and not as defined as a girl's.

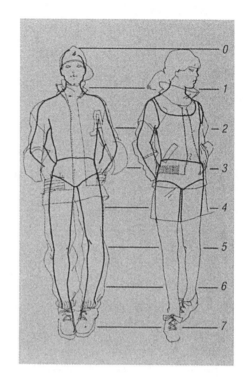

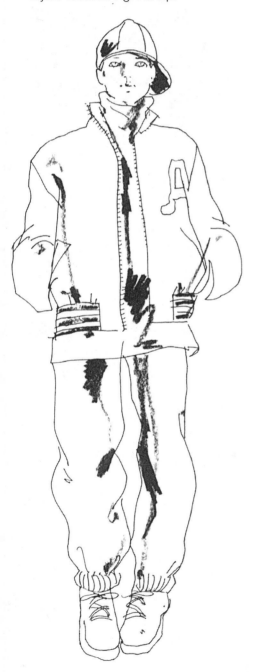

The Teenager and On

Teenagers begin to take on more of the qualities of an adult. Their growth develops at such different paces that the rules become more relaxed and mimic those of an adult figure. Teenagers reach a height of eight heads or more. The teenage girl has a high bustline, a defined waistline, and slim hips, while the teenaged boy begins to have a more developed upper torso, arms, and legs. However, the faces of both sexes begin to take on adult qualities.

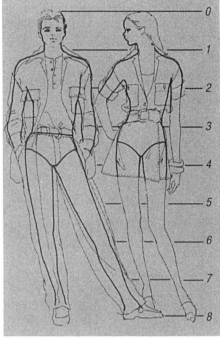

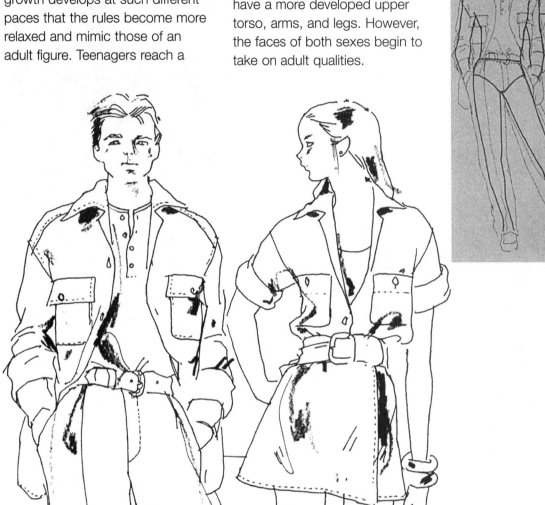

Have fun when drawing children. It can be a relief from all the good taste and refinement of drawing adults! To draw children well, you have to clear your head of adult attitudes. Think like a child would—even if it means watching cartoons on television while you work! Think like a child and you might even find your own foot twisting in a child's awkward position.

Keep the ages as general as possible. In reality, a two-year-old can be bigger than a three-year-old. Don't be overwhelmed by the categories. It is more important that the poses and gestures be correct. Wouldn't it look odd (and I've seen it done!) to have an infant in a walking pose!

Props are good devices to use when drawing young children. Balls, teddy bears, blocks, and so forth are useful to convey the playfulness of children. Just make sure that they are in the correct proportion to the child. Once again, any chic quality or facial expression that makes an adult drawing wonderful should be avoided when drawing children.

Children

Children's Garment Details

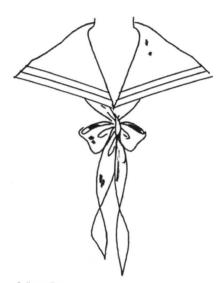

Appliqué

Embroidery

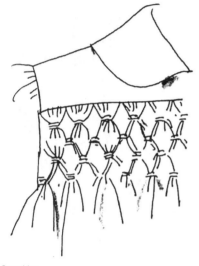

Smocking

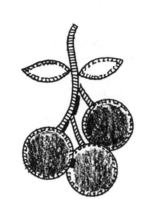

Sailor collar

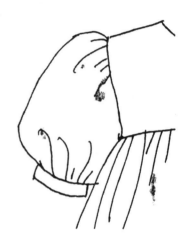

Puffed sleeves

Gathered yoke

Children's Fashions

Christening dress

Overalls

Coveralls

Jumper

Circle skirt

Eaton suit

Snowsuit

Bib

Emporio Armani 1995

For those of you that have ever sewn, your introduction to a flat was the back view drawing on the pattern envelope. It was a flat version of the garment drawn on the front, with all the seams and darts clearly indicated. That is what we are going to study in this section—"flats." A flat is a drawing without a figure. It is as if a garment is laid out on a table, to study its shape and construction details in their purest form.

A finished piece of fashion art will show the garment as it might appear in life, with the attitude, silhouette, and fabrication. On the other hand, a flat is drawn in such a way that anyone involved in the production of the garment can clearly see the silhouette and construction details accurately. Flats also allow the different items of a collection or group to be viewed singularly. Flats are used mostly in sportswear (both men's and women's), children's wear, and intimate apparel. In a sportswear collection, it would enable you to see each item, making it easier to coordinate the entire line.

Flats can be scaled down in size and used on line sheets. They are even used to design entire collections. They are included in presentation boards and are vital in a fashion design portfolio.

Generally, flats are drawn in black and white, but today—because of their many uses and the different needs they fill—they are rendered using color and showing fabrications as well.

Additionally, when a flat has measurements added, it is called a "spec," short for specification. With so much offshore production, it is possible for a flat and spec to eliminate any language barriers. When a pattern maker receives these sheets, an accurate sample can be made. So it is imperative that a flat or a spec be drawn with extreme accuracy and precision. It is vital each piece be drawn in exact scale to each other.

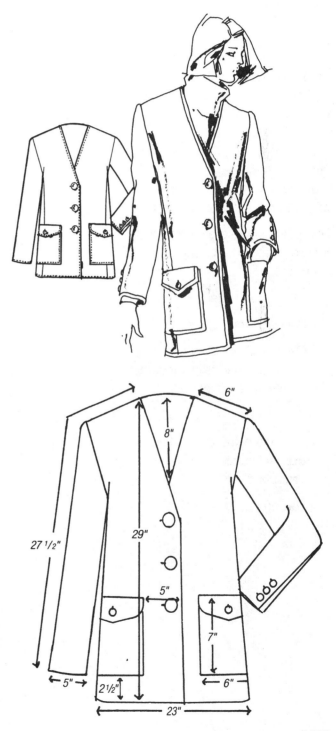

Drawing Flats

There are many ways and approaches to drawing flats, and most companies have their own particular look. We will begin by learning how to draw very precise flats with a ruler, a French curve, and templates. After you become proficient, it will be possible for you to just use a ruler for the straight lines and freehand for the rest. If you are particularly good at drawing flats, you may be able to draw them completely freehand!

Flats are drawn over a *croquis* figure that is shorter than a fashion figure. The *croquis* on the right is provided for you to use. The various arm and leg positions shown on the *croquis* figure allow for particular cuts and silhouettes.

Before starting to draw flats, the supplies that you will need to obtain are:

- 12-inch grid ruler.

- Simple French curve.

- Circle and oval templates (they are sold separately or together on one piece of plastic).

- Pencils and eraser.

- Fine and extra fine markers that feel comfortable in your hand.

- Tracing paper.

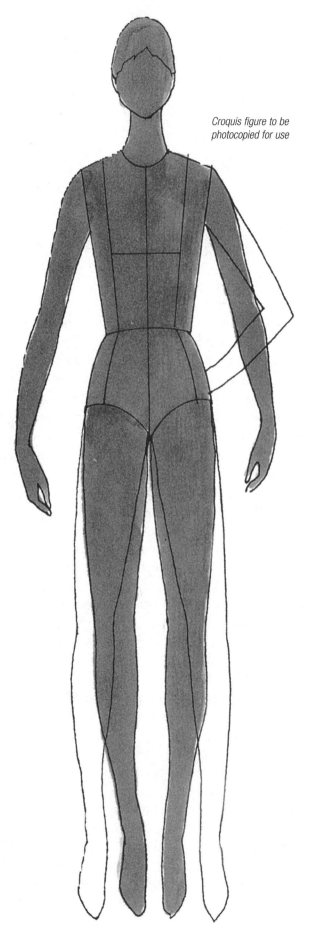

Croquis figure to be photocopied for use

Drawing Flats on a Croquis Figure

To begin, we will start with some sportswear pieces, which are:

- T-shirt.
- Skirt.
- Pants.
- Simple jacket.

When these pieces are drawn, you should be able to dress the croquis figure, layer by layer, to form a perfect outfit. It is exactly the same as cutting out clothes for paper dolls! Be aware of the ease the garment will have on the figure. Will it fit closely or will it be generously cut? Remember that the pieces will be layered, so a vest has to fit over a blouse and a jacket over the vest.

We will use the "fold over" method of drawing flats. This is a technique in which you will draw only one-half of the garment and then you will fold it on the center front line to trace the second half. It is a good way to learn the precision and accuracy that are essential to this type of drawing. All of the pieces that you draw in this section will be done in this manner.

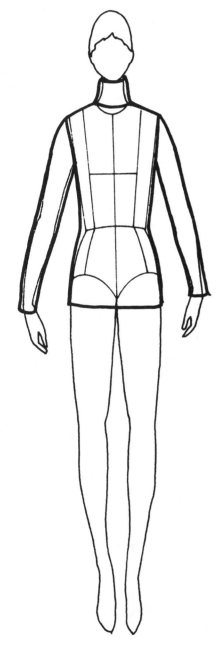

Little ease

Ample ease

T-Shirt

1 First, rule a line down a piece of tracing paper. This line will represent the center front of the garment being drawn. Lay the center front line of the tracing paper on top of the croquis figure. Lightly block in the T-shirt design, making sure that the proportions and details are acceptable.

2 On another sheet of tracing paper, rule in the center front line and lay the rough sketch under it, matching the center front lines. Use the ruler, French curve, and templates to draw precisely and accurately.

3 Once you are pleased with it, fold it on the center front line—wrong sides together—and trace the other half.

4 Finish by indicating the back neckline and by erasing the center front line.

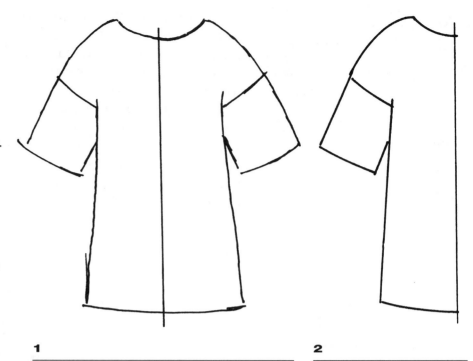

1

2

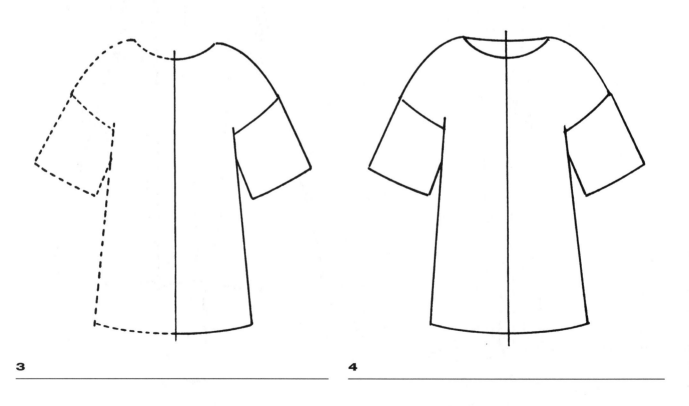

3

4

Skirt

We now have to establish the relationship of the T-shirt to the skirt. First, lay the T-shirt over the croquis figure. At the waistline and hem, draw a line to establish the proportion of the skirt. This should represent the way the skirt and top will look together. Continue by placing the croquis figure under a piece of tracing paper, blocking off the silhouette, and drawing a precise finish with the templates and ruler. If the skirt needs to be narrower, taper the lines more. Also, remember to erase the center front lines on all flats when you are completely finished with them.

Tops and Bottoms

The principles applied when drawing other garments is the same for pants, but now you will extend the lines from the waist to the pant hem. Be sure to indicate the crotch seam. Remember to treat the crotch area lightly—avoid drawing a "V." If the pants are wide, use the *croquis* figure with the open legs.

Next, design and execute some simple tops and bottoms, using this same method, but adding some freehand lines as well. If the garment has excess fabric, as in a flared or gathered skirt, imagine that in your drawing you are arranging the garment on a flat surface. This will help your drawing have dimension.

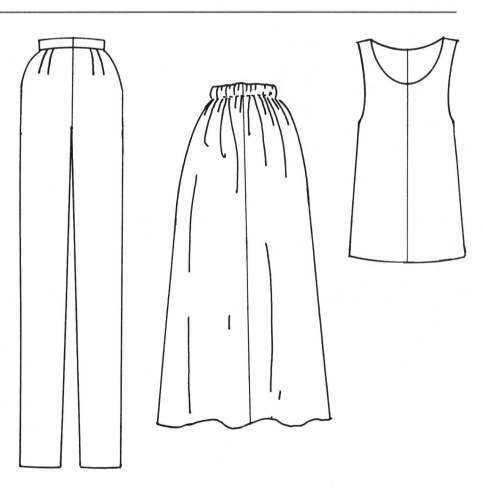

Single-Breasted Jacket

The jacket becomes a bit more difficult because of the addition of the closing to the center front. For a single-breasted jacket, first draw the neckline opening from the neck edge to the center front.

1 Establish the closing by placing the grid ruler alongside the center front and dotting in a line until you reach the neckline.

2 Place the ruler at the neck edge on the shoulder until it touches the closing. Next, place the buttons down the center front. Last, fold the drawing down the center front line to draw the second half.

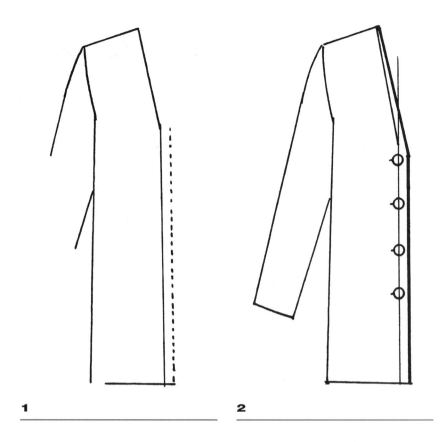

1   **2**

Double-Breasted Jacket

1 For a double-breasted jacket, establish the closing by placing the grid ruler alongside the center front and dotting in a line until you reach the neckline. The principles are the same as for a single-breasted jacket, but there will be a greater distance from the center front to the closing.

2 The center front becomes the distance between the buttons. For side closings, leave off the nonworking buttons. Remember erase the center front lines when you finish.

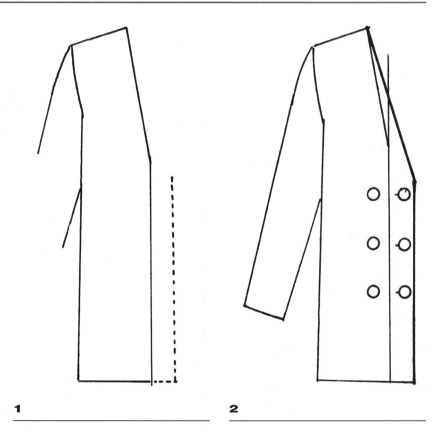

1   **2**

Some techniques to add and
enhance the basic flat are:

- Use number one gray magic
  marker to indicate shadows.

- Use a thicker marker for the
  outline, and a thinner marker
  for the seamlines and details.

- Draw a partial rendering to
  indicate patterns or textures.

Basic flat

Shadows indicated with gray marker

Thick and thin marker

Partial rendering

Collars

When drawing a rolled collar on a jacket, start by indicating the closing as you would in a collarless jacket. Establish the neckline shape to the center front. Dot the collar around the back of the neck and draw in the shape of the collar. Fold in half on the center front and draw the other side. Draw in the back neck and seam that joins the collar to the neckline.

For a notch collar, draw the opening, the top collar, and the lapel. Fold on the center front and draw the second half. Draw in the pockets and any details that appear on both sides.

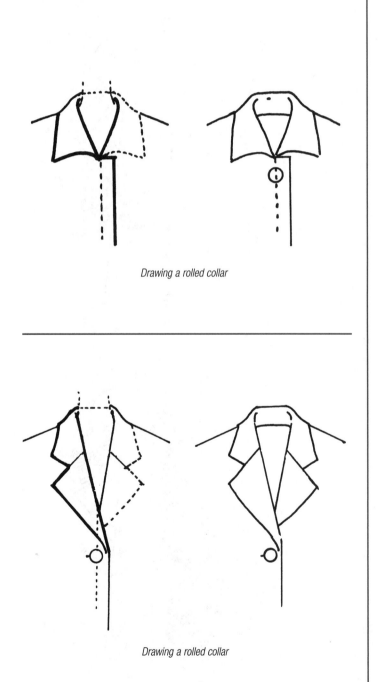

Drawing a rolled collar

Drawing a rolled collar

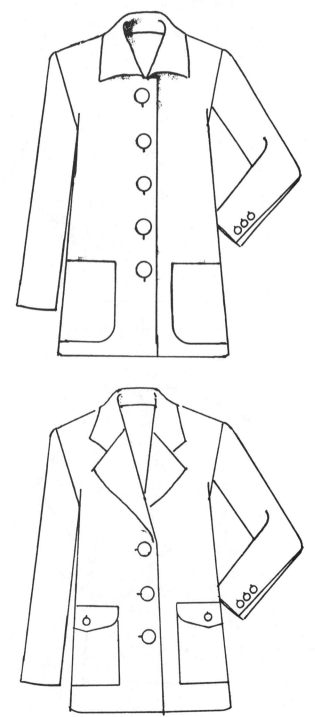

Topstitching and Other Details

When drawing topstitching, make sure that the distance from each stitch to the edge is exactly the same. If there is any detail that cannot be drawn directly on the flat (because of the scale or size requirements), draw an enlargement to the side. Such sleeve details as vents or cuffs are shown on the bent arm.

For a back view, trace over the front silhouette to duplicate the exact shape. Remember that the details in the back take a downward direction.

If you find it difficult to draw small, you can enlarge the *croquis* figure and after drawing, reduce it back down.

Some tips for beginners are:

- Most flats look better when reduced to a smaller size.

- If a marker is too difficult at the beginning, use a pencil and then photocopy it. It will have the look of ink.

- Small errors can be corrected with liquid paper or correction tape and then photocopied.

After you have achieved a certain skill in drawing them, flats can be done freehand, or with a combination of freehand, ruler, French curve, and templates. They can be tight or have a looser quality, depending on the needs of the fashion, the designer, or the manufacturer. However, when a flat has movement, it is called a "float."

One last word. Flats take practice. There is no simpler solution.

Enlargements show details.

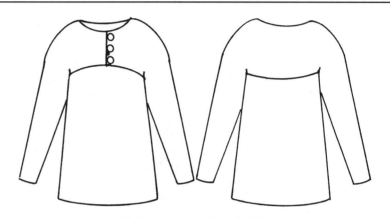

Back views are worked over front views.

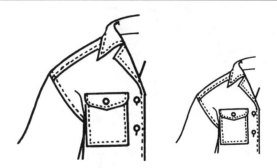

Flats can be drawn large and then reduced.

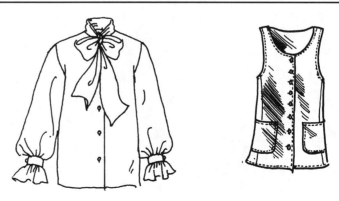

With practice, freehand can be used with other techniques.

Dior 1947

Think of a magnificent ballgown, a swashbuckling cape, or an extravagant caftan. The bulky shape the black Balenciaga coat creates over a slim body has a rich excess and an abundance of fabric. These types of garments are difficult to draw, requiring your utmost skill. Complete knowledge of the figure and the relationship to the clothing is necessary because not only is the clothing voluminous, but the garments are also making their own shapes. Both the extravagant cut and the amount of fabric appear to be overpowering the figure. Portions of the body seem to be lost within the shapes that the fabric is creating.

Earlier, you learned that the garment can take precedence over the figure, but voluminous clothing often brings this to its most lavish extreme. A perfect example of a voluminous garment is a bridal gown. The figure often is hidden under countless layers of crinolines and skirts. The bride's face barely shows through the veiling. The embellishments are extravagant and often there is a long train behind her.

Alexander McQueen 2002

Balenciaga 1965

Let's study four types of voluminous garments and see how their measurements relate to the measurement of the fashion figure.

By first examining the flat sketches, and then putting the body inside, we can see that the relationship between the body and the negative space is greater than that of the body and the garment. There is "air" between the garment and figure.

The first is a printed satin dress designed by Norman Norell in 1958 for Traina-Norell. The skirt has a sweep of 134 inches, which is gathered into a waist of 25 inches. The sweep is more than five times the waist measurement.

Dress from Mount Mary College, Milwaukee, WI

Traina-Norell 1958

134"

438

Volume allows skirt to move as its own unit.

The second is a gray flannel coat
with leather trim designed by
Bonnie Cashin in 1976. It is cut
with flared sections and has a
hem sweep of 180 inches, which
is seven times the waist
measurement. Because the
volume is created by flared shapes
rather than gathers, the top
remains small, and the silhouette
becomes more voluminous as it
reaches the hem.

Coat from Mount Mary College, Milwaukee, WI

Bonnie Cashin 1976

180"

440

The flared shape of the coat can create different movements.

The third is a ballgown designed by Sarmi in 1956. It has a very close-fitting, boned and draped bodice, with a skirt that has a hem sweep of 540 inches—21 times the waist measurement! The many-layered tulle skirt is cut with flared sections that are then gathered into the waist, creating a shape reminiscent of the gowns designed by Dior for his New Look in 1947.

Sarmi 1956

540"

The arms become a device to move the skirt.

The fourth is a silk crepe caftan designed by Madame Grès in 1982. The four sections in white, burgundy, deep pink, and purple have a hem sweep of only 55 inches, which is just about twice the waist measurement. Because the caftan has openings for each foot, it remains basically rectangular and the movement of the body will create dramatic shapes.

Madame Grés 1982

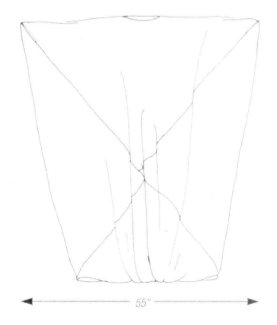

55"

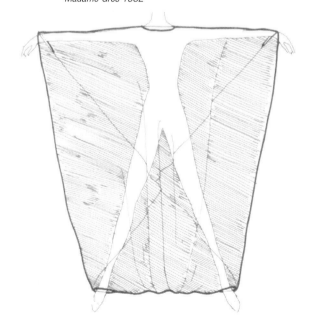

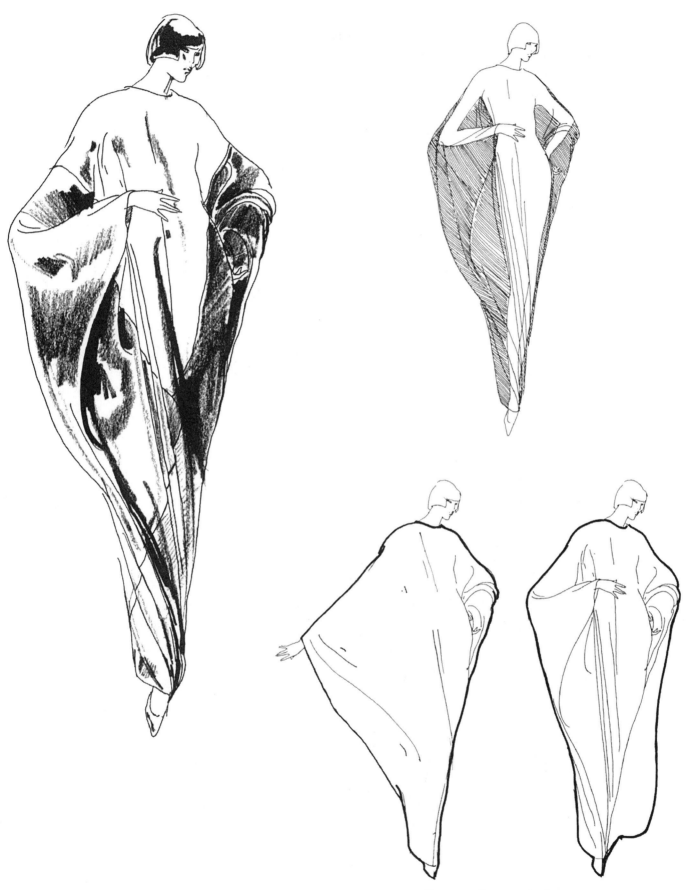

The arms and legs create the shape.

Because of the yardage, notice how dense the gathers are drawn at the seamlines and observe how they open out as they reach the hem. The negative space between the silhouette and the figure is crucial because those spaces help to produce the extravagant cut of the garment.

The first point to remember is not to lose the figure when drawing these clothes. The clothing could not come to life without the figure. The figure is a living hanger for garments with this much volume. Also, keep in mind that the arms and legs become more important because they are devices for manipulating the fabric.

Second, the expression of the face and the tilt of the head become a means of giving the garment the attitude that it requires. Additionally, poses must be more gestural and extravagant to match the drama of the garment.

Third, try to work the garment to its fullest potential. By shifting the garment detail with the most volume to a prominent place in your drawing, you will be creating the richest and most lavish possibility for the garment.

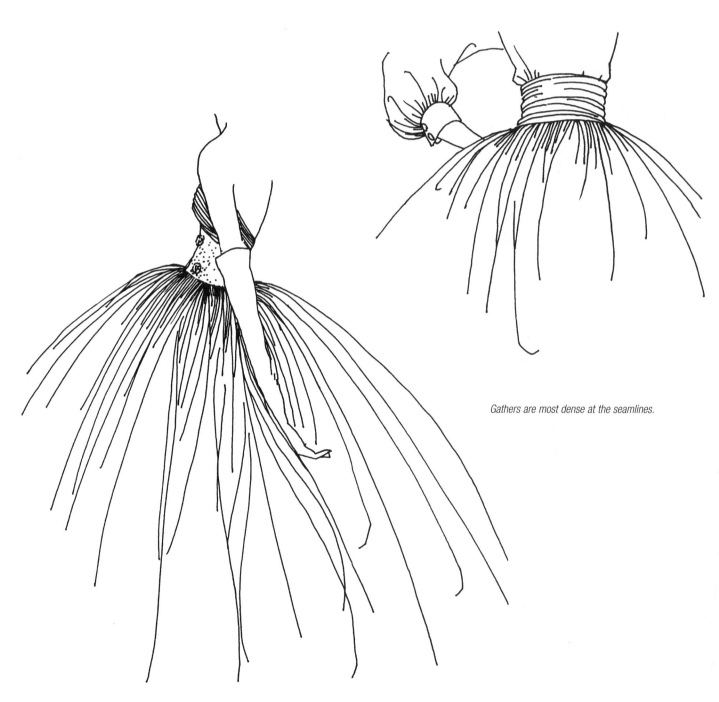

Gathers are most dense at the seamlines.

The last thing to remember is that this type of clothing is not easy to draw. You must work out the different possibilities before you begin the finished art. You have to combine the ability to move the garment so that it can make its own shape and still retain the figure underneath. But the dramatic results are endless!

Issey Miyake 1985

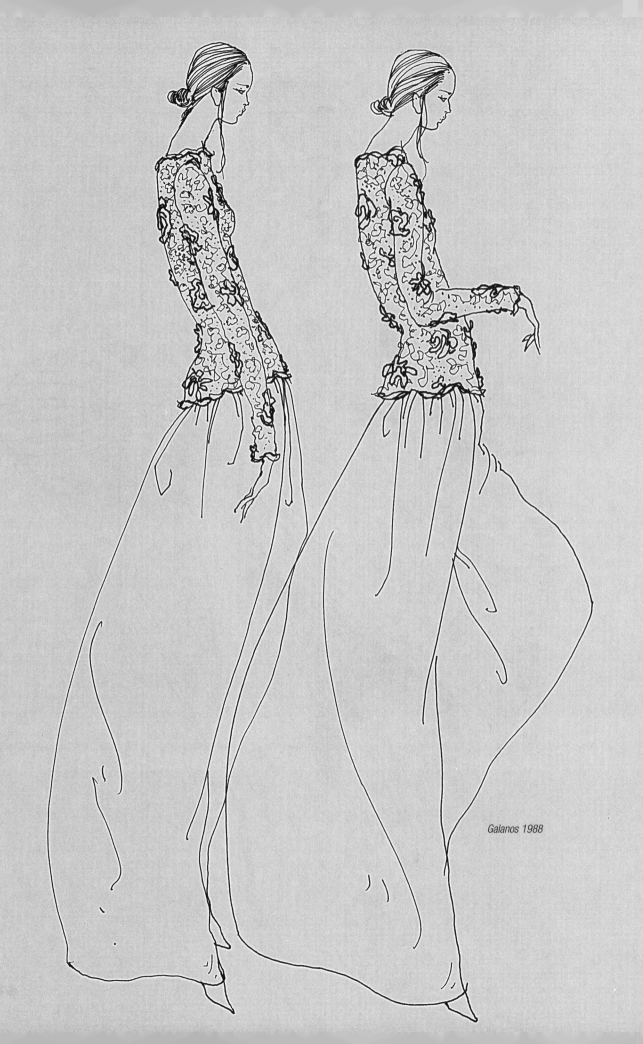

Galanos 1988

Manipulating the Figure

After all is said and done and after the facts are mastered, the most important thing is that you begin to draw with both accuracy and ease. Occasionally an unexpected accident might work for you, but you should have the control to draw the figure the way you want it to look, each and every time. Consistency should be your ultimate goal.

You have learned many rules and concepts by now. The creative and fun part happens when you begin to be able to manipulate the figure so it begins to work as one with the clothes.

I will show you how the different possibilities of a dress with a dropped waist bodice and full, gathered skirt can be interpreted in four different ways. First, let's analyze the dress and its relationship to the body. There are two focal points on the dress, which are:

- The long torso.

- The full skirt and its relationship to the head, arms, and legs.

In the first sketch, the figure is treated as a classic fashion drawing. There is an equality between the top and bottom of the dress. I used a fine marker and colored pencil. I selected a pose that shows the stretch of the torso and contrasted it with the puffiness of the skirt. I lightly blocked in the figure and exaggerated the gesture I want to achieve.

I thought about the stretch of the torso and made my line tense, to duplicate this feeling. When I drew the skirt, I lightened the line and tried for a more spirited quality. As I brought the line to the legs, the "S" curve became exaggerated.

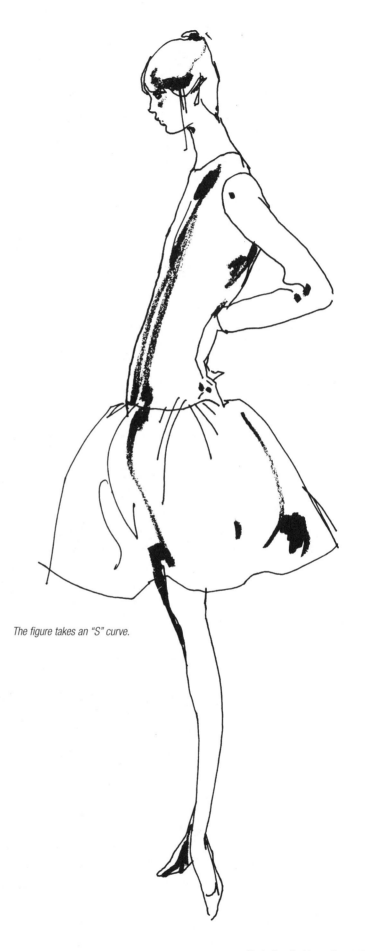

The figure takes an "S" curve.

In the second drawing, I wanted to work with more contrast and a more exaggerated flow. I worked in a medium marker and wash. I wanted the movement to have an exaggerated "S" curve to it with the skirt pushed back. I wanted the head and neck to sit a bit more forward, with the torso pulled back at the shoulders and pushed out at the hips.

The arm is used as a device to help swing the skirt back. The nonsupporting leg has been pulled backward. I worked the wash down the torso, following the movement and brought it only lightly into the skirt. I pulled down the supporting leg, almost putting it in the shadow.

An exaggerated "S" curve using the arm as a device.

In the third drawing, I approached the figure more graphically. I used an even heavier marker for the drawing and a thicker marker for the black areas. Rather than have some of the skirt in front as in the last drawing, I wanted the arms in front to push the entire skirt back.

I have blackened in the top of the dress with a heavier marker, keeping the graphic feeling, rather than a soft look. I extended a few dark areas into the skirt and made them flow in the backward direction, which emphasizes the skirt's movement. Also the legs serve as a means to balance the figure.

I selected a more blunt-cut hair style, which swings forward and exaggerates the movement of the head even more.

A more graphic approach

452

In the fourth drawing, I have still kept the "S" curve, but have put the hand in the pocket as a device to push the skirt forward. I worked in a medium marker with colored pencil. I also treated the face a bit more realistically, keeping the frizzy hair free of too much outline.

Because of the arm position, the movement is wider at the top and the skirt will be more centered. The nonsupporting leg is pushed forward. I treated the darker areas with a lighter hand, with the darks gently flowing into the skirt.

In the case of each drawing, you will notice that I have worked both the figure and the clothing together to best achieve the look I want.

Be very careful to distinguish distortion and exaggeration. Distortion is losing the true meaning of proportion. And proportion is what fashion is based upon.

On the other hand, exaggeration is manipulating the figure and clothing together to achieve a harmonious flow. This means picking and choosing and pointing up the most important parts, while downplaying the parts that are secondary.

This takes a lot of practice and can only begin when you have a solid and accurate knowledge of the figure, the clothing, and the figure in the clothing.

Remember, there is no fashion until the figure and garment become one.

Using the pockets to move the skirt forward

Style and Beyond

Many students concern themselves too much about the word "style." Style is not technique. Style is not how you draw something or with which art supply you draw it. Also, style is not whether the drawing is tight or loose.

Most important, style should never—under any circumstances—be based on a gimmick. Style is based on you and what you are about. Style is all of the things you gather and have gathered for your entire life, all of the things you are interested in, and all of the things you continue to learn about. Style is sum total of all your parts. Finding a style cannot happen overnight, and if it does, it isn't real.

Style is not about having a "singular" vision but rather about being open to all the things that relate to your life and profession. It is about always being curious, open minded, and involved. Locking yourself into a time and place and sticking to an established formula are the greatest enemies of style and art because great art always involves risk.

Being honest and objective about your work are essential. Learning, being curious and alive, and sharing your thoughts and knowledge will help you to find a style. Set high, but not impossible standards and your work will be successful.

Remember, if everything is good, nothing is great.

Balenciaga 1967

Index